People Populating

People Populating

DEREK LLEWELLYN-JONES
OBE MD MAO FRCOG

Illustrations by
AUDREY BESTERMAN

FABER & FABER
3 Queen Square
London

First published in 1975
by Faber and Faber Limited
3 Queen Square London WC1
Printed in Great Britain by
Butler and Tanner Ltd Frome and London

ISBN 0 571 09943 2

To
DAVID WALTER CLARKSON
a nephew
who was born on the 8th April, 1972.
In the hope that our generation
will meet the challenge
and act now
so that his generation may not be
crushed by disaster.

Preface

In the opinion of a large number of scientists the world is approaching a crucial period. The technological advances in sanitary engineering and in the control of infectious disease have increased the life expectancy of adults and have drastically reduced the deaths of infants and children. The result is that increasing numbers of young people are entering the reproductive era, and being normal, sensual, sexual humans, they are reproducing. The result is that a uniquely rapid rate of population growth has occurred in the past 25 years. Simultaneously with this, there has been an ever-increasing demand for consumer goods, with the result that non-renewable mineral resources are diminishing, and pollutants are making the rivers, the sea, the air and the environment increasingly unpleasant.

Mankind is approaching a time when decisions will have to be made. Can the current exponential growth rate of population be permitted to continue unchecked? Can man continue to add the waste of industrial processes into the environment without charging the cost of cleaning it on those who produce the pollution? Can the current evangelical faith in continued, increased economic growth as a 'good' be sustained?

Naturally there is disagreement, not only about the diagnosis of the disorders affecting mankind, but also about the solutions. Natural and behavioural scientists (and the latter include the economists) disagree almost as much as do physicians and politicians. But everyone admits that there are problems.

There are those who believe that we are probably doomed even if we change our demands from unlimited population

growth and unlimited economic growth to a stationary population and reduced, but better distributed, ecologically sound
economic growth. Their cause is championed in opposingly
divergent ways by the Americans, Dr. Paul Ehrlich and Dr.
Barry Commoner, and by the *Ecologist* in Britain. They are
called doomsday-men by their opponents, who imply that they
have identified a problem, but finding no solution, have gone
to the mountain top to pray for salvation, and spend their time
in exhortatory rhetoric but no real action.

There are those who are convinced that mankind's ingenuity,
coupled with scientific research and the huge injection of
resources, will enable technology to solve all the problems that
technology has created and that there is no need to control
population growth. They are called optimistic ostriches by their
opponents, as they seem to deny that there is any real need for
concern. In Britain, their cause is spearheaded by Dr. John
Maddox, the ex-editor of the prestigious magazine, *Nature*.

That both of these extreme views are likely to be in error is
clear, at least to me. I have faith in the survival of man, but I
believe that he will have to change his foolish ways, and will
have to discard as dated, irrelevant and dangerous, many current modes of thought. I believe that mankind can do this. I
also believe that people are central to our problem. The unexpectedly rapid rate of growth of the world's population is the
major danger facing mankind. To reach this opinion, I have
travelled in four of the five continents, I have had the opportunity to talk to many people and I have had the facilities of
several libraries open to me. I am neither a gloomy prophet of
doom, nor am I an optimistic, technological ostrich. I am a
Noah's man.

Noah, you will recall, was commanded to build an ark by
God when God had decided that the earth was filled with
violence through man, and when he determined to destroy man
and the earth. Noah built his ark, and by judiciously taking
only two of each animal and plant, ensured man's survival.

The old myth of Noah is relevant today. The earth is filled
with man's violence. He is violent to his fellow men, he is
violent to his habitat, he is violent and arrogant towards the
ecosystem which sustains him. But if he shows good sense, and
acts now, particularly by controlling his birth rate, by adopting

a new ecologically sane technology and by replacing greed with gratitude, he will survive.

The first, and essential, step in solving any problem is to identify what that problem is. This book shows how population growth has occurred, and how it may be measured. It shows what factors influence it, and how people influence the environment. It also offers information about how the present, abnormally high rate of population growth may be reduced.

There is so much data, that I cannot avoid the criticism that I have been selective. I have, but I have tried to be fair.

Finally, because I believe (all evidence to the contrary) that people are rational and would be concerned if they appreciated the problems, I hope that people will be stimulated to enquire further and search for possible solutions.

The most important age group in this search are those people aged 15 to 25, for the problem and its solution is in their hands. But I hope that people of other ages will find interest and information in *People Populating*.

Sydney, Australia   Derek Llewellyn-Jones
March, 1975

NOTE

Statistical information contained in many of the tables and figures originally appeared in Professor Llewellyn-Jones' more detailed analysis of demographic and social problems, *Human Reproduction and Society*, published by Faber & Faber, 1974.

Where the names of women have been used in case-histories, it is confirmed that the names are fictional, and bear no relation to any actual person alive or dead. The case-histories are based on fact.

Acknowledgments

This book could not have been written without the help of many people. In particular, I would like to thank Professor J. C. Caldwell and the members of the Department of Demography, the Australian National University; the officials of the Bureau of Census and Statistics, Commonwealth of Australia, Canberra; Mr. R. K. Nair and his colleagues in the Mauritius Family Planning Association; Miss Pamela Roberts and her colleagues in the Department of Social Work, the Women's Hospital (Crown Street); Miss Patricia Neill and her staff in the Department of Obstetrics and Gynaecology, University of Sydney. I must also thank my secretaries, Mrs. Shirley Pitfield and Miss Jennifer Robinson who typed and retyped the manuscript, prepared the index and helped me in many ways.

Contents

Tables

Figures

15

Figures

CHAPTER ONE

The Problem of People

There is a French riddle which, like many French things, is said to be for children but is really for adults. The riddle tells a story and asks a question. It is this.

A man owned a lily pond on which a water lily was growing. The lily plant doubled in size each day. If the lily were allowed to grow unchecked, it would completely cover the pond in thirty days, choking off all other forms of life, including the trout which the owner enjoyed eating. He also enjoyed looking at the lilies. So he was in a dilemma. How long could he keep the lily without cutting it back, and keep the trout healthy and plentiful? For a long time the lily plant seemed small, and there didn't seem any reason to worry. So he decided to wait until it covered half the pond; then he would cut it back so that he could look at the white flowers of his lily and still have his trout to eat.

The question in the riddle is this: On what day will the lily cover half the pond?

The answer is on the twenty-ninth day. The owner had only one day to save his pond.

Modified from 'The Limits to Growth',
D. MEADOWS, 1972.

I

For some years, demographers, who study population change, and human biologists, who study people, have been concerned that the rate of growth of the human population has speeded up, so that the time interval for population doubling has diminished progressively. This is exponential growth. The population is increasing at a rate proportional to its size, just like the water lily in the French riddle. Like the owner of the pond, mankind has reached the penultimate day.

Unfortunately, the exponential growth phenomenon is not just confined to people. Not only is the rate of population growth exponential, but so is the production of consumer goods, so is the production of waste, so is pollution and so is land occupancy. In no finite system is it possible for exponential growth to continue; eventually the limits to growth are reached. And planet Earth, which is a very small planet, is finite.

The limits to growth have been analysed recently by a team of scientists led by Professor Dennis Meadows from the Massachusetts Institute of Technology, with the help of models and computers. These models were constructed to investigate 'the five major trends of global concern—accelerating industrialization, rapid population growth, widespread malnutrition, depletion of non-renewable resources, and a deteriorating environment'. Dr. Meadows points out the trends are interconnected in many ways, and their exponential increase threatens our future. Population cannot grow without food. Food production is increased by growth of capital, which provides the needed inputs of water, fertilizer and new strains of seeds. Capital is produced by increasing industrialization, but this requires that more of the finite mineral resources of the world are used. These resources are converted into consumer goods which more and more people are induced to buy. The profits provide the capital to replace outmoded equipment, to finance research and to provide capital for food production. The discarded resources, the waste of the products of manufacture and the residues of food production, produce increasing pollution. Pollution interferes with the quality of life, with health, with the growth of population and the production of food. All have finite growth limits.

After studying the results of their computer studies, the M.I.T. scientists say, with some degree of concern, that 'under the assumption of no major change in the present system, population and industrial growth will certainly stop within the next century at the latest'. The transition from unlimited growth to rapid decline will not be pleasant. If it happens it will be within the lifetime of our children or grandchildren. There will be increasingly frequent crises, increasing disasters, and finally, collapse. The M.I.T. scientists show that scientific and technological discoveries can delay the date of the collapse, but alone they cannot prevent it. They admit that their model is simple, and that their conclusions are tentative, but they have made the first study which integrates the available information. For this reason alone, their study is important.

Scientists who have complete faith in technology to solve the problems of environmental pollution, of food supplies and, by substitution, of the increasing scarcity of finite, non-renewable, mineral resources, claim that the M.I.T. computer study is simplistic, biased and unscientific. Robert Boyd, recently, has articulated these views. Using the same data, he has added one extra parameter. This is the technological optimists' assumption of infinite technological progress. With this addition to the equation he claims that the computer then shows that technology increases productivity, reduces pollution, increases food production and increases the standard of living. The higher standard of living, it is assumed, will drive 'the birth rate down, until a stable population is reached'. He makes this assumption not on evidence, but on faith. However, the technological optimists accept that the exponential rate of population growth can create a considerable distortion, and accept, as Boyd says, that 'birth control allows the world to go through the demographic transition (so that births equal deaths) at a lower population level and greatly enhances the eventual equilibrium'. This statement shows that even the technological optimists accept that the current rate of population growth imposes a major constraint on our survival.

The main hope for mankind's survival is for us to change our attitudes so that we reach a state of global equilibrium, in which births and deaths are equal, and in which, simultaneously, industrial growth is reduced so that capital investment equals capital depreciation. This does not mean a dull, uniform society. Only population and capital need to be kept in equilibrium. Any human activity which does not use large quantities of non-renewable resources, or produce severe environmental pollution, can continue to grow. It means that technological advances to conserve, rather than to exploit, will be needed. It means that the stimulation of the spirit will largely replace the greed for goods. But it also means that there must be a more equitable distribution of the available goods. This, in turn, implies that the gap between the rich and poor nations must be drastically reduced. The rich nations must get poorer so that the poor nations can become richer. The rich nations must eat less and consume fewer goods, so that the poor nations may have more.

The greatest hindrance to this solution is the rapid rate of population growth. Dedicated economists are currently concerned to procure, in the shortest possible time, a state of capital equilibrium. Human biologists seek to achieve a state of population equilibrium. That is what this book is about.

2

About three million years ago, pre-man, a hominid, differentiated from the great apes, and leaving the forests went to live on the plains. Traces of his life have been found in East Africa, around Lake Rudolf. To look at, he was not so different from the apes, but his brain was bigger (although less than half the size of our brain) and his mechanical skills were greater. He made and used tools regularly.

The centuries passed, burning summers followed burning summers, drought was succeeded by flood, forests marched over the plains, and retreated as the climate altered. In the hot lowlands pre-man sweated, fearing the animals, unless he was with his group. With them he felt more secure. But the young and the old—and he was old by 25—were vulnerable. On the highland plains life was easier, but not easy. Life was short, death was near.

Slowly, imperceptibly, the hominids were evolving into man. They formed themselves into small gathering-hunting bands for mutual support, comfort and protection. They learnt to divide duties, and to communicate. They lived mainly by gathering fruits, nuts, seeds, tubers and grubs. The women stayed in the camp, scrabbling for the edible roots and fruits and caring for the children. The men moved further afield, mainly hunting small animals, but occasionally combining to hunt larger, fiercer beasts. The growth of the population was slow, and life expectancy at birth less than 18 years. It probably took over 100,000 years for the population to double in size.

About 40,000 years ago, man, who had discovered fire much earlier and used it when a natural source was found, discovered he could produce fire by friction whenever he wanted. He began to use fire regularly for cooking. Leopold and Ardrey have proposed that this was a monumental evolutionary step, and one which led to an increase in the rate of population growth. Plants contain a wide range of chemicals toxic to man, and the number which can be eaten raw with safety is limited. Cooking destroys or removes many of these toxic chemicals. When primitive man habitually cooked the plants he had gathered so laboriously he improved his diet, and more infants and children survived to reach the reproductive years. Fire used for cooking opened up a much wider food supply and was a necessary step preceding the cultivation of cereals. But 30,000 years were to pass before that happened.

Then 10,000 years ago, only yesterday, probably following an unexpected climatic change, primitive man learned how to cultivate the wild grains (whose seeds he had previously only picked when they were ripe) and how to domesticate wild animals. There is evidence that agriculture originated independently in three different areas: in the Yellow River area in North China, in the Tigris-Euphrates area in West Asia, and in Central America. From these centres agriculture spread outwards, so that developments occurred in South China, in the Indus and Nile valleys, and in South America. Man became an agriculturalist and a pastoralist.

With a better balanced diet—the cereals provided protein, vitamins and minerals as well as calories, and the meat provided additional protein—the population growth rate increased. There were, of course, considerable fluctuations. A succession of good harvests increased the birth rate and reduced the death rate of vulnerable infants and children. But when drought cracked the land, the growing crops withered and died; when floods swept through the river valleys, houses, plants and soil were inundated and the mortality rose.

The increase in population also led to tribal conflicts, over land or women or magic, with sudden death from the blow of a stone weapon as the ultimate sanction. But fights were probably uncommon, and most deaths were due to the effects of nature, for man was not naturally aggressive. Man was in ecological balance with his environment.

By the first year of the Christian era, the world's population had reached about 250 million. India had a population of about 100 million, China one of 70 million, and the Mediter-

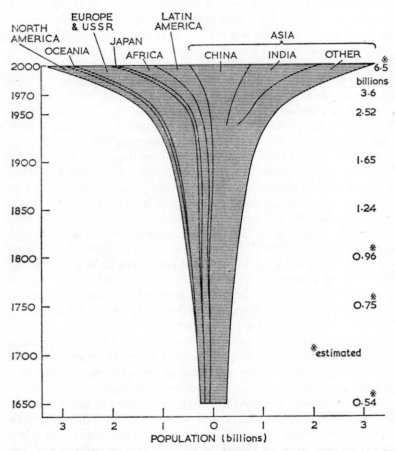

FIG. 1/1. The growth of human population since 1650 in U.S. billions. The estimates after 1970 are based on the U.N. population projection, medium variant. Note: a U.S. billion = a thousand million.

ranean seaboard, northern Europe and the other lands making up the Roman Empire, one of 50 million. The remaining 30 million are thought to have lived in Africa and America.

It had taken two and a half million years for the number of humans alive to grow to 250 million; it would take only the next 1,650 years for it to double to 500 million.

In 1650 reasonably certain estimates put the population of the world at 500 million. By 1850, 200 years later, it had passed 1,000 million. The exponential growth rate was taking effect. It took only 75 years for it to double again to 2,000 million; and

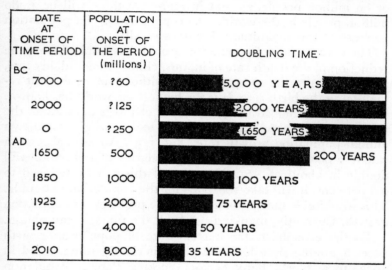

DATE AT ONSET OF TIME PERIOD	POPULATION AT ONSET OF THE PERIOD (millions)	DOUBLING TIME
BC 7000	? 60	5,000 YEARS
2000	? 125	2,000 YEARS
AD 0	? 250	1,650 YEARS
1650	500	200 YEARS
1850	1,000	100 YEARS
1925	2,000	75 YEARS
1975	4,000	50 YEARS
2010	8,000	35 YEARS

FIG. 1/2. Population doubling times since 7,000 B.C.

it will double again to 4,000 million by 1975 (Fig. 1/1). This implies an annual growth rate of 1·5 per cent per annum and a doubling time of only 50 years. If the current exponential growth rate continues, the population of the world will double again to 8,000 million by the year 2010, in only 35 years, which gives a population growth rate of 2·5 per cent per annum (Fig. 1/2).

At the moment, the rate of population growth is over 2·0 per cent per annum, about mid-way between the two rates just quoted. A growth rate of 2 per cent per annum may not appear serious until it is realized it is *exponential* and until the *scale* of the growth rate is considered. The population of the world in mid-1970 was 3,634 million. If the 2 per cent annual growth rate is applied, by mid-1971 the population had increased by 0·02 times 3,634 million, or 73 million people. This 73 million is added to the 3,634 million to give 3,707 million as a base in calculating the mid-year population for 1972, and so on. Thus at later dates, the increase will be even larger, even if the rate of growth is held to 2 per cent. For example, in 1975 the world population is expected to be 4,000 million. The annual addition in that year will be 0·02 times 4,000 million, or 80 million people, so that in mid-1976 there will be 4,080 million people in the world. The consequences of a population increase of this magnitude threatens us all.

The current rate of population growth has resulted from the reduction of the death rate of infants, children and adolescents, and the longer life span of adults, without an equivalent reduction in the birth rate. It is the highest the world has known. One way of demonstrating the effects of this is to estimate the time it takes the population of a nation to double, given a known annual population growth rate (Fig. 1/3). An annual growth rate of 2 per cent means that the population of any nation will double in about 35 years, but that if this can be reduced to 0·8 per cent, it will take 100 years for the population to double. This would give more time to solve the problems of population growth. Currently, mankind needs all the time we can obtain.

To the economist, the current rate of population growth poses a unique situation. This was succinctly summarized in 1972, in a World Bank Sector Working Paper, 'Population Planning'. The report states that 'There is no reason to believe that current rates of growth will fall fast enough to relieve the pressures on developing countries, arising from the need to use significant and rising proportions of their resources simply to maintain the average standard of living of growing numbers, leaving less for further improvement. . . . The decline of mortality in most developing countries has resulted in the survival of more adults, who would otherwise have had a shorter life span, and an increase in the number of surviving infants. The respective contributions of these two groups to the post-war population increase cannot be accurately calculated, but probably they are about equally significant. The economic impact of their survival is quite different, however; more adults living longer increase the potential labour force and create an immediate demand for jobs and supporting services. They also add to the numbers in the reproductive age group with a potential impact upon fertility. More children surviving mean a rise in the dependency burden and, at a later stage, a further relative increase in the reproductive age groups. Thus, while

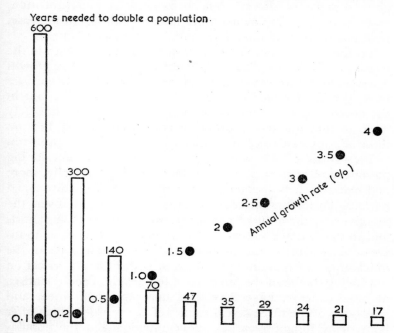

Years needed to double a population.

FIG. 1/3. The calculation of population doubling times given various annual reproductive growth rates. Note: The doubling time approximately equals 70 divided by the growth rate.

any fall in the infant mortality rate is to be welcomed on humanitarian grounds, it adds burdens to weak economies which can be lessened only by reducing fertility. To do so, and thus lessen the dependency burden, leads to large economic benefits. This is the heart of the economic case in favour of programs to limit fertility.' To the ecologist the needs of the 'growth' economists will mean increasing environmental pollution, increasing aggregation in urban areas, increasing congestion of roads,

houses and lungs; and increasing threats of an ecological doomsday. To the demographer the consequences of this growth rate
are that the children born today will themselves start having
children in the next 15–25 years, and a multiplier effect on
population will result. To the physician the population growth
imposes strains on the provision of preventive health care and
of medical care. To the politician the population growth rate
gives promise of dissent and turbulence as undernutrition,
malnutrition, unemployment and under-employment increase,
with potential revolutionary situations in many countries.

To the affluent nations the rate of population growth in the
world offers a further threat. As will be seen, the rate of growth
is not uniform throughout the nations. The developed countries
have already reduced their growth rate considerably, but in
the developing countries the growth rate is disproportionately
high, so that the great burden of population growth falls on
those nations least able, economically, to cope with the problem.

Two-thirds of the world's people live in the developing
nations, and as their population increases exponentially, more
and more do they threaten the current values of the developed
nations. Possessions become threatened by people. Even the
aid given by the affluent nations (as much to aid their exports
and to damp down dissent in the developing regions, as to increase employment and productivity), is swallowed up in the
quicksands of expanding populations, with little real effect on
improving the lot of the majority of the people. Food scientists,
at huge expense, have developed new strains of wheat and
rice—two of the three cereal staples of the world—which offer
hope of avoiding increasing under-nutrition. But the populations are increasing as, or more, rapidly than harvest yields, so
that little progress is being made in the battle to increase the
calorie intake of the people. And more than calories are needed.
The intake of the most important constituent of the diet,
protein, has also failed to increase. The situation is such that
'continued malnutrition mocks the basic aim of development
and hinders its effective realisation . . .', to quote the Director
of the Food and Agriculture Organization, speaking in 1971.

At this time, environmental pollution is mainly a problem of
the developed nations. In the industrial nations of the Atlantic
seaboard and in Japan the skies over the cities are becoming

increasingly contaminated with industrial smog. Open land is being swallowed up to be covered with concrete to make highways on which cars can travel, discharging pollutants as they speed between new, raw suburbs of brick and concrete. Rivers, and the ocean, are being increasingly polluted with the industrial effluent resulting from the manufacture of products which custom and advertising induce an acquisitive society to believe it needs. The need to possess more material goods dominates the need to live in harmony with the environment. Forests are cut down and minerals are dug up to satisfy the insatiable demand for paper and packaging which add considerably to the cost of the goods and are discarded haphazardly over the land. The disposal of this garbage is becoming an increasing problem. The need for water is outstripping the water resources, so that in many developed nations water restrictions appear to be inevitable, unless all water is re-used again and again. Despite a multiplicity of consumer goods, and affluence, the diseases of maladjustment are increasing, as is the consumption of drugs, whether these are alcohol, tranquillizers, narcotics, tobacco or sedatives, and as is the shortage of housing. A basic cause, although not the only cause, of these problems is the current exponential growth rate of the population of the world.

3

The problem of the rate of population growth becomes even more serious, when the regional differences in the rate are studied. It at once becomes obvious that the greatest growth rate is taking place in those nations economically and organizationally least able to cope (Fig. 1/4).

In 1971, Africa had a population of about 354 million. Between 1961 and 1970 the growth rate was calculated to be an average of 2·5 per cent, but because of the unreliable statistics from many African nations it is likely that both the population and the growth rate are higher. This supposition has been confirmed by those nations which have made a census recently. These have shown that previous population estimates were too low. For the continent, as a whole, in the period 1961–70, the annual birth rate was over 45 per 1000

of the population and the annual death rate about 22 per
1000.

After a period of colonial rule, the African nations, south of

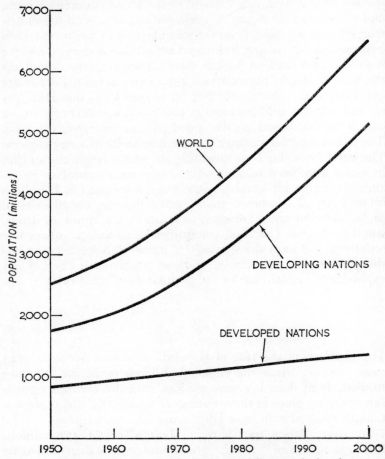

FIG. 1/4. The expected growth of the world's population between
A.D. 1950 and 2000 showing the disproportionate growth in the
developing nations.

the Sahara, are anxious to increase health measures to reduce
the high death rates of infants and children, but in general
show little enthusiasm for reducing the birth rate. With the
world's highest infant and childhood mortality rates, and with

tribal societies, large families are a source of pride, and high fertility a cultural norm. As the continent has one quarter of the earth's surface, but only one tenth of its population, many African leaders find difficulty in believing that population growth poses a problem. As far as density of population is concerned there is no problem; however, the urban population is growing at a rate of 5 per cent per annum, and in rural areas the available land has very limited agricultural potential. The fertile lowlands are relatively small in area, and apart from Australia, Africa is the driest continent. In addition, an increase in the reproductive growth rate is inevitable, due to the age structure of the population and to better death control. Economic development and the expansion of social services are lagging increasingly behind the population growth rate, with potentially severe problems likely to arise, unless a massive investment programme can be mounted. In the present climate of African opinion control of population growth is unlikely to be accepted except as a part of a programme of maternal and child health; and the population growth rate may be expected to rise to about 3 per cent per annum during this decade. Professor Caldwell, who has made a particular study of sub-Saharan Africa, is cautiously optimistic that changes can occur. He writes, 'There can be little doubt that most of the "ideological" resistance to family planning will crumble as enough African precedents are established to demonstrate that family planning is compatible with the African way of life or government.' The unanswered question is, will the change in attitude come about quickly or slowly? Major determinants of change are probably the increasing rate of urbanization and the increasing demand for education.

Africa is not the fastest-growing region at this time. This dubious distinction must go to Latin America, which includes South America, Central America and the Caribbean area. With the exceptions of Argentina, Cuba, Jamaica and Uruguay, every Latin American nation has a high rate of population growth. In 1971 the population of South America was estimated to be 291 million, an increase of 72 million over the 1961 estimate. This equates to an annual growth rate of 2·9 per cent. Although the birth rate of 40 per 1,000 is lower than that found in Africa, the death rate of 11 per 1,000 is also lower, so that the annual population growth rate exceeds that of Africa. The population problems of Latin America are far greater than those of Africa, for more and more Latin Americans are migrating to the cities, seeking jobs which do not exist and adding to the congestion of the insanitary urban slums. The social problems arising from this internal urban migration, coupled with uncontrolled fertility, are immense. Both within the cities and in the rural areas, social programmes in health, education and welfare are unable to meet the basic needs of the population, as the rate of population growth outstrips the investment in social services.

The situation in North America is different. Population growth in Canada and the U.S.A. is steady but not excessive; however, in an intensely consumer society, which survives only by importing raw materials from the developing nations, environmental pollution problems are increasing rapidly, and are causing considerable concern. It has been calculated that one American child will consume, and pollute, in his lifetime, twenty-five to fifty times the quantity consumed and polluted by one Indian child.

Asia, excluding the U.S.S.R., contains 56 per cent of the world's population. In 1971 over 2,000 million people lived in Asia, and the annual population growth rate between 1961 and 1971 was 2·1 per cent. This means that over 40 million people are added to Asia's population each year. The birth rate has tended to remain constant since 1950, at about 36 to 38 per 1,000, but the death rate continues to decline, so that the annual growth rate is increasing slightly. Within Asia the reproductive growth rate varies between 1·2 and 2·8 per cent per annum. There is a ray of hope in Asia. The world's most populous nation, the People's Republic of China, seems to have made considerable headway in reducing its rate of population growth to less than 1·4 per cent per annum, which is a remarkable achievement. Japan, too, must be excluded from the general statement about Asia. In fact, Japan is now classed, together with Israel, as a developed nation. Asian Governments face increasing problems of land hunger, under-employment and unemployment, increasing inequalities of income and increasing urban growth.

Europe, including the U.S.S.R., with 711 million people, has the lowest birth rate of all the regions, a low death rate and the lowest annual growth rate. The problems facing Europe are those of urbanization and environmental pollution rather than population growth, but these problems are of considerable magnitude, and currently defy resolution. At a meeting held in the Netherlands in 1971, the degree of pollution of the North Sea and its effects on the ecology of the region provoked an intense argument; but no action was taken.

Oceania is the least populated region, with 20 million inhabitants, and one in which land is available. But in the largest nations of the region, Australia and New Zealand, 85 per cent of the people live in towns of 25,000 inhabitants or more, and 66 per cent live in the six largest metropolitan conglomerations. In Australia the problems of urban congestion and environmental pollution are beginning to be serious.

The problem of the non-Caucasian nations in Oceania are considerable. Papua–New Guinea, which achieved semi-independence in 1972, has an estimated 2·4 million inhabitants. The birth rate is unknown, but estimates range from 38 to 53 per 1,000 of population. The death rate is falling, so that a reproductive growth rate of over 3 per cent per annum is anticipated. The next largest nation, Fiji, has a population of 500,000, and the next, Samoa, one of 160,000. In both these nations family planning measures have been implemented, as population growth presses on land, jobs and resources.

It can be seen that in all the continents, population growth and the distribution of the population are creating problems which threaten the well-being, perhaps the survival, of all mankind, and these are compounded by the current desire of most nations to increase economic growth.

There are, of course, solutions which may or may not work. They are suggested in this book, and if they are accepted, and if they do work, this will be known within the lifetime of most readers. If the solutions are wrong, or fail to work, a disaster of unprecedented magnitude will sweep the earth, and the readers of this book or their children will not be spared.

4

Lying 700 kilometres west of Madagascar, Mauritius rises out of the ocean, an island 40 km long and 25 km broad, its mountains wreathed with cloud, its beaches separated from the long swells of the Indian Ocean by coral reefs. Until 1721 Mauritius was uninhabited by humans. It had been visited, from time to time, by Phoenicians, by Malays, by Arabs, by Portuguese and by Dutch sailors, but no permanent settlement had been established. The Dutch, between 1638 and 1658, had established a small colony of 25 men, but it had not prospered and had been abandoned. They made two other attempts to settle the island, and both failed. In 1721 the French occupied the island to exploit the ebony and ambergris found there, to provide a source of food for French ships voyaging across the Indian Ocean and to grow spices. They brought in African slaves from Madagascar and Mozambique, a few artisans from French India, and some landowners from France. The colony prospered, particularly when, in 1790, it was decided to expand the sugar industry, and by 1821 the population had grown to 80,000. Meanwhile, in 1810, the British had replaced the French as colonial rulers of Mauritius, and in 1835 they abolished the slavery on which the economy of the island depended. Within four years of the abolition nearly half of the 70,000 slaves had refused to work the sugar plantations, and had moved into the tree-clad mountainous interior, to set up their own small farms. Faced with a labour shortage for a burgeoning sugar industry the British encouraged the large-scale migration of Indian workers, with the result that the population quadrupled to 320,000 by 1871.

The Indian immigrants, who were coming in at a rate of 10,000 a year, brought with them malaria, cholera and enteric fever. As a result population growth slowed, the population reaching 370,000 in 1891, at which level it remained until 1921. The three post-war years had been boom years for sugar, the 1920 crop having realized £20 million, and the taxes raised were used to improve water supplies and sanitation, with the result that the infant and childhood mortality fell, and the population growth rate rose to reach 420,000 in 1944.

Again, after World War II, sugar prices rose, and the increased wages meant that childhood nutrition improved. At the same time malaria was eradicated, and a vigorous campaign was mounted to reduce infectious disease, with the result that the infant mortality rate fell from 140 per 1,000 in 1944 to 80 per 1,000 in 1954, and the crude death rate from 27 per 1,000 to 16 per 1,000 over the same period.

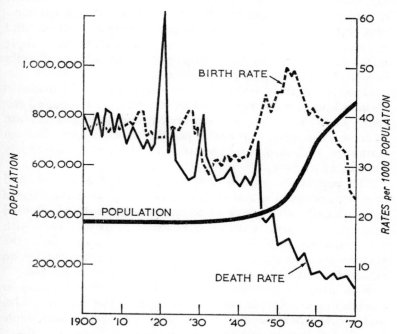

FIG. 1/5. The growth of the population of Mauritius, 1900–70.

Mauritius was at the take-off point for a spectacular population explosion. The health measures of the 1930s and 1940s meant that many more children survived to reach puberty, and as they married and had children, the birth rate rose. By 1950 the population growth rate had reached more than 3 per cent per annum, which implied that the population of Mauritius, then 500,000, would double in 24 years (Fig. 1/5).

The alarming rate of population growth led to the appointment of a committee to consider its effects on the economic resources, the employment problems and potential production of the island. The report was sombre. The committee calculated that the island would have a population of one million by 1975 unless action was taken urgently, and noted that the growth of population was exceeding the expansion of the island's productivity. It contended that at least 15,000 more people would need to be employed each year, and that housing and the primary school population would grow to unmanageable numbers. To solve the problem the committee rejected emigration, as they could see no possible accepter nations, and recommended that the Government should make the people aware of the problem by a propaganda campaign, and offer family planning as part of the social services.

However, nothing was done. The population of Mauritius is divided into four racial groups: 53 per cent are Hindu, 28 per cent white or creole, 16 per cent are Muslim and 3 per cent are Chinese. The white and creole population are mainly Roman Catholics and, supported by the Muslims, they effectively blocked any action.

The population growth continued. By 1958 Mauritius had over 600,000 people, and even more serious, the percentage of children under the age of 14 in the population had increased from 38 per cent in 1952 to 44 per cent by 1958. Faced with the alarming implications of these demographic facts the Government set up two further studies, each headed by an eminent scientist. In 1961 the two reports were published.

Both strongly recommended urgent Government action in establishing family planning as an integral part of the health and welfare programme. It was the 'most important single measure' that they had to propose.

'Had the Government started such a service in the early 1950s the future of Mauritius might have looked less sombre than it did at that time.' The author of the socio-demographic report, Professor Titmuss, also declared that 'no alternative presents itself but action, immediate and sustained, to develop population policies on as broad a scale as possible designed to slow down the rate of population growth'. Families had to be limited in size by voluntary measures, information and assistance being provided by the Government as an integral part of the health and welfare services and within the reach of every

mother and father in the island. The economic report by
Professor Meade concluded: 'The scheme would not make much
sense to the people nor have much success unless the family
planning measures were accompanied by vigorous economic
and social planning.' Unless all these measures were initiated
Professor Titmuss saw 'economic, social and political disaster'.
That disaster would occur was emphasized by Professor Meade.
He foresaw the 'terrifying prospect' of a population of 3 million
by the year 2000 unless action was taken urgently. He declared
'the economic future of Mauritius is dominated by its population problem. . . . Unless resolute measures are taken to solve it,
Mauritius will be faced with a catastrophic situation. Even
with the "optimistic" assumption that the 3–child family will
rapidly become the general pattern in Mauritius, it will be
necessary to find work for a 50 per cent increase in the population of working age over the next 15 years and to find school
accommodation etc. over the same period for a 20 per cent increase in those under 15 years of age.'

The debate on the report was long and bitter. The proposal
to introduce family planning was opposed by the hierarchy
of the Roman Catholic Church, who instructed all Roman
Catholics, inside and outside Parliament, to oppose the measure.
In Parliament one member declared: 'The philosophical
principle is well known: God blesses big families.' But a change
in attitude was occurring, particularly as the population in
mid-1961 had reached 655,000. Time was running out. The
Government, and many Roman Catholics, accepted that the
rate of population growth could lead to disaster, and urgent
action was needed in checking population growth and improving the economy.

From 1965, slowly initially, but lately with increasing
momentum, a campaign to educate, to inform and to offer
contraceptive measures to the people of Mauritius has been in
progress. The Roman Catholic 'Action Familiale' teaches the
'rhythm method', and by 1971, 6,200 couples had enrolled.
The Mauritius Family Planning Association sends field workers
to every newly married woman and to each woman after
childbirth to explain the purpose of family planning. In 1970
50,000 visits were made to women. Talks are given over radio
and television. Discs have been cut which can be played at

weddings. Film shows are given. By 1972 20 family planning centres, and 62 clinics, using existing Maternity and Child Health facilities, were open. In 1972 over 25,000 women, or one woman in every 5 at risk of becoming pregnant, were receiving advice and appliances, and nearly three-quarters had chosen the Pill.

The effect of all these measures has led to a decline in birth rate, despite the fact that increasing numbers of girls are entering the reproductive era. It has been calculated that 10,600 females enter the reproductive era and 3,500 leave it annually—a net gain of 7,100 potential mothers.

The campaign is in progress. The battle has not yet been won; but the people of Mauritius have shown an awareness of the problem, and the courage to tackle it.

The history of Mauritius in the last 20 years is a model of what has happened in many nations. Firstly, there is a reluctance to believe that a problem exists. Secondly, there is a belief that increased economic growth and increased food production will solve the now identified problem of the rate of population growth. Thirdly, when it has been realized that economic policies must be related to population policies, the resistance to birth control by large and influential groups on ideological grounds is found. Fourthly, public opinion begins to accept that action is needed to slow the rate of population growth. Fifthly, there is a sudden awareness that, because of the delay which has occurred, the problems have multiplied, have become more complex, and perhaps defy solution. Sixthly, the hope arises that population policies based on humane principles will succeed, before the inhuman solutions of famine, pestilence and civil or international war reduce the population, by increasing deaths rather than by decreasing births.

The peace of nations, and the dignity of man, is dependent on how Mauritius and other nations, particularly the giants—China, India, Indonesia, Brazil, Bangladesh, Nigeria and Pakistan—solve the problems of acute population growth. There is no other way.

CHAPTER TWO

Population Dynamics

I

In 1796 Thomas Robert Malthus left Jesus College, Cambridge, where he was a Fellow, and took a curacy in the village of Albury in Surrey. He was said, by the local villagers, to be a good clergyman, rather 'high church' but kind and helpful to his flock, when they could get him out of his study. This was difficult, for he spent a lot of his time either reading or writing. Observers said that the books he read were not theological tomes but works of philosophy. Thomas Malthus was, in fact, writing a book, and writing it in some haste.

The book was in answer to a revolutionary book which had been published three years earlier, in 1793. William Godwin, its author, had written a book called *Political Justice* which envisaged a glorious future for mankind because of technological and political progress, and because of his belief that man was perfectible. All that was needed, Godwin claimed, was for man to follow the principles of the Marquis of Condorcet and other French philosophers. They advocated political anarchy, the reign of reason, social justice and the abolition of private property. When all this occurred society would be perfect.

Malthus was appalled. Although he had been brought up at home by his father, who was an intellectual, and a friend of Rousseau, his whole background was that of a landowner. He firmly believed in a society in which the haves and have-nots were clearly defined, and in which each man knew his place. It was, Malthus held, the only possible society 'that can consistently with individual freedom, equally promote cultivation and population', as he wrote later to Godwin. Yet in *Political Justice*, a man of the property-owning class, who had had a similar upbringing to Malthus, was advocating the abolition of private

39

property and claimed that the labouring poor were the equals of men of substance. It was not only dangerously revolutionary, it was against the will of God.

Malthus determined to counter the pernicious doctrine by writing an answer which he called, in the ponderous fashion of the time, *An Essay on the Principle of Population as it Affects Future Improvement of Society, with remarks on the speculations of Mr. Godwin, M. Condorcet and other writers.*

To answer Godwin's claim that man and society were perfectible, and to prove that the perfect society was a mirage, Malthus chose an illustration. It was not a particularly original illustration, and Malthus had found it in a primitive form in one of the books he had read so assiduously in the evenings in the Rectory at Albury. But Malthus had thought about, and had elaborated, the terse statements of Wallace into a principle, which he termed 'The Principle of Population'. It was based on two observable facts and a questionable deduction. Malthus stated: 'First, that food is necessary to the existence of man. Second, that the passion between the sexes is necessary and will remain nearly in its present state.' Those were the incontrovertible facts. From them he made the questionable deduction. 'Assuming then, my postulata as granted, I say that the power of population is infinitely greater than the power of the earth to produce subsistence for man. Population, when unchecked, increases in a geometrical ratio. Subsistence increases only in an arithmetical ratio. A slight acquaintance with numbers will show the immensity of the first power in comparison of the second. . . . By the law of our nature which makes food necessary to the life of man, the effects of these two unequal powers must be kept equal. This implies a strong and constantly operating check on population from the difficulty of subsistence. This difficulty must fall somewhere; and must necessarily be severely felt by a large portion of mankind.'

According to Malthus, population would double every 25 years, provided no factors impeded its growth, but food production would only double in the first 25 years. Population grew geometrically, or exponentially as we now say (1, 2, 4, 8, 16), but food supply only increased arithmetically (1, 2, 3, 4, 5). Malthus held it was the race between population and the food supply which helped keep down the standard of living and gave rise to famine, pestilence and war. And since these outcomes were inevitable, man could never be perfect. His argument was made with deep concern and sincerity and was based on his belief that the society in which he lived was the best possible. Since man could only hope to achieve a balance between population and subsistence by misery and vice, 'the argument is conclusive against the perfectibility of mankind'.

If he had stopped there his book would have been merely a philosophical exercise fashionable at the time. But Malthus went further. He was much worried by the increased turbulence of the labouring poor, and had observed that they married early and had large families. Since this increased the rate of population growth, it hastened the corrective of misery, which, as a Christian, he could not tolerate. There was another way of avoiding misery, and that was by the preventive checks of late marriage, and of sexual continence before marriage. He therefore recommended that the preventive checks should apply particularly to the labouring classes and that the *status quo* of society, ordained by God, should remain inviolate. He even announced that society need have no concern with the hungry and the poor in its midst. He wrote: 'A man who was born into a world already possessed, if he cannot get subsistence from his parents, on whom he has a first demand, and if the society do not want his labour, has no claim of right to the smallest portion of food, and, in fact, has no business to be where he is. At nature's mighty feast there is no vacant cover for him. She tells him to be gone, and will quickly execute her own orders, if he does not work upon the compassion of some of her guests.'

This was a satisfying philosophy for the growing entrepreneurial classes who were replacing the old feudal landowners. It added authority to their belief that man's first, and only, duty was to himself. It confirmed their belief in the puritan ethic of work, in the superiority and immutability of their English society and in their own status.

His book was a wild success. It was published at a most appropriate time, for the small landowners and shopkeepers of England feared that the revolutionary ideas, which were being propagated in France, would infect the labouring poor of England, and property would be in danger. In describing the principle of population, Malthus not only denied the perfectibility of man, but defended the principle of private property. The poor were poor because of God's will and of defects in their character. None should marry until he could support a family. He should practise moral restraint. No property-owning citizen had any moral obligation to help the poor. This was an argument for reducing taxation levied to give money to the poor, under an Act of Elizabeth I. If money was given to the poor, it would only encourage them to marry, and this would increase misery and the pressure of population.

So successful was Malthus that his *Essay* went through seven editions in the 27 years to 1825. For each edition he collected new data, and in each he advanced further views to support his 'Principle'.

In many ways Malthus was wrong, at the time, although what he wrote is much more applicable now. He ignored, for example, the technological advances in food production which were accelerating. He ignored emigration to the empty lands of North America, and the recently discovered Australia. And he ignored birth control, or, more accurately, considered it a 'vicious' method of preventing population growth.

For the past two centuries his views have been attacked and applauded. For the past two centuries there have been recurrent complaints by the rich of the improvidence of the poor. For the past two centuries population has continued to press on food resources, but today the lid has blown off, and the population growth rate has escaped control.

2

Although philosophers from Confucius to Aristotle and Plato had been concerned about population growth, the scientific study of demography really began when bubonic plague swept Europe, decimating the population. Just before the last of the great epidemics in England, which was that of 1665—The Poores Plague—John Graunt had studied the Bills of Mortality which were published weekly to record the deaths in each parish, so that the onset of a new epidemic might be detected. Graunt analysed the Bills of Mortality and was able to detect patterns of death, and even more surprisingly, considering the novelty of the method, he drew up the first 'life table'. In this he was able to calculate the chances of death occurring to a member of a population at any particular age. The study of demography had begun.

But demography—or the scientific analysis of population dynamics—cannot exist without statistics. The more accurate the statistics, the more accurate the studies.

There are certain essential bits of knowledge required about populations, so that Governments can plan ahead to improve the welfare of the people, so that business can anticipate demand and so that hospitals, schools and other facilities may be placed in the most appropriate place. The essential questions to ask are: what is the size of the population, what is its composition by age and sex, and where do the people live. These questions relate to people, but questions are also asked about events, which are equally important. The events which most interest demographers are births and deaths (termed vital events), for they will affect population dynamics to the greatest extent. But, as well, it is important to know about marriages and divorces and about the movement of people in and out of the country.

If these data can be obtained accurately, demographers can provide information about several matters which are of social, economic and political importance. Firstly, the information provides an inventory of the human resources of the country. Secondly, the data on the composition of the population enable a demographer to describe the population. Thirdly, the information about births, deaths, marriages, age and sex are essential for any analysis of probable changes in the population. Finally, the information can be used to effect social change.

With all this talk of population it is essential to be clear what population is. A crowd of 120,000 filling the football stadium at Wembley is not a population in a demographic sense. But the 160,000 people living in Samoa—only 40,000 more—are a population. They are a population because they are living in a specific area at a special time and they can marry, have children, move to another area or die. These dynamic influences make the population one in a demographic sense. The events make it a living, changing organism, and any analysis of

43

population change—population dynamics—demands that demographic data are obtained.

Demographic data come from three sources. Most countries in the world have realized the need for a periodic counting of their population. This is termed a population census. It takes place at 10-year intervals in most developed nations, and in a few developing nations. In the census a series of questions is asked which have been worked out by various interested committees and approved by the government, to provide the most information with the least intrusion on the privacy of the individual. Every effort is made to ensure that the information remains confidential, particularly as some of the questions relate to matters frequently considered private.

On the appointed day, at an appointed time, the head of every household, whether that is a household of one person or one which has a large family, either fills in the form giving information about all other members of the household or is interviewed by an official who fills in the form. The completed forms are collected, checked and sent to the census office, where the data are processed, and over a period of months or years statistical information about the population on census day is published.

One of the characteristics of the last half of this century is the intrusion of privacy by an increasing number of governmental and private agencies, such as credit bureaux, security agencies and the like. Information from the U.S.A. has shown that the Armed Forces have a large amount of data, about a considerable number of citizens, on magnetic tape. These data are constantly updated and are added to the existing information retained in computer information banks from which they can be retrieved. What information is in the bank, its accuracy and its quantity is not disclosed to the citizen.

Because of this, many people fear that census information may be used, later, to the disadvantage of some individual or to persecute a minority group. Their fears are more imaginary than real. Firstly, each nation has strict laws about the confidentiality of the data. Secondly, no information is disclosed about individuals, and only aggregate data are published.

The second way in which demographic information is collected is by the registration of events, that is births, marriages, divorces and deaths. This is a fairly sophisticated procedure and requires well-trained staff and a well-motivated people if completeness and accuracy are to be obtained. Such accuracy is only obtained in the developed nations, and in not all of them. In most of Africa, Asia and Latin America, between 30 and 40 per cent of births are not registered, infant deaths are not notified, whilst statistics for marriage and divorce are ignored. Because of this, many estimates of world population changes are 'guess-timates', and more accurate information is needed badly.

The third way of collecting demographic data is by making sample surveys. These require careful planning to make sure that the sample surveyed really represents the population, and they are time consuming. One problem is the number of questions to be asked. If too many are asked, in too limited a time, the person being interviewed may get bored or confused, and give wrong answers, or the interviewer may not complete the form at the time, and complete it later using imaginary data. Despite the disadvantages, sample surveys are the only practicable method of obtaining information about population dynamics in many nations.

From the data obtained by a National Census, and by the registration of vital statistics, information about the composition of the population can be obtained. This is usually reported in the form of *ratios* and *rates*. A ratio indicates the relative size of two numbers. For example, the more children there are in the population, the more rapidly is it likely to grow, for the children will grow up, marry and have children of their own. This information can be obtained by finding the child-woman ratio, which is defined as

$$\frac{\text{The number of children aged 0 to 4 in the population}}{\text{The number of women aged 15 to 49 in the population}}$$

For convenience, the fraction is usually multiplied by 1,000 (Fig. 2/1).

In Britain in the 1971 census, the child-woman ratio was 336. This means that there were 336 children under the age of 5, for every 1,000 women aged 15 to 49. Contrast this with the child-woman ratio in Iran which was 746, or over double that of Britain. Twice as many Iranian children will reach the

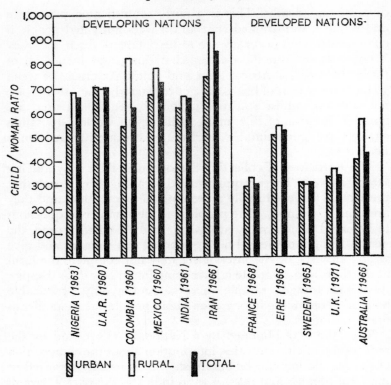

Fɪɢ. 2/1. Child-woman ratios in selected nations, various years.

Child-woman ratio

$$= \frac{\text{No. of children aged 0–4 in the population}}{\text{No. of women aged 15–49 in the same population}} \times 1,000$$

Source: *Demographic Yearbook*, 1969, U.N., New York.

age of 15 in the next 10 to 15 years, and since early marriage is normal in Persia, they are likely to add to the population explosion in that country, whilst in Britain a much smaller population growth rate may be expected.

One special form of ratio is a rate. This measurement has the additional characteristic of referring to what happened during a certain period of time. The most commonly used rates in population dynamics relate to births and deaths, and since these are vital events, the rates are called vital rates. Vital rates answer the question: how much per unit of what per year. Since the rates relate to the whole population, they are pretty crude. In fact, they are so termed. For example, in 1971, the crude birth rate in Australia was 21·67 per 1,000 of the population. This was obtained by the calculation:

Crude birth rate =

$$\frac{\text{Total births registered during the calendar year}}{\text{Total estimated population at mid-year}} \times 1,000$$

The crude death rate and the crude marriage rate are calculated in a similar manner.

The crude rates are valuable as they are fairly easy to obtain and give an indication of the rate of reproductive change—which is the difference between the crude birth rate and the crude death rate. The greater the difference the more rapidly is the population growing; the smaller the difference the more stable is the population (Table 2/1).

For many demographic analyses, however, crude rates are inadequate, and more precise measurements need to be computed. This applies particularly to births and deaths. For example, since only women aged 15 to 49 are likely to bear children, a more accurate measure of the fertility of the population would be to make the calculation:

$$\frac{\text{Live births to women aged 15 to 49}}{\text{Mid-year female population aged 15 to 49}} \times 1,000$$

The result of this calculation produces what is termed the *general fertility* rate. In demography, fertility has a special meaning and is defined, not as the ability of a woman to become pregnant, but as her ability to give birth to a live-born child.

The general fertility rate is a much more informative index of population dynamics, and can be refined even further by computing age-specific fertility rates. Age-specific rates (and they apply to deaths and marriages as well as births) give even more information. For example, it is well known that more women have children under the age of 30 than after that age. If women are divided into age groups (5 years are usually chosen) it is possible to find out in which 5-year age group women are most likely to give birth to a live-born child. In other words, you can determine their age-specific fertility rate.

TABLE 2/1

The birth rate, death rate and reproductive growth rate for the five or six largest nations in the four main continents

Country	Population in mid-1970 (millions)	Birth rate 1965–70 (per 1,000 population)	Death rate 1965–70 (per 1,000 population)	Reproductive growth rate 1965–70 (per cent)
Africa				
Nigeria	64	50	25	2·5
Egypt	34	37	14	2·5
Ethiopia	27	52	26	2·7
S. Africa	20	40	16	2·4
Zaire	17	43	20	2·3
America				
U.S.A.	203	18	10	1·1
Brazil	94	42	11	3·0
Mexico	51	45	11	3·5
Argentina	24	22	9	1·5
Canada	21	18	7	1·8
Colombia	21	40	13	3·2
Asia				
China	750	34	11	1·4
India	534	42	23	2·5
Indonesia	120	43	22	2·5
Japan	102	18	7	1·1
Bangladesh	70	44	20	2·1
Pakistan	56	46	18	2·0
Europe, USSR				
U.S.S.R.	241	17	7	1·1
Germany	59	15	12	1·0
Britain	56	17	11	0·6
Italy	54	18	10	0·8
France	51	17	11	0·9

The calculation is made by:

Age-specific fertility rate =

$$\frac{\text{Live births to women aged x years}}{\text{Mid-year population of women of x age}} \times 1,000$$

Population Dynamics

In Table 2/2, the age-specific fertility rates of Sweden and of the Philippines are shown, and this Table also shows the general fertility rate, which it will be realized is the sum of all the age-specific fertility rates. If these figures are plotted, the differences in natality (or the actual births of children) between the two nations can be seen (Fig. 2/2). Age-specific rates are of great value in demography, as they give an indication in current trends of fertility.

TABLE 2/2

Age-specific fertility rates for Sweden and the Philippines, 1967

Sweden 1967

Age group	Births to women of age	Females of age	Age-specific fertility rate
Total 15–49	121,360	3,700,473	58
15–19	13,823	608,423	25
20–24	43,254	632,182	135
25–29	35,956	490,430	146
30–34	17,855	442,285	82
35–39	8,133	468,312	35
40–44	2,177	522,300	9
45–49	162	536,541	0·6

Philippines 1967

Age group	Births to women of age	Females of age	Age-specific fertility rate
Total 15–49	828,015	7,574,000	86
15–19	73,854	1,802,000	19
20–24	204,427	1,472,000	185
25–29	230,432	1,208,000	194
30–34	164,795	996,000	141
35–39	112,480	822,000	139
40–44	35,675	689,000	52
45–49	6,352	585,000	11

49

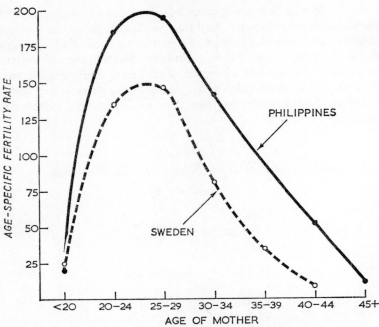

Fig. 2/2. Age-specific fertility rates, Sweden and the Philippines, 1967.

4

An important demographic analysis is to determine the *age and sex composition of a population* since this will have considerable socio-economic impact on the community. In a society where the birth rate is high and the death rate is low, and where people are, in general, living longer, there will be a considerable proportion of the population dependent on others. Children require to be housed, fed and clothed. They require, or are required to have, education. During this period they produce no income, but consume part of that which is produced by people of working age. Similarly, old people cease work, and require to be cared for until they die eventually. These two groups, the youth and the aged in the population, are dependent (for most things) on the producers, who are usually considered to be aged between 15 and 64. The dependency ratio of a population measures the impact of the age composition on the economy of the nation. It is:

Dependency ratio =

$$\frac{\text{Population under 15 or 65 years of age and over}}{\text{Population aged 15 to 64}}$$

It can be seen that the ratio has two parts, each of which can be calculated separately. The first measures the dependency load of youth, the second the dependency load of the aged.

The youth dependency ratio is calculated by dividing the number of people aged 15 to 64 into the number of people under the age of 15. The aged dependency ratio is calculated by dividing the number of people 65 and over by the number of people aged 15 to 64.

In Fig. 2/3, the total, the youth dependency and the aged

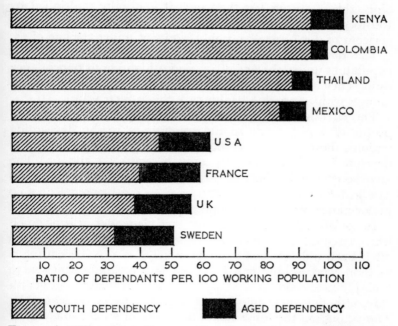

FIG. 2/3. The dependency ratio of certain nations. Source: *Demographic Yearbook*, various years, U.N., New York.

dependency, are shown for certain selected nations. One feature is at once obvious. The developed nations of the world tend to have a lower total dependency ratio, a lower youth dependency ratio and a higher aged dependency ratio than the developing nations.

A percentage is derived from a proportion, which in turn is a kind of ratio. A proportion can be defined as showing the ratio of one part to the whole. It is found by dividing the whole number into the part number. Thus the proportion of the population of Australia under the age of 15 is found by dividing the number of those under the age of 15 by the total population. The 1971 census showed that the population was 12,728,461, and the number under the age of 15 was 3,670,052.

The calculation $\dfrac{3,670,052}{12,728,461} = 0\cdot288$ gives the proportion.

Since this is always less than one, it is usually multiplied by 100 to give the percentage value. In the example given 28·8 per cent of the Australian population was under the age of 15.

The developing nations have a high proportion of their population under the age of 15, and a high youth dependency ratio. They also tend to have a low aged dependency ratio, although with improving health care this is increasing.

The effect of the population structure is that for every 100 people of working age in the community in the developing nations, there are between 80 and 105 dependants, but in the developed nations there are only between 50 and 65. The adverse economic effect of this higher total dependency ratio can be deduced, and is one of the reasons for the poor economic performance of many developing nations.

In social and economic terms aged dependency is of much less consequence than youth dependency. Old people have often been able to save a bit of money, or may be getting a pension, and usually can be taken into a family unit where their physical needs are few, apart from food, shelter and health care, although their emotional demands may be considerable. The young, on the other hand, are more of an economic drag as they require far more expenditure for food, and for education, make far greater demands and have greater expectations.

The economic cost of a high youth dependency ratio has been stressed by the World Bank:

'The most certain, immediate and measurable benefit of slowing population growth is the increase in per capita income. The immediate impact of falling fertility is a decline in average family size, reflected throughout society in a smaller dependency ratio. In the short run there is no change in the labor force or other resources, so that the same national income will be available to a smaller number of people. At the same time, proportionately less of the national income will have to be used to maintain the capital stock per person at a constant level, making it possible to apply more resources to increasing capital per worker, thus raising productivity and per capita income. . . . Problems of unemployment and inequality in the distribution of income will always be eased by reductions in fertility. Continuing high fertility results in large numbers of young people entering the labor force each year. Employment opportunities have to expand fast enough to absorb them. At high rates of growth of population, where the numbers involved may be doubling every 25 years, the absorption problem is severe.'

5

The age composition of a nation can be refined a bit further by calculating the age and sex structure simultaneously. This information is most often given, and is certainly more explicit, in graphic form. One commonly used representation of the age and sex composition is the *population pyramid*. By convention population pyramids are made by using 5-year age groups and by plotting each age group on a horizontal axis. Males are conventionally plotted on the left and females on the right.

A population pyramid gives the demographic picture of a population at a fixed point in time. If you want to observe the effects of health control, of birth control, of wars or of famines, a series of population pyramids have to be drawn, which can then be compared to obtain a dynamic view of the population of a nation. But without knowledge of historical events the differences in the shape of the pyramids are meaningless. When major disasters are avoided, and when migration is minimal,

Population Dynamics

the shape of the pyramid is determined principally by the current patterns of births and deaths in the nation. When the birth rates and death rates are high, as is usual in the developing countries, the pyramid has a broad base and gently sloping sides (Fig. 2/4). As preventive health measures are instituted,

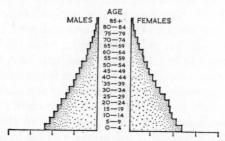

FIG. 2/4. Population pyramid—pre-transitional. This population profile, or pyramid, is typical of developing nations with a high birth rate and a high death rate. It could be that of any one of a number of nations in Africa today. In fact, it is that of England and Wales in the year 1851.

with purification of water supplies, improved infant nutrition and inoculation against infectious disease, the base of the pyramid becomes even broader and the slope steeper (Fig. 2/5).

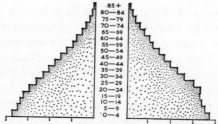

FIG. 2/5. Population pyramid—transitional. This population profile is typical of nations which have reduced the deaths of infants and children but have not yet controlled fertility, so that they are beginning to grow rapidly. A number of developing nations fall into this category, particularly in Latin America. In fact, this profile is that of England and Wales in 1901.

If a campaign for fertility control is now started and is successful, the birth rate will fall, with the result that the base of the population pyramid will become pinched in the 0 to 4 age group cohort. However, the 5 to 9 and the 10 to 14 age cohorts will not be affected and will overhang the base. As health care becomes more effective, the age of death is delayed and the upper steps of the population pyramid become proportionately wider (Fig. 2/6). The effect of the health measures on control

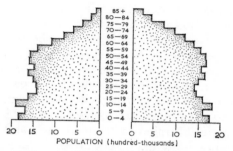

FIG. 2/6. Population pyramid—late transitional. This population profile is typical of nations which have done much to control both fertility and mortality before the age of 65. It is typical of most developed nations. It is, in fact, that of England and Wales in 1961.

of mortality in infancy also has the effect that more children reach the reproductive age, which will increase fertility—more children being born with a resulting broadening of the base of the pyramid.

These findings are illustrated in the accompanying population pyramids, and show the use of the technique in the study of population dynamics. It will be noted, for example, that the population pyramids illustrated give the proportion of young people and that of old people in the community, and that the dependency ratios for each sex can be derived from the information given.

6

The 1960s have been characterized in western countries by an apparent increasing permissiveness in sexual matters, a greater openness in discussion of sex and an apparent increase in extra-marital sexual intercourse. Despite this changed attitude in western countries, both in them and in the rest of the world, most conceptions which end in the birth of a child lead to, or occur within, marriage. In studies in Australia, Britain and the U.S.A. it has been found that only between 6 and 10 per cent of babies are born to single girls, although it is likely that between 15 and 35 per cent of conceptions occur outside marriage, the couple marrying before the child is born. Other cultural patterns are found in other areas. In Central and Southern Africa child marriage (before the age of 16) is usual. In India most girls are married between puberty and the age of 18. In Islamic countries early marriage is usual and conceptions outside marriage exceptional. In the Caribbean and South America a married category in which the partners live together without a formal marriage is not uncommon and between 5 and 20 per cent of marriages fall into this category. It is termed consensual union or 'conviviente', and is similar to *de facto* or common-law marriages of Anglo-Saxon nations.

It is apparent that marital status has a considerable influence on population dynamics. In fact, the key-index to population growth is not the number of fecund females (that is women potentially able to bear a child) but the number of cohabiting fecund females.

Of course, a proportion of men and women never marry. As far as population dynamics are concerned, the proportion of women who do not marry is the more important. In most nations, whether developed or developing (with the exception of Ireland), over 80 per cent of women have married by the age of 30, and 90 to 99 per cent by the age of 35. In Western nations divorce is common, but many divorced women either remarry or form a semi-permanent relationship with a man. In all nations, because of better health care, and a lowered mortality, widowhood is becoming less common. For example, in 1920–30, between 10 and 20 per cent of women aged 30 in India and Sri Lanka were widowed. Today the percentage is less than 5. The fall has been less marked in the developed nations, where in 1920–30, because of good health care, only between 1 and 2 per cent of women were widowed at 30. Today the proportion is less than 1 per cent.

As well as celibacy and premature widowhood, a proportion of married couples fail to have a child, despite the desire. It

56

has been calculated that in the developed nations between 10 and 15 per cent of wives who want to become pregnant have not done so after one year of marriage. Investigation and treatment of infertility permits about 4 out of every 10 infertile married couples to achieve the desired pregnancy. Although the incidence of involuntary infertility is higher in a few developing nations (mainly because of infection of the internal female genital organs, or of the male, due to gonorrhoea), in most the proportion of infertile couples is similar to that found in the developed nations.

Once the never-married women, the infertile couples, and the women widowed prematurely are excluded, over 75 per cent of women of reproductive age in a population are at risk of becoming pregnant or are delighted to be able to become pregnant (depending on their point of view). And in the absence of birth control or of induced abortion, most will become pregnant at fairly frequent intervals. This clearly plays an important part in population dynamics. It is therefore quite obvious that the number of pregnancies, and of live births, which occur to a woman is influenced by the age at which she marries. The earlier she marries the more children is she likely to have.

Age at marriage is considerably influenced by cultural attitudes. In India it is customary for Hindu girls to be formally married at puberty, although the first coitus is usually delayed for 2 to 4 years. In Central and Southern Africa child marriage is usual (that is marriage when the girl is less than 16). In these societies coition is not delayed as in India and the girl's fertility is proved whilst she is still less than 18. In Islamic countries custom encourages an early age of marriage for females. In the industrial or post-industrial nations of Europe and North America the age of marriage has become earlier for both males and females in the past 50 years, and this has been more marked since 1940. In part, this is due to the greater affluence of the country, with higher wages being obtainable by men of 18 years and over; in part, it is due to a consumer society and the availability of many goods on hire-purchase. The necessity to save to purchase furniture is thus reduced, and marriage becomes economically feasible at an earlier age. There is also a factor of imitation; if other members of the peer group tend to marry earlier the custom spreads. In China it would appear from the limited information available that early arranged marriages are discouraged and that the age at first marriage is rising, partly in deference to the wishes of the Government and the Chairman of the Communist Party.

The study of population dynamics, and the understanding of the effects of the current, exceptional, rate of population growth, is clearly of vital importance to the survival of mankind. It is only when the majority of the people become aware of a problem, and are able to determine its magnitude, however incompletely, that positive political action is likely to be taken, and the co-operation of the people obtained. People can be forced to take measures which they oppose, but for success in any venture, their willing support, given voluntarily, is the major ingredient. An informed co-operative people can alter cultural patterns quite radically. And mankind needs to alter its attitude to uncontrolled fertility. This chapter has opened the discussion on population dynamics. In the next chapter the crucial matters of the increasing birth rate and the diminishing death rate, particularly of infants and children, are considered in greater detail.

CHAPTER THREE

Births . . . and . . . Deaths

Birth and copulation and death
That's all the facts when you come to brass tacks.

'Sweeny Agonistes',
T. S. ELIOT.

I

Births . . .

The rate of population growth depends on the annual excess of births over deaths, and on the age-specific patterns of fertility and of mortality. If the excess of births is large, for example, if the crude birth rate exceeds the crude death rate by 20 or more, and if the age-specific mortality of the age groups 0 to 4 years, 5 to 9 years and 10 to 14 years is falling, or has fallen, the nation can anticipate it is going to have an unprecedented reproductive growth rate, which is likely to cause a variety of unpleasant complications.

The main question today is, can the desire of man and woman to reproduce excessively be changed? Animals copulate in response to certain physiological alterations in their bodies, and in some species these are controlled by environmental factors. Unless the female is 'on heat', the male is sexually uninterested in her. The human animal has the same urge to copulate in response to physiological stimuli, but the female is much more often at risk of becoming pregnant. The human animal also has a cultural desire for many children, which has developed in the 10,000 years since man learned to cultivate grain and to

59

domesticate wild animals. Prior to that stage man limited the size of his group, probably largely by killing unwanted children, rather than by preventing conception. But once he had ceased to be a gatherer and hunter, and had become an agriculturalist, children became a valuable commodity to be cherished. Children on growing added to the labour pool of the family, or the tribe, for agriculture or for hunting. Children provided security, shelter and food for their parents when they became too old and feeble to work. Children, when adolescent or adult, added to the strength of the family or tribe should fighting break out. These intellectualized needs were mythologized, and in almost all religions children—particularly male children—became needed to ensure that their parents were given help after death. The rites, duties and prayers of a son were needed to ensure a safe passage into another world and a comfortable sojourn there. If the proper prayers were not said, if the proper rites were not carried out, the journey of the soul might be hard, its rest or re-incarnation unpleasant. And since the rituals could only be carried out by blood relatives, a man wanted many sons, so that they would have many sons, and the rituals would continue for all time.

The fertility of a woman, and its most obvious expression, the birth of a living child, has been a matter of vital concern for all peoples. Only in the last 50 years have men accepted, and then reluctantly, that a woman's inability to conceive might be the fault of her husband. Previously this concept seemed ridiculous. If a male copulated, and on reaching orgasm, ejaculated, it was obvious that he had introduced the necessary ingredient to ensure that a child would result. If the woman's belly failed to swell, if a child failed to appear, it was clearly the fault of the woman. Since between 5 and 15 per cent of women in a society failed to become pregnant, rites were devised, astrologers and wise men were consulted, diets were instituted to ensure fertility and to make the barren woman fertile. In the society the pregnant woman was given special status and the birth of the child was surrounded by ritual.

Despite the glorification of fertility, practices were evolved, at specific times when hardship or famine was present, to control fertility so that the available supply of food, and land, could be more readily shared. When the circumstances changed, and when more children were needed, for example, after war, famine or pestilence, the practices were dropped. In many societies abortion was permitted. In some, infanticide was practised, especially of defective-looking babies and twin births, or of surplus female infants. In other societies fertility was reduced by social customs. Women were segregated for long periods after childbirth for ritual reasons. Many societies observed that breast feeding reduced fertility and so they encouraged prolonged lactation not only for the sake of the existing child, but also to prevent a new conception. Still other societies encouraged the belief that copulation was weakening to the male, and that ejaculation removed a vital essence from him. This is developed to extremes in Rajputana where the men believe that a drop of semen takes 40 days to make at a cost of 40 drops of blood, and it is better to avoid coitus if you can. The obvious implication is that copulation should only take place infrequently.

But despite the restraints, the fertility of a woman was of vital concern to the society in which she lived. Today, as death control has become increasingly effective, fertility is of concern, not only to the individual, but to the nation and to the world. Sanitary engineering, by providing pure water and by eliminating insect-borne diseases, and medical science have drastically reduced infant and childhood deaths, so that more and more children reach the reproductive years. These are conventionally described as being from 15 to 49. It is true that a few girls become pregnant before the age of 15, but this is balanced by the low fertility of women aged 45 to 49.

2

The impact of fertility cannot be assessed unless it is measured. Demographers have agreed that six measurements are of value in analysing the fertility of a nation. Each measurement requires accurate information, and as the measurements become more sophisticated, so does the information required. For this reason, not all the calculations can be done for every nation.

The simplest measure is the *crude birth rate*. It will be recalled that this is obtained by dividing the number of live births, registered in the population during a year, by the total population at mid-year, and for convenience, multiplying the result by 1,000. It is called crude, and it is. But even using this relatively simple measure of natality it is probable that in 1970 only 60 per cent of the world's births were registered. In the 209 nations in the world, birth registration is thought to have been complete in 87, to have been incomplete in 68 and in 54 nations no birth data were recorded. This is the reason why demographers can only estimate the world's population within a range of plus or minus 10 per cent.

The crude birth rate pays no attention to the age structure of the population, which may contain a disproportionate number of young or old people. This will have a considerable influence on future fertility so that the value of the crude birth rate in the analysis of population dynamics is limited.

When he can obtain the necessary data a demographer uses more refined measures of fertility. A commonly used index which is of value in analysing population dynamics is the general fertility rate. This rate was mentioned in Chapter 2 and is obtained by dividing the number of live births occurring in a year by the number of women aged 15 to 49 in the population at mid-year. As with the crude birth rate, the result is multiplied by 1,000.

Age-specific fertility rates are even more refined and were described in Chapter 2. Unless age-specific fertility rates can be calculated, other, more precise, measurements of fertility cannot be computed. It will be recalled that age-specific fertility rates are obtained by dividing the number of births to women in each age group (and these are usually 5-year age groups) by the total number of women in that age group in the population at mid-year. Once again, the result is multiplied by 1,000. The age-specific fertility rate for Sri Lanka (Ceylon) for 1963, and the other measurements of fertility are shown in Fig. 3/1.

Age-specific fertility rates give a great deal of information about trends in fertility between nations and over a time period within a nation. In Fig. 3/2 the age-specific birth rates for Australia between 1921 and 1971 are shown graphically.

If the curve is followed it can be seen that throughout the period the age-specific birth rates of women aged 35 and older have tended to fall, that of women aged 30 to 34 have remained

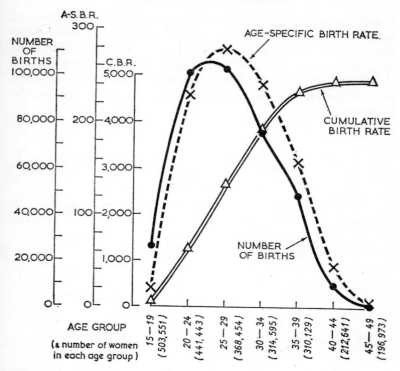

FIG. 3/1. Calculation of birth (fertility) rates, using Sri Lanka (Ceylon) as an example (1963 census).

$$\text{Crude birth rate} = \frac{\text{Total births}}{\text{Total population}} \times 1,000$$

$$= \frac{364,472}{10,595,116} \times 1,000 = 34\cdot4$$

$$\text{General birth rate} = \frac{\text{Total births}}{\text{Total women aged } 15\text{–}49} \times 1,000$$

$$= \frac{364,472}{2,347,786} \times 1,000 = 155$$

$$\text{Age-specific birth rate} = \frac{\text{No. of births in age group}}{\text{No. of women in age group}} \times 1,000$$

Cumulative birth rate = A.S.B.R. × 5, cumulated by age

$$\text{Total birth (fertility) rate} = \text{Sum of A.S.B.R.} \times \text{interval}$$
$$= 981\cdot5 \times 5 = 4907$$

63

relatively unchanged, whilst the age-specific birth rates of women aged 15 to 19 and 20 to 24 have risen spectacularly since 1941. From these changes it can be determined that Australian women marry earlier and have children at an earlier age than 50 years ago. The figure also shows that they have fewer children, but this is better calculated from age-specific birth rate tables.

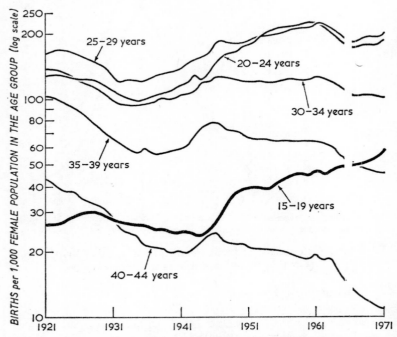

FIG. 3/2. Age-specific fertility rates in Australia, 1921–71. Note how women have decided to have children at an earlier age over the fifty-year period. Source: Australian Bureau of Census.

An informative calculation is that of the *total fertility rate*. This gives an estimate of the number of births that 1,000 women would have if the age-specific birth rates of a given year persisted. It is made by adding the individual age-specific birth rates and by multiplying the result by 5. The total fertility rate for Sri Lanka is shown in Fig. 3/1, p. 63; and that for Australia at various years can be calculated from Fig. 3/2.

The total fertility rate indicates the total number of children the women will have. But only female children can have babies, so a more sophisticated measure of the fertility of the population, the *gross reproduction* rate, is made, determining the number of female children born to the 1,000 women. This is obtained by multiplying the total fertility rate by the percentage of births which are female in the year.

3

Thomas Malthus' belief that the pressure of population could only be reduced by sexual continence outside marriage, and delay in marriage, has some substance. However, most people in most nations resolutely refused to do what Malthus expected. The two exceptions amongst western nations were Ireland and France, where for different reasons, either marriage was delayed or sexual continence was practised.

Between 1770 and 1840 Ireland had experienced a surge of population growth. The population had increased from 3 million to 8 million, which made Ireland one of the most densely populated nations in Europe. The people were miserably poor. Travellers to Ireland who could be objective were appalled. The Frenchman, de Beaumont, writing in 1839, found the 'extreme of human misery worse than the negro in his chains', and even the Duke of Wellington, ultra-conservative as he was, remembered his Irish origins enough to write in 1838, 'There never was a country in which poverty existed to the extent it exists in Ireland.' In the census of 1841 the Commissioners found that nearly half the families in the rural areas lived in single-roomed, windowless, mud-walled cabins. Pigs and chickens lived in the cabins and shared the floors with the children. There was no furniture. In 1837, in Tullahobagly in County Donegal, there were 9,000 inhabitants who had between them 10 beds, 93 chairs and 240 stools.

The misery and poverty were the direct result of the land tenure system. The land was owned by Englishmen, who had obtained it following the English occupation of Ireland which began 700 years earlier, and had added to their holdings after subsequent rebellions, by confiscations and by punitive laws.

The absentee landlords regarded Ireland as a desolate, despicable place in which no gentleman could live, but which, through rents, could provide an income for a gentleman to live in England. The land was farmed out to middlemen at a fixed rent, and they exploited the peasants to get all they could from them. In their own country the peasants were landless, they had no security of tenure and any improvement that they made to the land increased the rent they paid. The power of the landlord—and more particularly of the middleman—was so great that, according to John Stuart Mill, 'the whole agricultural population can be evicted by the mere will of the landlord, either at the expiration of a lease or, in the far more common case of their having no lease, at six months' notice'.

Despite the oppression, despite the poverty and despite the malnutrition, the Irish peasants had an unexpected gaiety. When there was work they worked. On their own plots, which rarely exceeded half an acre (0·2 hectare), they grew potatoes. Potatoes require little attention, so much of their time, particularly in winter, consisted in sitting around the turf fire, telling stories and drinking poteen, whilst outside the cabin the wind howled and the rain fell. They were, moreover, hospitable and had a cultural courtesy. If a stranger came he was made welcome, a stone was rolled that he might sit near the fire, and he was given a bowl of potatoes and buttermilk. The poverty was intense, but the spirit was great, and the opposition of the Irish to, and hatred of, the English was deep, lasting and binding.

There is no explanation why the population grew so rapidly in the 60 years after 1780. Sanitation was rudimentary, medical care non-existent and there was little migration to the towns. Yet the population of Ireland grew at double the rate of England and Wales, and for a while reached today's critical growth rate of 2·5 per cent per annum. It could have been due to the good potato harvests and an abundance of buttermilk, for every peasant had his cow. The Irish also married early. Girls married at 16, boys at 18—and as the Bishop of Raphoe told the Irish Poor Enquiry of 1835, 'They cannot be worse off than they are . . . and they may help each other.' With a high infant mortality, and no prospect of saving for old age, children were a safeguard, a comfort and insurance against destitution.

With few prospects, with no security of land tenure, with a sullen hostility towards the foreigners who oppressed him, the Irish peasant retreated into his warm cabin where the turf fire burned all year. He told tales of a mythical golden age when the Irish were free of domination. He drank poteen and buttermilk. He sired children. And the entire family existed on a diet of potato. It was not an idyllic existence, but it was all that the peasants knew, and they survived and multiplied.

Unemployment was high. Apart from the thirty weeks of the year, between planting and harvesting the potato, over three quarters of the Irish peasantry had no work. They could survive if they had sufficient land to grow the ubiquitous potato. Without that the peasant and his family starved. As the population increased, land became more precious than gold. Legally, and illegally, the small peasant plots were divided and further subdivided, and rents rose as the middlemen took their profits. Eventually, most peasants had less than a quarter acre (0·101 hectare), and it needed an acre (0·405 hectare) to provide food for a family, the cow, the pig and the fowls. But if there were potatoes there was hope of survival.

In 1844 the summer started well. The weather in July was dry and hot, the potato crop was flourishing. Then in late July it changed. For three weeks 'chilling rain, and some fog' swept over Ireland. Despite this the crop appeared to be thriving. In September the bad weather continued. Then in England, in Europe and in Ireland, the plants began to wilt and the wilt coincided with further bad weather. By October, which was the time for harvesting, it was clear that the crop would fail. It was not due to the rain, but to potato blight—brought in from North America. When the potatoes were dug up they looked healthy, but within a few days they had become a rotting, stinking mass, which even the pigs refused to eat. The great famine had begun.

It was to continue for four years, during which time one and a half million Irish peasants were to die of starvation or disease, mainly typhus, and one million were to emigrate, mostly to North America. America sent the potato blight, and in return took the turbulent Irish!

In 1851, when it was all over, the population of Ireland had fallen to 6·5 million. In the Province of Connaught, 29 per cent of the population had died or migrated, in Munster 24 per cent, and in Leinster and Ulster 16 per cent of the population had gone.

The effect of the famine on the Irish was extreme. No longer did the peasant welcome the stranger, no longer did he enjoy his children in his cabin. In place, a hatred overwhelmed him, and he vowed that such a disaster would never again occur. He knew what had happened. He knew he could no longer sire a child annually. The sight of children slowly wasting away, of children whimpering from hunger, of children dying from fever or diarrhoea, had cut a jagged gash into his consciousness. And he knew the potato crop might fail once more. Land could no longer be divided and divided again, until there was insufficient for each family to survive. Men could no longer marry young, they must be sustained by their faith, and remain abstinent, only marrying when they had land of their own. Migration must continue.

The cultural change occurred rapidly. Within 10 years of the famine the birth rate in Ireland declined precipitously and the growth rate of the population was markedly reduced, finally ceased and there became a decline in population. It came about by a simple device. Land tenancy passed to the eldest son, who postponed marriage until his father was too old or feeble to work. For the other sons there was nothing, and no reason for staying in Ireland. So they, and the girls who saw no hope of marriage, emigrated, or else remained single. Between 1845 and 1940 the birth rate fell from 30 to 21 per 1,000, and the death rate declined to 11 per 1,000. But with a high rate of emigration there was a negative population growth, averaging 150,000 a decade, so that in 1940 Ireland had a population of less than three million.

In Ireland Malthus' solution to population growth had occurred. The Irish, uniquely amongst the nations, had adopted sexual continence and late marriage, allied with emigration, to solve their population problem, but they had only done this after a disastrous famine, which had brought misery to an entire nation.

In France the potato famine of the 1840's was avoided, but the population failed to grow at the rate of the rest of Europe. Between 1770 and 1870 France's population growth rate of

1·0 per cent per annum was half that of the rest of Europe, and over the period declined to become almost zero. The reason for this was not due to environmental causes but the intense feeling of the French peasant for land, and to Napoleon's Civil Code. This law ordained that parents had to bequeath a determined portion of land to each child. As the French peasant landowner was conservative, and suspicious of others, but a realist, he saw that his hard-won property would be dispersed and would disintegrate as an economic entity if he had too many children. So he didn't. It is likely that coitus interruptus, rather than sexual continence, was his solution, but there is no real evidence.

4

Although the examples of Ireland and France do not apply to most nations, a study of fertility, on a world-wide basis, does uncover certain facts. Thomas Malthus' view that early marriage favoured large families has been confirmed. For example, in England, if the wife was under the age of 20 when she married in 1957, she was likely to have had 2·47 live births by 1967, in ten years of marriage; whilst if she married at 30 she was only likely to have 1·25 live births. The effect of age at marriage on fertility is now less than it was in the past because of contraception, but it continues to have an effect, especially in the developing nations.

The social status of the husband also has an effect on the fertility of the couple. If the population is divided into groups which depend on the socio-economic status of the husband, it is found that the higher the social class the fewer are the number of children in the family. This applies in western nations irrespective of the income or place of residence of the couple. It is not so obvious in the developing nations. For example, in India, rich rural women have more children than poor peasant women living in the same area. The difference may be due to the better health of the rich women, to the fact that peasant women breast feed their babies for longer or to the fact that, quite often, their husbands are away from home seeking work in another village or in the towns.

It has also been observed that rural women are more likely to have large families than urban women. This was observed in England in Malthus' time, and is still found in most developing nations today. In the rural area a child is an advantage, for once it is old enough to walk it can help by looking after the geese, or chickens, by carrying water from the well, or by bringing in dung or wood for fuel. In the urban areas a child is a disadvantage, for he requires to be cared for at all times, and is an economic liability.

Throughout the world there is a strong inverse relationship between educational attainment and the number of children a couple decide to have. The higher the proportion of the population which is illiterate, the higher is the birth rate, although there are variations. John Smith, who has been to University, is likely to marry later and to have fewer children than Joe Bloggs, who left school at 15, who impregnated a girl at 17, who was forced to marry her at $17\frac{1}{2}$, and who has had five children by her by the time he is 28. It is not quite clear why this should be so, particularly in western nations, where contraceptives are reasonably readily available. It may be because of ignorance about sexuality, reluctance of the woman to seek a reliable contraceptive from a middle-class doctor or to fatalism. Whatever the reason, the difference exists in every nation which has been studied. The information has been particularly well quantified in the U.S.A. and is shown in Fig. 3/3. The figures are taken from the 1960 census, and the trend is obvious.

In summary: women of the lower socio-economic groups, living in non-urban areas, who have left school at the earliest opportunity and who marry early, are likely to have more than the average number of children. Women whose fathers or husbands belong to the upper socio-economic groups, who complete secondary, and often tertiary, education, who live in urban areas and who tend to marry later, have less than the average number of children, and today are tending to the two-child family.

The distinction is becoming rather blurred as efficient contraceptives become more readily available, but it persists. It has led to concern that the disparity will lead increasingly to a poorer genetic pool—the unintelligent tending to swamp the intelligent. This fear is unfounded. Firstly, there is no definite

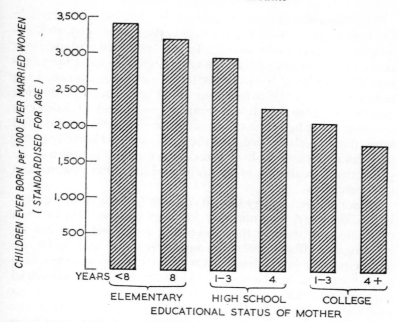

FIG. 3/3. Educational attainment and fertility in the U.S.A. The more years of education, the smaller is a woman's completed family. Source: U.S. Bureau of Census and Statistics, Census of 1960.

relationship between income and intelligence; and secondly, there is a desire, as evidenced by social surveys, by poorer women to limit the size of their families.

5

. . . and Deaths

The 'population explosion' of today would not have occurred if there had not been changes in the pattern of mortality, and particularly in age-specific death rates. No one has yet found a way to avoid death. Inevitably a person dies, and the inexorable journey towards death begins at the moment of conception. Good nutrition, good sanitation and good medical care have had the effect of delaying the moment of death, so that, statistically, a person's life-expectancy at birth has increased.

Births . . . and . . . Deaths

The particular impact of death delay has been observed in the past 75 years, with a more rapid effect since 1945, particularly in the developing nations. In the developed nations, since 1900, the death rates of infants and of children have been falling. This has been due to better nutrition which has raised the resistance of the child to infection. It has been due to a reduction of overcrowding which encouraged the spread of infectious diseases. It has been due to the provision of safe water and good sanitation, which has reduced the incidence and severity of the diarrhoeal diseases. It has been due to the medical control, by protective inoculation, of the childhood infectious diseases and of tuberculosis.

If modern technology has given these benefits to one group, it has increased the mortality in other groups. Deaths from accidents, particularly those involving motor vehicles, are increasing and affect mainly men aged between 17 and 35. Deaths from coronary heart disease, again particularly amongst men aged 35 to 55, are increasing. They appear to be associated with modern life, and an over-abundant diet taken by an under-exercising male. Deaths from lung cancer, whether due to tobacco pollution or to environmental pollution, and from other respiratory diseases, which are certainly aggravated by increased environmental pollution, are increasing. These particularly affect men and women in the 55- to 75-year age groups.

On balance, however, there has been a considerable reduction in the death rate in the past 50 years, with a considerable prolongation of life. This reduction in the death rate has been particularly found amongst infants, children and adolescents. The result is that increasing numbers of children now reach the reproductive years and have children of their own. An example of this changing pattern of mortality is given by comparing the deaths for every 1,000 conceptions occurring in England and Wales in the 100 years between 1860 and 1960 (Fig. 3/4). You can see that deaths in infancy have been reduced sevenfold, those in childhood fourteen times and those in the reproductive years fivefold. The table also shows that in 1860 only 530 of the 1,000 children conceived reached the age of 15, whilst in 1960 796 of them did. The importance of these observations in population dynamics is obvious. It is even more

72

marked because the reduction in infant and childhood deaths is occurring in all nations.

The death of an infant, or child, has a far greater social economic and demographic effect than the death of an old person. When an old man dies, it does little demographically except reduce the population by one, although it may be the occasion of joy, or sorrow, for his relatives. The death of an in-

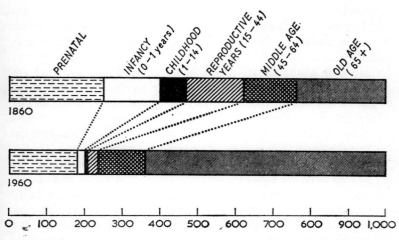

FIG. 3/4. Mortality per 1,000 conceptions in England and Wales in 1860 (partly estimated) and 1960. 'Prenatal' includes abortions and stillbirths. Life expectancy at birth has increased from 43 years in 1860 to 72 years in 1960.

fant or young child, on the other hand, means a reduction not only of one person, but of the many descendants the child might have had if he had lived. The death of an adolescent has the same demographic effect, but also represents the economic loss of a person in whom an investment has been made (by the cost of care and feeding, by that of schooling and further training) but who has scarcely begun to give an economic return.

Mortality is measured from information obtained from death certificates, which are needed in many nations before burial is permitted. In most of the developed nations the death certificate is completed by a qualified doctor and gives details of the age, the sex, the race and the cause of death. Because of a shortage of physicians in most developing nations, particularly in the rural areas, certification of death, when it is required, is made by a government official, a village headman, or a policeman, and the data, especially the cause of death, are often speculative. In addition, many deaths are not registered. This is especially so of infants, dying soon after birth. The parents see little point of going to the police post to register the birth, and the death, of the infant at the same time. It is worrying to have to give information, bribes are often required, and to many peasants the death of an infant is essentially a private matter.

An example of under-reporting can be deduced from information deriving from Indonesia. In 1967 a social and economic survey was undertaken. One of the measurements made was to record the deaths of infants by their age at the time of death. From these data the infant mortality rate, that is the number of deaths of infants aged less than 1 year per 1,000 live births, was estimated. The figures reported an infant mortality rate of 40·6 for urban areas and 78·4 for the rural areas of Java–Madura. The islands of Java and Madura are the most densely populated in the Indonesian archipelago and over 85 million of the 125 million Indonesians live in them.

The infant mortality rates of 40·6 and 78·4 for the urban and rural areas were suspiciously low, and are only half of what might be expected from the recorded numbers of children ever born and surviving. As well as this, the proportion of infants dying in the first 28 days of life (the neonatal deaths), which were recorded as 36 and 26 per cent for the urban and rural areas respectively, were very much lower than those reported from other nations at a similar stage of socio-economic development.

This has led one demographer, Dr. Ruzicka, who is an ex-

74

pert in the population problems of South East Asia, to 'venture that some 35 per cent of neonatal deaths in urban areas and about 50 per cent in rural areas were missed'.

For this, and other reasons, the measurement of mortality, and particularly of infant mortality, tends to be less accurate than that of fertility. It is likely that only half of the births occurring in the world are recorded and notified, but only one-third of the world's deaths are notified to the department of government which deals with vital statistics.

The effect of this under-reporting makes accuracy in population projections difficult, as I mentioned in Chapter 1. Luckily, two measures of mortality are of some value. One of them is the *crude death rate*, which is calculated in a similar way to the crude birth rate and is

$$\text{Crude death rate} = \frac{\text{Deaths in a given year}}{\text{Population at mid-year}} \times 1,000.$$

The second is *age-specific death rates*. Once again these are calculated by obtaining the ratio of deaths occurring in a year to people of a precise age group divided by the total number of people in that age group in the country at mid-year. Because the result is less than 1, for convenience it is multiplied by 1,000, to represent the age-specific death rate per 1,000 population.

Births only occur to women in the reproductive years, but death can occur at any time. Age-specific death rates are more extensive than age-specific birth rates, although with one exception, 5-year age groups are used for convenience. The exception is in the 0 to 4 age group. Because of the relatively high mortality in the first year of life, the group is split into two parts. The first is the period 0–1 year. As has been mentioned, deaths in this period are computed separately and are reported as infant mortality. This is calculated as the number of deaths per 1,000 live births (rather than the number of deaths per 1,000 children alive at mid-year, but the difference is small).

The age-specific death rates, when plotted, tend to follow a 'U' shaped curve both in the developed and in the developing nations. Mortality tends to be high in the first year of life but then falls rapidly reaching a trough by the age of 10 to 20 in the developing nations, and from 5 to 40 in the developed nations, after which it rises. Using age-specific mortality rates it is possible to compare the mortality of two nations and of the two racial groups within the most affluent of all nations, the U.S.A.

In Fig. 3/5 the age-specific mortality rates of India and Sweden are compared. The figure shows clearly how, at all ages up to 60 but especially in infancy, far more Indians die than do Swedes. This is a measure of the better socio-economic conditions under which Swedes live.

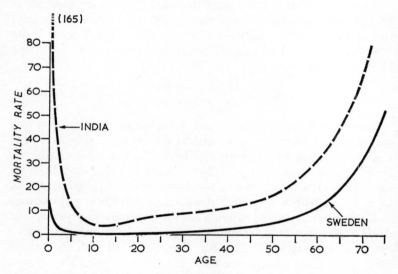

FIG. 3/5. Age-specific death rates, India and Sweden, 1961.

Figure 3/6 shows how socio-economic conditions affect the mortality of citizens of a nation. The age-specific mortality of Black Americans exceeds that of White Americans at all ages up to 65. But although Black Americans are disadvantaged when compared with White Americans, they have relatively low age-specific death rates when compared with Indians, and indeed with the citizens of all large underdeveloped nations, particularly those of Black Africa.

But this should not obscure the fact that age-specific mortality differences do exist even in the richest nation in the world. It emphasizes the problems facing the poor nations, who are currently trying to reduce age-specific death rates and to increase longevity.

The reasons for the higher age-specific mortality rates in the developing nations of the Third World are many and complex. Most are preventible, or reversible, provided the essential resources of manpower, materials and money are available. A different strategy may be required to effect change in different countries and when the mortality at specific ages is considered.

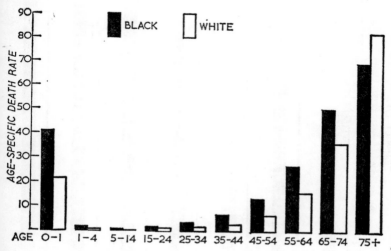

F<small>IG</small>. 3/6. The racial differences in age-specific death rate, U.S.A., 1964. Source: U.S. Public Health Service, *Vital Statistics of the United States*, 1964 Report.

There is ample evidence, for example, from many sources to show that age-specific mortality, particularly in infancy and childhood, is considerably affected by poor sanitation, lack of education of the parents, ignorance of hygiene, malnutrition, overcrowding and inadequate medical care. There is also evidence that deaths in the reproductive years increase if the same conditions permit the spread of infectious disease, especially tuberculosis, and when poor obstetric care and inadequate nutrition increase the deaths of women in pregnancy and labour. In fact, in some nations, the increase in maternal deaths has caused a reversal of the usual finding that women live longer than men. This is conveniently calculated by the actuarial 'life table' in which life-expectancy at birth is recorded. In Fig. 3/7 the longer life-expectancy at birth of the developed nations is shown, and the reversal of the anticipated life-expectancy of females in India is demonstrated.

In the study of population dynamics, the deaths of infants aged 0 to 1 are of particular concern. As we have seen, this

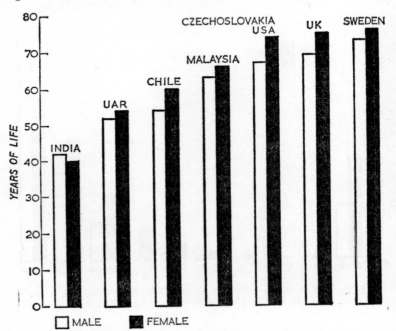

FIG. 3/7. Life expectancy at birth, selected nations. Source: *Demographic Yearbook*, various years, U.N., New York.

group has the highest age-specific mortality until old age is reached. It is also the group in which mortality is most easily influenced by preventive health measures and specific health programmes.

If such programmes are successful infant mortality will be reduced and an increasing number of children will reach biological maturity, and add, within a few years, to the population explosion by their sexual activity. On the other side of the coin, there is evidence that unless the infant mortality can be reduced significantly in the countries of the Third World, the women will not readily accept birth control. Unless a woman can be sure that her existing children will live she will not accept family limitation.

There is a very considerable difference in infant mortality rates between the developed and developing nations. No developed nation has an infant mortality rate above 35; no developing nation has an infant mortality rate below 35, and in most cases the rate is very much higher.

The reduction in infant mortality has been occurring in the developed nations over the past 150 years. Sweden, uniquely,

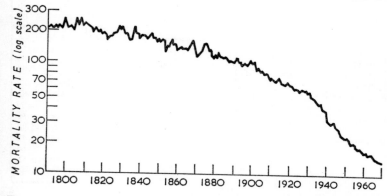

FIG. 3/8. The decline in infant mortality in Sweden since 1800.
Source: Statistiska Centralbyran, Sweden.

has kept accurate statistics about infant mortality since 1750. Until 1850 the rate was between 250 and 150 and over the century the trend was downwards (Fig. 3/8). Between 1850 and 1900 the infant mortality rate dropped to 100. These changes were not due to better medical care, for advances in paediatric care were rudimentary, but were due to improvements in living conditions, to better food and to control of water-carried infections by providing pure water. But after 1900 medical science added to the decline, by the provision of preventive inoculations and by drugs. Since 1935 the downward trend has been even steeper. This is due to better training of physicians in child health and to the development of potent antibiotic drugs.

There is a lower limit. It is unlikely with our present knowledge that the infant mortality rate will ever drop below 8 per 1,000 live births, and will probably not drop below 12 per 1,000 live births. If this is the outlook for Sven Svendsen born in 1974 it is the prospect which national leaders would like to be able to offer N'gumbo or Raju or Chinnathamby, or Maria or Fatimah. They, too, are children born in 1974 in nations where

VERY HIGH	HIGH	MODERATELY HIGH	INTER-MEDIATE	LOW
250 — 150	149 — 100	99 — 50	49 — 25	24 or less
Angola 230	Morocco 149	Rhodesia 95	Venezuela 45	Canada 21
Mali 190	Malawi 145	Algeria 86	Caribbean	USA 20
Zambia 190	Cameroon 140	Tunisia 84	islands 40	
Up.Volta 180	Kenya 130		Cuba 40	Austria 24
Ivory C'st 180	Nigeria 130	Guatemala 94		W. Germany 23
Uganda 160	Sudan 120	Chile 92	Poland 35	Czecho-
Tanzania 160	Zaire 120	Ecuador 86	Hungary 34	slovakia 23
Ghana 156	Malagasy 120	Colombia 78	Bulgaria 31	Belgium 22
	UAR 115	Mexico 65	Greece 31	E.Germany 20
		Peru 65	Italy 30	UK 19
Brazil 170	Haiti 130	Argentina 54	Spain 30	France 16
	Bolivia 110		USSR 25	Switzerland 15
		Portugal 56		Denmark 15
		Yugoslavia 55		Finland 14
		Romania 54		Netherlands 13
				Sweden 13
	Turkey 155	Philippines 80		
Bangladesh 180	India 140	Thailand 70		
Pakistan 150	Cambodia 140	Malaysia 70	Taiwan 25	Japan 16
Indonesia 150	N.Korea 135	S. Korea 60		
	Iraq 120	Sri Lanka 55		Australia 17

FIG. 3/9. Infant mortality per 1,000 live births in some nations of more than 5 million population, 1970–71. Source: *Demographic Yearbook*, various years, U.N., New York. Note: Some of the infant mortality rates of the developing nations are probably underestimated.

the infant mortality rates are high. In Fig. 3/9 the infant mortality rates of nations with more than 5 million people are shown. As was mentioned when the example of Indonesia was given, it is probable that many of those reported from the developing nations are underestimated by between 30 and 50 per cent, but the extent of the problem can be seen.

It is a problem which should concern people. The lesson is that as more and more nations seek to reduce infant and childhood mortality, more and more children will survive to reach maturity.

Since no sane person would welcome a dramatic increase in infant and childhood mortality as a means of reducing the rate of population growth, it is clear that all our efforts must be directed to reducing the birth rate, so that in the shortest possible time birth control will be as effective as death control has been in the last half century. This objective is more likely to be achieved if the deaths of infants, and particularly those which occur around the time of birth and which account for over two-thirds of infant deaths, can be reduced. The deaths of infants around the time of birth is termed perinatal mortality. At this moment, in many nations, perinatal mortality is being investigated in considerable depth.

CHAPTER FOUR

Don't Let My Baby Die!

I

Mrs. Smith had always wanted a boy. Ever since she was a child she had wanted to have a large family and the children were to be boys. She had married at the age of 18 and by the time she was 25 had had five pregnancies, one of which had ended as a spontaneous abortion, and the rest had gone on the full time. All the children had been daughters. Now Mrs. Smith was pregnant once again. She was a sensible woman and had gone to see her doctor early on. She had done all the right things during the pregnancy, too. When she had been told to diet, she had dieted; she had watched her weight gain, she had taken her iron tablets, she had attended her doctor's clinic regularly. It was surprising after all this care that one night, when she was 34 weeks' pregnant, she had been woken up by a severe pain in her abdomen and had found she was bleeding. She woke her husband up, and he called the doctor. The pain persisted, and so did the bleeding from her womb, which was particularly tender. Her doctor came, examined her quickly, and at once arranged for her to go into hospital.

'I will be all right, won't I?' she asked.

'Yes, but you will have to be seen by the specialist obstetrician, and I think you will need a blood transfusion,' he replied.

Mrs. Smith could appreciate this. She felt giddy and the walls of the room tended to recede and approach.

With great efficiency and gentleness the ambulance attendants moved her on to the stretcher, and she was driven in to the maternity hospital and put in a bed in the labour room.

Doctors came. A blood transfusion was set up. She heard them talking.

'It appears certain that it's a moderately severe abruptio,' a voice was saying, 'I've checked the fetal heart with the doptone, and it's there, but it's rather rapid.'

She remembered the doctor palpating her abdomen gently and she recalled the machine which had picked up the noise of the baby's heart, and of her happiness when the doctor had told her that he was alive. It was a he, of that she was certain.

A new voice was speaking, new hands were gently palpating her abdomen.

'I'm going to examine you internally,' said the voice. 'Do you think you can relax? It won't be painful.'

Mrs. Smith nodded. She felt doped from an injection she had been given, and the pain in her abdomen was much less. The new doctor examined her internally. He must be the specialist, as the other doctors sounded quite deferential.

'What have you found, sir?' asked one of them.

'The cervix is uneffaced and not ripe,' said the specialist. 'It's certainly a moderate abruptio,' he went on, 'and you said the baby was alive, didn't you?'

'Yes, but the heart rate was rapid.'

Mrs. Smith pulled herself out of the warm mist which was surrounding her. 'Doctor,' she said, 'please don't let my baby die.'

'We don't intend to, Mrs. Smith,' answered the specialist, 'but I'm afraid that you will have to have a Caesarean section'.

'I don't mind, but can I see my husband?'

'Of course you can. We'll call him.'

Mr. Smith was in the delivery floor waiting room, sitting on the edge of a chair, anxiously twining his hands, when the specialist came in.

'I've seen your wife,' he said. 'She has had some bleeding inside her womb, behind the afterbirth, and I think that I should operate. You see, the baby may die if it's left where it is. But I have to say that it is very premature, so we can only hope that it will pull through.'

'I don't mind too much,' said Mr. Smith. 'As long as my wife is all right.'

'She will be. You can be sure of that. And you may see her now whilst we prepare for the Caesarean section.'

Twenty minutes later Mrs. Smith was delivered by Caesarean section of her fifth child. It was a boy, and he weighed 1500 g (3¼ lb.). He was taken to the premature nursery for special care, because of his prematurity and because he had suffered from an oxygen lack after the bleeding had started to separate the placenta. The paediatrician was concerned that the combination of prematurity and oxygen lack might have affected the ability of his lungs to expand fully. And this is what occurred. Richard Smith developed a lung condition called hyaline membrane disease, and despite all the efforts of the nursery staff, he died when only three days old. In the hospital records his death was recorded as due to hyaline membrane disease, due to hypoxia, due to prematurity, due to abruptio placentae. His death had occurred in the perinatal period, that is the period around the time of birth, and it added to the perinatal mortality.

2

The concept of perinatal mortality is fairly new. It arises from the observation that many of the complications of pregnancy which lead to the birth of a stillborn baby are the same as those which cause the death of the newborn baby in the first week or month of life. Previously in many Western nations, stillbirths and neonatal deaths were recorded separately by law. Today an increasing number of nations record the stillbirths and neonatal deaths together and call them perinatal deaths. If the number of perinatal deaths is divided by the total births, alive and still-born, and the result is multiplied by 1,000, the perinatal mortality ratio is obtained. For example, in the year 1970 88,820 births occurred in the State of New South Wales, Australia. During the same year 1,684 babies weighing 1,000 g or more were either stillborn (the actual number was 680) or died in the first week of life. By the calculation

$$\frac{1,684}{88,820} \times 1,000 = 18\cdot8 \text{ per 1,000 births,}$$

the perinatal mortality ratio is obtained.

As will be shown, this ratio is a very good indicator of the health of the nation, or the part of the nation being examined, and perinatal mortality studies are now being conducted increasingly. Altogether, 41 of the 132 nations who form the World Health Organization report national perinatal mortality ratios, and most of these are in Europe, North America or Oceania. Perhaps the most ambitious investigations have been made in Britain, where in 1958 all the perinatal deaths which occurred in one week in March were analysed, and where a further study is in progress.

The time, energy and money expended in recording perinatal mortality statistics, in analysing them and in publishing reports, would be wasted unless some use were made of the results. And use is made. At the level of the hospital, although the statistics can be very misleading if extrapolated to the nation, they are valuable as a method of improving obstetric and paediatric care. Many hospitals have established committees and arrange regular meetings at which the perinatal deaths which have occurred during a given time period are discussed by the medical and nursing staff.

The purpose of these meetings is not to punish the medical attendants for failing to prevent the death of the baby, but to educate administrators, doctors, nurses and other staff in methods of preventing avoidable deaths. It also enables the health workers to identify and correct potentially dangerous procedures. Because of these meetings, problems have been identified and research has taken place to find out ways of preventing the death. One disease which is currently receiving a lot of attention is hyaline membrane disease, which led to the death of Richard Smith.

Perinatal mortality studies have value at a national, or state level, for they give factual information which enables health planners to identify avoidable factors and to suggest corrective action. The information may show that in certain areas the perinatal mortality is higher than the average, and this can lead to further investigations and the deployment of resources to correct the problem.

If women are to accept that birth control is necessary for mankind's survival, they have to be sure that each child they bear has a high chance of survival to adult life. Population control depends to some extent on the knowledge that the perinatal mortality will be low.

3

As far as Mrs. Smith was concerned, she couldn't really care less about statistics. She had lost the son she had so wanted. She felt empty, restless and physically exhausted. She kept on thinking about the pregnancy to see if there was anything she had done which could have caused the bleeding; something for which she was being punished by God. She could find nothing; she had gone to see her doctor early in pregnancy, she had done everything he had told her. Yet she had a feeling of failure; she had failed her husband by failing to give him a live son; she had failed her daughters by being unable to give them a little baby brother.

Luckily, Mrs. Smith was looked after by sympathetic, humane doctors, who knew that the sense of grief following the loss of a newborn baby is no less strong than that which follows the death of an older child or of a husband. They also knew that the recovery from the bereavement is slower in women who suppress their grief.

Psychiatrists are aware that women who deliver a stillborn baby or whose baby dies in the neonatal period need support, reassurance, explanation and help. Discussing the problem of grief, the British Medical Journal in 1967 suggested that 'a willing ear, tolerant of confusion and anger, is probably more important than tonics or sedatives'. Unfortunately, all too often doctors are not prepared to face possible hostility, or resentment, by giving the bereaved mother, and her husband, a simple, rational explanation of the cause of the death as soon as possible after the baby has died. Instead, they prescribe heavy sedation and avoid all talk about the infant's death.

But Mrs. Smith was lucky; the paediatrician who had looked after Richard came to her room and told her quietly and unemotionally about his fight for life, and to a large extent relieved her anxiety. Later, the obstetrician talked with her and with her husband, and answered their questions. Mrs. Smith still wanted a son and had many questions to ask about the chances of the same disaster occurring in the next pregnancy. The obstetrician was able to reassure her that abruptio placentae was unlikely to recur, and that she had every chance of having a live and healthy baby next time. But he couldn't promise what sex it would be! Because the doctors had been prepared to talk frankly and openly and had treated Mrs. Smith as an intelligent human being, she was reassured and her loneliness and guilt disappeared. She felt full of confidence that her next pregnancy would be successful—and that she would have a boy.

4

The perinatal period, that is from about 12 weeks before birth to the end of the first week of life, is one of the most dangerous periods for survival. If age-specific mortality ratios are calculated, a higher proportion of lives are lost in this 13-week period than at any other time of life until the 60 to 64 group is reached. It is for this reason that many research workers are studying the perinatal period to find out ways in which the perinatal mortality ratio can be reduced. Over the past 40 years the ratio has been falling in most affluent developed nations (Fig. 4/1). In most of them the perinatal mortality ratio now lies between 15 and 35 per 1,000 births. The lowest recorded rate is that of Finland, where in 1971, it was 14 per 1,000.

It is likely, with existing knowledge, that a ratio of less than 10 per 1,000 will not be achieved, but the reduction in the past 40 years is in itself remarkable, when one realizes that today, in the developed nations, over 980 out of every 1,000 pregnancies reaching the end of the 28th week after conception, result in a baby which survives the perinatal period. In the developing nations the perinatal mortality ratio is much higher, and in several African countries it exceeds 250 per 1,000 births.

One of the most exhaustive and sophisticated investigations into perinatal mortality is being conducted in Britain, as has been mentioned, as part of a continuing study. In most published statistics the death of the baby is classified in a list of over 160 'causes of death' which have been defined by committees of experts, at meetings organized by the World Health Organization, and which are revised at intervals. These tables give a single cause of death, but as was the case of Richard Smith, the matter is more complicated. Richard died from a disease of the lungs which is almost exclusively associated with prematurity, and the premature birth was necessary to attempt to save him from dying in the uterus as a result of an unexpected, unanticipated separation of the afterbirth from the wall of the womb.

Because of the complex causes leading to perinatal death, Sir Dugald Baird, the Regius Professor of Midwifery in Aberdeen at that time, suggested another classification which was based

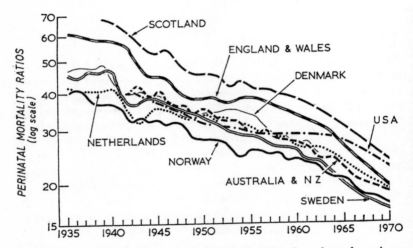

FIG. 4/1. The decline in perinatal mortality in selected nations between 1935 and 1970. Source: *Demographic Yearbook*, various years, U.N., New York and W.H.O. publications, various.

on *how* the baby died, rather than on the actual cause of death. He, and his colleagues, felt that the information obtained from this type of investigation would help research workers to discover ways of reducing the death rate. As the material mounted, and was analysed, it was possible to identify two main groups of causes: those due mainly to environmental factors, and those due mainly to obstetrical factors.

A list of the causes and the number of babies which were included in each category is shown in Table 4/1 for the State of New South Wales, Australia, in 1970; and for the survey week in Britain in 1958.

TABLE 4/I

Clinical causes of perinatal death
(*N.S.W., Australia, 1970 and U.K., 1958*)

Cause	N.S.W. 1970 per cent of total	U.K. 1958 per cent of total
Environmental		
1. Unexplained, low birth weight	23·3	17·4
2. Antepartum haemorrhage	14·2	13·1
3. Malformations	14·4	18·0
4. Maternal disease	5·9	2·4
Obstetric		
5. Toxaemia	6·1	13·1
6. Mechanical/Trauma	14·0	13·1
7. Unexplained, normal birth weight	10·5	15·1
8. Serological incompatibility	4·0	4·8
9. Infection	3·4	1·1
10. Miscellaneous	4·0	2·0
	100·0	100·0
	n = 1,684	*n* = 2,210
Rate	19·4	Rate 30·5

It will help to explain the matter if each of the categories is considered further. The *mainly environmental causes* are ones in which a change in the management of the pregnancy or labour would have had little effect, and in which social or economic factors were considered more important.

The largest sub-section of this category was *unexplained, low birth weight*. This group accounted for about one-fifth of all perinatal deaths. In all of the cases the pregnancy had been normal until the birth occurred prematurely, when a baby weighing 2,500 g (5½ lb.) or less was born after a normal labour. Despite investigations no cause could be found for the low birth weight, and when an autopsy was done on the baby only the immediate cause of death could be found, but there was no indication of how that event occurred. About 14 per cent of the babies are lost because of *antepartum haemorrhage*, that is, bleeding in late pregnancy due to separation of a normal placenta (as occurred in the case of Richard Smith) or bleeding from a low lying placenta, which is called a placenta praevia. *Congenital malformations*, which currently cannot be prevented, caused the death of about 15 per cent of all the infants lost. We know very little about why certain babies fail to develop normally, and are born with severe or minor defects. Thalidomide, as is well known, was one cause, but the drug is no longer used and no other commonly used drug has been found to cause malformed children. The principle is clear, however, and that is that women should avoid all unnecessary medication in pregnancy. An important cause of congenital abnormalities in past years was infection by German measles (or rubella) in early pregnancy. Although many infected women obtained legal abortions, others delivered malformed babies. A safe vaccine is now available. If this is given to all girls by the age of 14 all rubella-induced malformations will cease. The final sub-section of mainly environmental causes of perinatal death are those due to *maternal diseases*, such as diabetes, heart disease or infections. In the developed nations these conditions account for about 5 per cent of all perinatal deaths; but in the developing nations the proportion is higher, because of the widespread prevalence of anaemia in pregnant women.

The other main group of perinatal deaths are those which are due to *mainly obstetric causes*. Since these deaths are due to abnormalities occurring in pregnancy and labour, better obstetric care should prevent many of them. The reduction oi deaths in this group by improved maternity care is a major factor in the lower perinatal mortality in the developed nations. '*Toxaemia of pregnancy*' is defined as a raised blood pressure which occurs for the first time in the second half of pregnancy, and which is often associated with the presence of protein in the urine. 'Toxaemia' accounts for 10 per cent of all perinatal deaths. Although the cause of this disease is not known, it is known that its early detection, and active treatment, reduces its severity, and prevents the perinatal death of the baby. One of the purposes of prenatal care is to prevent the development of severe 'toxaemia'. *Mechanical causes, and birth trauma*, are defined after a careful scrutiny of the labour records. These babies die during labour because the umbilical cord becomes entangled, during a difficult delivery of a breech baby, or from mechanical obstruction in labour. The better the quality of the obstetric care, and the more skilful the medical attendants, the fewer will be the deaths in this group. In New South Wales, and in Britain, 14 per cent of all perinatal deaths were thought to be due to mechanical causes.

A number of babies of normal birth weight (that is, more than 2,500 g), which either die in the womb before delivery without any warning or fail to breathe properly after delivery, are entered in the sub-section, *unexplained, normal birth weight*. About 12 per cent of all perinatal deaths fall into this unsatisfactory category—unsatisfactory because so little is known about the cause of the death. A small sub-group accounting for fewer than 5 per cent of all deaths are those due to the effects of *blood incompatibility* between the mother and her baby—the so-called rhesus problem. Oddly, the rhesus problem is only a problem amongst Caucasians, that is, whites. It is uncommon in Indian and Malayan races and almost unknown amongst Chinese. It will diminish as a problem in the future now that all women who are rhesus negative and have a rhesus positive baby, can be given a protective injection of anti-D gamma globulin within 72 hours of abortion or childbirth. The final sub-group is that in which *infection* in the first days of life caused the death of the baby.

The use of this type of investigation is shown by Professor Baird's experience in Britain. In their study the investigators divided the country into three zones—North, Central and South (Fig. 4/2). The Northern zone included north and northwest England, Wales and Scotland. This zone is characterized by dependence on heavy industry and coalmining. The proportion of people living in substandard housing is high. It is an area which is particularly affected during an economic recession, when the rates of unemployment tend to be the highest in Britain. The standard of nutrition is poorest in this zone, and more women are in the lowest two socio-economic groups, or to put it more bluntly, more women are poor. They also tend to have more children. In the study period in 1958 the perinatal mortality was 35·4 per 1,000, or 9 per cent higher than that in the Central zone.

The Central zone included most of Yorkshire, the Midlands and the South West of England. The zone is more prosperous

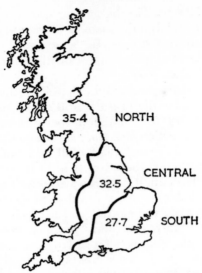

FIG. 4/2. The different perinatal mortality in the three zones of Britain in 1958. Source: *Perinatal Mortality Survey*.

than the Northern zone, there is more light industry and less poverty. The perinatal mortality in this zone was 32·5 per 1,000, which is 9 per cent lower than that in the Northern zone, but 17 per cent higher than that of the affluent Southern zone.

The Southern zone, which is dominated by London and includes all of East and South East England, is the most prosperous part of Britain. It has the lowest unemployment rate, the best nourished people, and the smallest number of poor people. The women in this zone have the smallest families in Britain, and the perinatal mortality was the lowest, 27·7 per 1,000, which is 28 per cent lower than that in the Northern zone.

5

This type of investigation, which has now been made in Australia, in Britain and in the U.S.A., has enabled research workers to identify certain socio-economic factors which affect perinatal mortality. Some details are given in Table 4/2. It can be seen that in the group of mainly environmental causes,

The socio-economic factors influencing perinatal mortality related to the clinical causes of perinatal death

Cause of death	High risk mothers
1. *Unexplained, low birth weight* (20 per cent of all deaths)	Low socio-economic status Shorter height than average Women under the age of 20 or over the age of 35 Women pregnant for the 5th time or more Heavy cigarette smokers (more than 20 per day)
2. *Antepartum haemorrhage* (14 per cent of all deaths)	Women pregnant for the 5th time or more Low socio-economic status
3. *Malformed babies* (15 per cent of all deaths)	
(*a*) Malformations of the central nervous system (e.g. spina bifida)	Increased incidence in lower social groups First pregnancies, especially if the mother is aged less than 20
(*b*) Other malformations	Increased incidence with increasing age and increasing numbers of previous children
4. *Maternal diseases* (5 per cent of all deaths)	Increase with increasing age
5. *'Toxaemia of pregnancy'* (10 per cent of all deaths)	First pregnancies, especially if under the age of 20 or over the age of 30 Women aged more than 30 History of toxaemia in a previous pregnancy
6. *Mechanical or trauma* (14 per cent of all deaths)	Short stature First pregnancies, especially if mother aged 30 or more Women pregnant for the 5th or subsequent time
7. *Unexplained, normal birth weight* (12 per cent of all deaths)	First pregnancies in women aged 30 or more Women pregnant for the 5th or subsequent time Pregnancies lasting 42 weeks or more, especially in older women pregnant for the first time
8. *Rhesus problems* (blood incompatibility) (5 per cent of all deaths)	Increasing incidence with increasing previous pregnancies

the major factor was low socio-economic status. This in turn often implies poor nutrition in childhood and poor obstetric care in pregnancy. The major factor in the group of mainly obstetric causes was increasing age of the mother and increasing numbers of previous children.

These findings are of considerable importance, and indicate ways in which the perinatal mortality can be reduced. There is, of course, considerable interplay between two groups of factors. For example, Mrs. Sugden is at high risk. She was born in the depression years before World War II, and was the seventh child. Her father had been unemployed for three years and spent what money he could extract from his wife on alcohol. By the time she was 16, the war was over, and she started work in a clothing factory. She was a fat, synthetic blonde who ate too many sweet things and smoked incessantly. By the time she was 18 she was pregnant. The family forced her to marry, and over the next eight years she had four children and obtained two induced abortions. She also developed varicose veins, a raised blood pressure and a foul temper. Her husband was weak and easy-going. Between the ages of 26 and 30 she had three more children, two of whom died in the perinatal period; and then luckily she found out about family planning. Mrs. Sugden is a typical high risk mother, and despite family planning she may become pregnant again. She started life at a disadvantage. She was malnourished in childhood. She had frequent pregnancies at short intervals. She was an irregular attender at antenatal clinics, and two of her seven children died in the perinatal period.

The perinatal mortality ratio increases with increasing age and with increasing numbers of previous children; and at all ages the rate is higher if the expectant mother smokes cigarettes. The reason for this appears to be that nicotine causes a spasm of the blood vessels which supply the afterbirth, so that the baby cannot obtain all the nourishment he needs and becomes chronically starved in the womb. The ratio is also higher amongst short women, which is a curious finding. The explanation is that short women tend to come from lower social groups and to have had poor nutrition in infancy and childhood. This is what has caused their short stature (although of course genetic inheritance plays a part), and tends to perpetuate the woman's underprivileged status. As she is less intelligent, less educated and less able, she tends to eat an inadequate diet in pregnancy and her baby is less likely to survive. The effect of social status is considerable and operates either directly or indirectly. In the British Perinatal Mortality Survey the overall perinatal mortality ratio rose from 24 per 1,000 births in the highest social group (in which the husbands were professional people, executives or managers) to 42 per 1,000 in the lowest social group (in which the husbands were unskilled labourers).

One important factor is the interval between births. This has been studied extensively in the U.S.A., where it has been found that if the interval between the birth and the next conception is 12 to 36 months, the perinatal mortality of the new baby is half that if the interval is less than 12 months. This finding makes a strong argument for the use of family planning to 'space' the births of wanted children.

Another important factor is the availability of good quality prenatal care, and its acceptance and use by women. If a woman fails to obtain prenatal care her baby has a 30 per cent increased chance of dying in the perinatal period. Since, in many nations, the high risk mothers—those who are poor, tired by childbearing and prematurely old—are the very women who fail to obtain prenatal care, the significance of this observation is clear. Prenatal care is particularly important if the mother is carrying twins. Twins have three times the perinatal mortality of singletons, and are more likely to die in infancy. This may be the basis of the old habit in Central Africa, which is now changing, of abandoning twins when they are born, and leaving them to die. Provided a mother seeks prenatal care, and follows instructions, the perinatal mortality due to a multiple pregnancy can be reduced considerably.

The information collected by studying perinatal mortality statistics provides a framework by which concerned women, and indeed men, can seek to bring about changes which will reduce the perinatal mortality, and will do much to ensure that every wanted child will survive. It is also hoped that it will generate interest, so that additional funds are made available to those clinical research workers who are seeking new and better methods to treat diseases such as the hyaline membrane disease which killed Richard Smith.

6

The analysis of the causes of perinatal mortality shows clearly that the number of deaths in any community is influenced by two main, but interrelated factors. These are, firstly, the health, physique and reproductive habits of the mother, and, secondly, the quality and availability of obstetric and paediatric care available to her.

It also is obvious that the measures required to reduce perinatal deaths will vary, depending on the sophistication of the people, their nutritional status and the type of health services available. For example, in the developing nations, maternity care is provided to over 80 per cent of the population by trained or traditional midwives. In these countries, where anaemia amongst women is usual, a considerable reduction in the perinatal mortality could be achieved by simply making sure that every pregnant woman received iron and vitamin tablets. The midwives, too, could be (and are being) trained to give instruction in nutrition, in family planning and in child health. In the developed nations a greater proportion of maternity care is given by doctors. In those nations where a well-organized national health service has been established, for example Scandinavia, the U.S.S.R., Britain and New Zealand, there are no financial barriers to obtaining proper health care throughout a pregnancy. In the U.S.A., and to a lesser extent Australia, the quality of care offered depends on the income of the woman. In both nations the majority of affluent women are attended in pregnancy and labour by a doctor. For the poor it is different. In the U.S.A. the poor receive a much inferior service, as do the submerged 10 per cent of the Australian population and, particularly, the Aboriginals. Indeed, there is great concern that the perinatal mortality of black Australian children is between 3 and 7 times that of white Australians. Poor nutrition of Aboriginal expectant mothers, and especially of their infants, leads to an increased death rate of Aboriginal children, and to impaired intellectual capacity, in later life, amongst the survivors.

But there is no need to despair. There are measures currently available which will reduce perinatal mortality in all nations, although the extent to which any one nation has introduced them will depend on many factors.

These measures should start at school. It is becoming increasingly realized that most educational systems are currently geared to produce men and women who will fit easily into existing industrial processes. Too little time is given to educating the child to obtain the most fulfilling life within his intellectual range. Since the majority of people marry, it is more than surprising that so little attention is given to preparation for family life, and to the study of human biology, including sexuality. Education in family life, in the physiology of human reproduction, in human sexuality, in family planning and in the impact of nutrition and hygiene on health, should begin in primary school, even if it means that the time given to nationalist-history, to rote-mathematics and to religious studies is reduced. The course should continue through the entire school years, and since most children in the developing nations, and some amongst the least affluent in the developed nations, leave school as early as possible, continuing health education should be made available through health and community services. Such continuing education should offer information on sexual responsibility, family planning and child care, and stress good nutritional habits. For example, the dependence on sweets and sweet drinks by Australian schoolchildren, promoted by very persuasive television advertising and parental culturally conditioned indulgence, could well be corrected to the advantage of the teeth and physique of the average Australian. Contrary to the popular myth of a bronzed, sunburned god and a shapely goddess the average Australian is physically unfit and edentulous by the time he, or she, is 25 years old.

The instructional programmes need to be supplemented by optimal care in pregnancy. The aim should be to make sure that prenatal care is readily available to all pregnant women. This is currently not the case in many developed nations and in most developing nations. Once again the division between rich and poor is clear. Mrs. D'Arcy-Rigby, whose husband has a position of some importance, and who has received good nutrition since childhood, decided to have her second child after four years of marriage. Her husband, Anthony, wanted a son and heir, and Amanda needed a brother. Mrs. D'Arcy-Rigby was able to purchase the services of a very competent obstetrician, and since she was well nourished and informed, had no problems at all. Her visits to see him were all by appointment, and although he was an uncommunicative man she had confidence in him. And she supplemented the information he didn't give by reading books about pregnancy and childbirth. By contrast, Mrs. Williams had been brought up in a lower working class area. Her second child was conceived a year after marriage and she went to the local clinic where she spent an average of two hours waiting to see a doctor (it was rarely the same one), for about two minutes. No one gave her information about nutrition, about baby care or about birth control. The staff all seemed to be busy and, as she said, 'didn't seem to care'. By the time she had added in the travelling time, which included taking her son, Len, to her mother's house, each prenatal visit consumed three and a half hours. Yet Mrs. Williams was far more likely to have problems in pregnancy and labour than Mrs. D'Arcy-Rigby. The priorities seem to have become mixed up.

In the developing nations, the key person in providing care in pregnancy and childbirth is the midwife. Her personality in motivating pregnant women to seek prenatal care as early as possible in pregnancy is crucial. Her importance in educating the woman during pregnancy in nutrition, hygiene, childrearing and family spacing is as great as is her traditional role of detecting abnormalities which may arise in pregnancy.

In all nations the provision of a network of interlinked prenatal clinics, doctors' clinics and health centres is merely a matter of organization. It is relatively easy to make sure that each woman has the best available prenatal care. What is needed is the will to do it and the financial resources. But since such measures will reduce the perinatal mortality, and may consequently lead to fewer conceptions, because of a greater use of family planning, the economic benefits will be positive.

To most women the 10 hours of labour are felt to constitute a greater danger than the 10 months of pregnancy. In fact, if the prenatal care has been good, problems are less likely to arise in labour. However, it must be recognized that most women do fear labour, and that danger to the baby can arise. Once again the care of the women in labour needs reorganization if the perinatal mortality is to be reduced. Medical science can identify women who are at particular risk of losing their babies in pregnancy and labour; and constant vigilance in labour can spot those women whose baby is at risk because of complications in labour. These women only form a minority of all pregnant women, and in the developed nations, at least, are best cared for in hospitals with highly qualified obstetrical and paediatric staff, and sophisticated equipment.

Efforts to achieve this goal will encounter opposition from conservative doctors, who have been brought up to believe that they are competent to undertake the total care of a woman, including surgery if necessary. Whilst this was possible 50 years ago, the dramatic advances of medical science make it a ludicrous concept today. Doctors will have to relinquish their believed God-like omnipotence and refer their problem patients for more sophisticated care in specialized intensive fetal care units. And such action will reduce the perinatal mortality rate. In the British Perinatal Survey the perinatal death rate fell as the quality of obstetric care rose. Aberdeen, in Scotland, has a highly organized obstetric service with an excellent two-way communication between midwives, general practitioners and the specialist staff in the hospital. The university staff and the specialists are enthusiastic about the continuing education of doctors and of midwives. Patients with problems can be easily and readily transferred to the main maternity hospital. The family planning services are excellent, and in fact tubal ligation as a permanent method of birth control was pioneered in the area. The results of this co-ordinated approach to the problem of perinatal mortality is shown by the fact that in 1958 the perinatal mortality rate in Aberdeen was 40 per cent lower than that of the rest of the country. If Aberdeen can achieve this, so can other areas, and there will be fewer tragedies like the death of little Richard Smith.

CHAPTER FIVE

Off to Philadelphia

I

That winter was terrible. But then it had been a terrible year. After the potatoes became blighted there wasn't much food at all. But we did what we could, and at least in the cabins the women tried to be cheerful, and give the little ones something. In Sligo Town it was worse, so I stopped going there. There wasn't any point.

The winter started early that year. There was snow in early November, and you don't get snow then in the west of Ireland. And the frost was worse than the snow. A man couldn't keep warm, not with him half starved. And worse than both the frost and the snow were the winds. They weren't the decent gales that came out of the Atlantic, hurling the clouds across the sky towards England, and spattering the land with rain. These gales came from England, and like most things English, they were bad. The winds blew from the north east, and they brought icy rain, and hail, and sleet and snow, and they cut right through into your bones. Christmas in 1845 was no season of comfort and joy. We huddled around the turf fire in the cabin and prayed that the cup might pass. But it didn't. It got worse.

Others were suffering more than we were. Didn't I meet that decent man, Mr. Cummins, who had come over from Cork to see how the famine had affected the district. He was telling me that in the hamlets down in West Cork, things were really bad. He went to a cabin near Ballydehob and found six famished and ghastly skeletons lying on a heap of filthy straw in the corner, huddled to each other, and naked except for a horse-cloth. He thought that they were dead, until he heard a low moaning. They were all alive—just—four children, a woman, and what had once been a man, he said. I knew that man. We had taken poteen together, and we had cut turf together, before the famine. Now he is dead, for Mr. Cummins said he died. And he saw worse. On a bitter day in December he went to a hamlet, and found most of the people dead. In one house were two frozen corpses, half eaten by rats. Oh yes, it was bad.

There was nothing we could do. We had no food and we couldn't get any for love or money. The gleanings had run out, even the nettles were dead. All the turnips had gone, eaten raw by women and children who had gone over the fields like a flock of famished crows. Didn't we try to help Shelagh O'Mara, and she bursting with a child, and her man dead of the famine and the fever. And didn't my wife help her have the baby, and it turned Shelagh's mind. She went off from the cabin into the night, when we weren't looking, the baby in her arms. We found them next day in a boreen, naked and frozen. It was bad: herself, her man and the child all dead, and she only seventeen.

Then Michael died. He was never strong, and he wasted away in front of us. His eyes sank back in his head, and his skin was thin and white like the parchment on a drum. He had no flesh on his arms, but his legs were swollen. Then he got the fever, and he lay in the corner of the cabin, his eyes dull, and said not a word, nor did he moan. He just lay and couldn't move. He didn't seem to see us, his eyes were blank, as if he was in some other place. I hope it was a happy one, for it wasn't happy with us. The women no longer talked cheerfully, and the tales were no longer told in the evenings. We sat silent, and the hunger had us in its grip. Our people were dying. Dying of famine and of disease. There was no help, it seemed.

Two of the other children died that terrible winter, and we saw no end to it. But with God's will it had to change.

It didn't. We couldn't pay the rent. I had been a good tenant, a good farmer and my father before me. But the agent didn't help. Oh no, he said, Lord Palmerston had to have his rent. And him a rich man. He wasn't here in County Sligo, he was in England, and he had to have his money when we were starving, and could plant nothing for the potatoes had the blight. But the agent had us evicted. All of us. He was a hard man.

They came in the dawn in March that year. On St. Patrick's Day it was, God curse them. The agent wasn't there. But the bailiff came with the police, and the men with the crowbars. They were Irishmen, too, but they were going to destroy us. I suppose that some men, hungry men anyway, will do anything for food.

We were dragged out. We tried to resist, and the children were crying, and the women were screaming, and my mother who was over eighty and starved and half blind, was dragged out, keening and crying, to sit on the roadside in the rain. They tore down the thatch and they battered in the walls, till there was nothing but the chimney stack, and the turf fire still smouldering away on the hearth, as it had done for a hundred years or more. Oh yes, they tumbled our home, where I was born and my father before me. And they left us, huddled in shawls in the rain. The agent came, and if I had had a loaded gun I would have fired it at him and damn the consequences. He said that Lord Palmerston was a decent man, and as I had been a good tenant he would give me money and I should go to America.

So we did. With all the others we went down the stony road to Sligo Town. We left our own place, our own hills, the talk of the women in the evening, the warmth of the turf fire and its honest smell, and the songs and the life we knew. And we went to America.

We sailed on the *Larch* out of Sligo, me and my wife and the three of the children who were still alive. My mother, God rest her soul, had died, after the tumbling. There were over 400 of us, crowded into the between decks space. There were drivelling old men and tiny babies. We were huddled together, without light, without air, sick, whilst the ship was lifted to the stars and fell into the pit of the Atlantic waves. Sure, we couldn't wash, there wasn't any water. We didn't get much to eat. The captain gave us rations each day, and they were little enough, God knows. We had to cook on a stove made from a large wooden case lined with bricks, on which we put the coals. But there were too many of us, so we ate half-raw food. Then the water began to get short as the casks had leaked.

Soon after that the fever came. In the hold the air was thick, and the straw in the berths became filthy from excrement. And the deaths began. First the old and the young, then the others. And the smell got worse. We wanted air and we wanted water and we wanted food and we wanted medicine. We sent a deputation to the captain, and he turned the guns on us and told us to get below or he'd shoot us. In the six weeks we were at sea 108 of us died. And when we got to America, half of the rest had fever. My wife, Maureen, had the fever. Oh yes, she had gone through the famine, and the tumbling, and the voyage, sick as she was from the moment we left Sligo Bay. And when we got to the smooth waters of America she went down with the fever.

She died. She died before she put a foot in America. And I buried her, God rest her soul. And as soon as I can earn the price of a passage back, I swear I'll go home and I'll shoot the men that murdered her—and that is the agent, and Lord Palmerston. Oh, a great man that, they say. An English leader, the Queen's friend. A great man, him, and his agent, and between them they murdered my wife.

2

Famines have occurred throughout history. In 1878 Cornelius Walford recorded 350 from historical reports. In Ireland there was a famine in A.D. 192 'so that the lands and the houses, territories and tribes were emptied'. Five hundred years later famine again struck Ireland, and 'men ate each other'. In Europe, between 1193 and 1196, famine caused many to perish and more to leave. In India the famine of 1770 killed over 3 million people; and one hundred years later 9 million people were destitute in North China. Children were sold in the markets so their parents could buy food. In this century famines have occurred in Bihar, Biafra and Bangladesh.

The description of the famine of 1845–49 in Ireland is that of famine in India or China, Biafra or Bangladesh. Many die from starvation or from disease; others try to escape by migrating.

Movement of people either singly, in groups or in masses goes far back into history. The earliest information we have about man is that he was a nomadic gatherer and hunter. He lived by collecting roots and fruits and by hunting animals. He had few possessions but was able to endure extremes of heat and cold. He was the prey of other animals, and because of his defence-lessness, having no claws and being weakly muscled, he used his superior intelligence to form hunting bands. It is unlikely that these ever exceeded 50 people and probably were usually smaller. The band would consist of 10 or so adult and sub-adult males, and between 20 and 30 others: women and small child-ren. If the band grew too large and outstripped its food supply, it is likely that newborn babies were left out to be eaten by the animals. The men hunted, the women scrabbled for edible roots and watched the children. When his traditional hunting grounds were invaded by another tribe he became aggressive, but because of the small population density such contact was usually avoided. His way of life was nomadic, although it is likely that the range of his migratory journeys was limited in most cases. He followed the animals wherever they ate: if they moved, because of drought, he moved; if they stayed grazing on the lush grass, he stayed. A few tribes moved on into un-known lands, where sexual liaisons between them and tribes living in the new lands took place, so that the variants in the genetic pool spread and found phenotypic expression in the offspring of the unions. This type of nomadic society exists today amongst the Australian aboriginals, the Kalahari bush-men and the Sakai peoples of Malaysia.

After at least 2·4 million years of this kind of existence, a change occurred, about 10,000 years ago. At about the same time in three distinct areas man learned how to cultivate cereals instead of merely gathering the seeds. The areas were the foothills adjoining the valley of the Tigris–Euphrates; the foot-hills bordering the Hwang-Ho river in North China and an area in Central America. For the next 5,000 years he continued to obtain meat by hunting so that his diet was better balanced. He ate meat which he hunted, and cereals which he grew, and such fruits and roots as the women gathered. Over this period he learnt to domesticate wild animals, and by so doing became a pastoralist. No longer requiring to hunt to obtain meat, the tribes followed their flocks through traditional grazing areas, and only supplemented their diet by hunting when the opportunity arose. Hunting had become easier with the invention of the bow and arrow, which enabled man to kill at a distance, a matter of some importance for the puny, thin-skinned, light-framed biped. With the better diet the infant mortality began to fall, but population growth was slow and was further slowed by inter-tribal fighting, which now became increasingly common, and by drought and epidemics which decimated the people at unpredictable intervals. To some degree, societies at this stage of development continue to exist in Central Asia, Mongolia and Arabia.

In certain areas where water was plentiful and constant, the pastoralists found that the grass was sufficient for their flocks throughout the year and it was no longer necessary to move to find pasture. The cultivation of grain and the domestication of animals produced a ready supply of food, so that the necessity to hunt diminished still further.

The settled tribes increased in size, as a more ready supply of food reduced the mortality. But as the tribes became larger and land became scarcer, it became necessary for some people to leave the tribal lands, which could no longer support the population. It is unknown whether these migrants were the most intelligent and the best physical members of the tribe, or the worst; but whichever it was, man's migratory movement led to the exploration of greater and greater portions of the earth's surface. In the most fertile river valleys the population pressures leading to migration were slow to develop and migration was delayed. But such rich areas attracted the more war-like tribes from the wilderness, with resulting turbulence, and the forced migration of the weaker tribes.

It can be seen that two factors influenced migration. The first was the necessity to find new land and new food sources when population pressures became too great in a particular area. The second was the forced migration of some or all members of defeated tribes after inter-tribal war. The relative influence of these two influences cannot be assessed, but both are of importance today. In the first, economic, social or political influences induce people to leave their homes and seek better conditions in an alien environment. These may be called the attractive (or pull) forces. In the second, political or military events impel the weakest, the most vocal or the most fearful, out of their homeland into new territories. These are the impelling (or push) forces.

3

It is obvious that migration can affect population dynamics quite considerably. Not only does the new emigrant bring his physical presence, but he brings his psychological and cultural life style. This affects, and is affected by, the prevailing norms in the community, and in general has a beneficial effect. In Australia, for example, post-war European immigration immeasurably improved the quality of city life, altering it perhaps from a dull, pedestrian model of working-class England of the late nineteenth century, to a more vital, exciting way of life. The impact of migration is greatest with international migration, but occurs also from migration within a nation, from region to region, or more particularly, from the country to the city.

As a generalization, it can be stated that the two groups most likely to migrate are the intellectually strong and the physically weak. The majority of people resist moving from their home, and from familiar surroundings, even when conditions are becoming increasingly unfavourable. In Ireland, prior to the great famine, emigration did not come easily. The Irish peasant had a deeply-felt warm attachment to the locality in which he had been born and brought up; and only a few made the painful decision to emigrate. When they did, their departure was marked with scenes of sorrow, reminiscent of an Irish wake. The neighbours wept, the family keened for the departing migrants as if they were dying.

Whilst this attitude is perhaps extreme, most people weigh the advantages of the psychological security of living in a familiar environment, amongst familiar people, against the real and imagined dangers of moving to another land, or another area of a country. Only when the familiar area ceases to satisfy physical or intellectual needs, or when continuing to live there imposes danger of physical or intellectual discomfort, does the urge to migrate exceed the urge to stay.

In real life the decision to migrate is far more complex. In all the nations of the world there is an increasing mobility of people. Radio, television and cheap 'packaged' travel are diminishing the fear of strangers, and the increasing contact between different peoples encourages further mobility. In these ways the crude influences of the 'push' and 'pull' factors are being modified by intervening factors, one of which is the increased information about other nations available through the mass media.

There are two main influences which 'push' people into leaving their homes and familiar environment. These are economic and political forces, although the two are often interrelated in causing an individual to make the decision to migrate. Economic forces alone may lead to this decision. Out-migration will be considered if there is a lack of opportunity for continued employment, because of a reduction in the demand for a particular product or commodity, or because the supply of a particular resource is reduced. An over-supply of labour may also have the effect of encouraging the decision. At this time of technological change and innovation, and particularly of automation, an individual may be unable to adjust to the new conditions, and this may lead to migration. In most cases, economic push factors merely cause internal migration, which has no effect on the nation's total population, but which does cause problems of urbanization and population density. The drain from the north and north-west of Britain to the south east is an example of this. Of course, economic considerations can lead to international migration, either temporarily, as is occurring increasingly in the European Common Market nations, or permanently. The permanent emigration of Europeans to the then empty nations of the U.S.A., Canada, Australia, Brazil and New Zealand, did much to aid in the economic and social development of those nations, and to reduce problems in the donor nations. Since the sixteenth century, over 60 million Europeans have emigrated overseas, and the greatest exodus was in the hundred years from 1845. (Over the same period, at least until 1865, it should be pointed out that there were 15 million involuntary immigrants to the Americas. These were the black African slaves).

The political factors which induce emigration have been

particularly important in the past century. They include alienation from the community because of the different beliefs, or mode of behaviour of the individual, or because he believes that there is a lack of cultural facilities in the area. These factors can cause internal migration to another area of the country where facilities are more to the individual's taste. The drift, in many nations, of young, unmarried people from the rural areas to the provincial towns or to the major cities is a continuing and easily observable example of this factor.

Oppressive, or repressive, acts by the majority on a minority group, because of the latter's racial origins, or its religious or political beliefs, is an even stronger 'push' motive for migration, and in this case the person usually emigrates if it is possible. Examples abound in the past century. The exodus of the 1·6 million Irish after the famine was as much political as economic, and had lasting effects on Anglo-American relations. The Irish, as will be understood from the beginning of this chapter, were forced to emigrate because of starvation, and the knowledge that they had no land tenure. In their own nation they were tenants of overseas owners and could be dispossessed without notice. In their emigration to America they brought no resources, except their muscle power. They brought that at a time of industrial recession and had to be 'content to live together in filth and disorder with a bare sustenance, provided they can drink and smoke and gossip and enjoy their balls and frolics and wakes without molestation'. But beyond their difficulty in becoming assimilated in their new nations, the Irish had the bond of hatred of the English and a burning feeling of indignation and resentment at their treatment.

The attractive, or pull forces, which lead to a decision to migrate, often operate in conjunction with the push factors. As has been mentioned, they include the lure of greater recreational, cultural, scholastic or intellectual activities in the chosen area. These are strong pull factors in the decision to leave small country towns to move to larger centres. In other cases the pull factors are personal, because of a close relationship with the wage earner, and a knowledge of the new habitat is unimportant. For example, if a man moves, his family usually migrates with him. As far as children are concerned, the new area is as good, or better than the old, and nostalgia for the latter soon goes; but the 'forced' move may lead to a sullen resentment by the wife and to domestic hostility. The 'pull' factors, being value judgements, are many and varied, and merge into the third group of factors: the intervening factors.

A decision to migrate is rarely made only after evaluating the attractions of the new home and the disadvantages of the existing home. The decision is inevitably influenced by intervening factors, many of which are difficult to identify, and are related to the psychological make-up of the individual. The same factors, which appear insuperable to one individual, appear trivial to another. Examples of this are the refusal of one migrant family to leave Britain when they found that in Australia there were no kippers; and the return of another because the wife missed her mother, whom she had always visited three times a week. In both cases the opportunities offered in Australia, on considered thought, far outweighed the intervening factors. It is clear that when migration is voluntary, emotions often replace reason in making a decision. A wet, grey summer in Britain increases by 20 per cent the number of enquiries to travel to Australia.

The importance of intervening factors are not felt only in migration between the developed nations. Java, with 132,000 km² of land and 80 million people, has sought to encourage migration to Sumatra, an island of 474,000 km² and 18 million people. In the past 20 years only 420,000 people have migrated, although land in Sumatra was given to the migrants, there was no real language barrier and the predominant religion in both islands is Islam.

4

Although throughout history there has been a movement of people from one nation to another, or from one continent to another, until the nineteenth century the movement was mainly of families escaping from persecution or seeking better living conditions. The initial colonization of the western coast of North America was largely by people escaping from religious persecutions; in Europe the Huguenots fled from France after 1560 to settle and to bring their skills in the wool trade to England.

Spain, in the sixteenth, seventeenth and eighteenth centuries, sent migrants and soldiers to South America to exploit the riches found there for Spain's benefit. The numbers migrating permanently probably did not exceed 500,000, but their effect on the cultural development of the area was considerable.

In the nineteenth century sea transport became safer and more regular across the Atlantic, with the consequent migration of Europeans to the Americas. The United States was the main recipient, and in the early years most of the migrants came from Britain, although after the Irish famine in 1846 increasing numbers of Irish migrated. Towards the end of the century migrants were leaving Poland, Italy, Greece and Scandinavia in considerable numbers.

The earlier immigrants were mainly ill-educated peasants who had insufficient capital to buy land of their own in Europe or had been cleared from feudal lands they had tilled, and whose main objective in migrating was to obtain the cheap land available in the U.S.A., and, to a lesser extent, Canada. The 'pull' effect of cheap land was backed by the 'push' effect of dear or unobtainable land in Europe. The migrants had very limited capital but much muscle power. They knew how to clear and to cultivate land, and they cleared and cultivated it. They opened mid-western America, and because their efforts were labour intensive, but required little capital, they were readily absorbed. After about 1880 most of the land had been settled, and increasing numbers of migrants went to the cities, where they took the lowest paid, least skilled work. Wage rates were low, and it was possible for manufacturers to use sweat-shop techniques, which again limited capital expenditure. The migrants had high fertility rates, usually higher than those of the earlier settlers, but this was in part an artefact, as so many migrants were young and in the peak reproductive ages, and in part due to their abnormally high infant and childhood mortality rates. Health care was rudimentary for the poor, housing conditions inadequate, families crowding into decaying, insanitary dwellings; public education was elementary and minimal, so that the social costs of absorbing migrants were limited, and were less than the social value of cheap labour readily available. The consequence was that capital accumulated.

Between 1820 and 1920 about 33 million migrants went to

the U.S.A., the largest numbers migrating between 1880 and 1919. After 1920 immigration quotas were imposed, which favoured migration from North West Europe and Mexico, at the expense of Southern Europe, West Asia and East Asia, so that immigration slowed, only 3·5 million migrants crossing the Atlantic between 1920 and 1940.

On a reduced scale, migration was taking place from Russia into the relatively empty lands of Siberia. Between 1800 and 1912, 8 to 12 million settlers crossed the Urals, and since that date another 12 to 15 million probably have joined them.

Chinese, from the several provinces of Imperial China, also migrated to neighbouring countries from the middle of the nineteenth century, and by 1950, 11 million Chinese lived overseas, mainly in Indonesia (4 million), Malaya (3·5 million), Thailand and the Philippines.

As a consequence of the social, economic and political upheavals which convulsed Europe during and after World War II, European emigration increased. With the division of Europe into Communist and non-Communist blocs, those who disliked or feared one regime attempted to move to a nation which had adopted the other. Between 1945 and 1960 4·5 million migrants went to North America, and Oceania (mainly Australia and New Zealand) had a net migration of 1·6 million people, Australia taking more than 85 per cent of the total. Europeans, mainly from Southern Europe, also migrated to South America, particularly to Argentina and Brazil, which had a net gain from migration of about 1 million.

By 1960 the large migrations had diminished. Europe was not only rehabilitated but was booming economically, with the result that central and north western Europe was seeking immigrants, although usually only on a temporary and seasonal basis. Between 1961 and 1970 fewer than 1 million migrants have gone from Europe to North America, Australia has had a total net immigration of 547,000, and very few people (less than 20,000 per year) have migrated to South America.

Migration has continued in Africa but is largely undocumented. It tends to be seasonal and temporary, as, for example, the workers recruited in Mozambique and Malawi for work in South Africa.

Perhaps the largest movement of people in this century has

occurred in the Indian subcontinent. Partition of India in 1947, which established the predominantly Hindu state of India and the largely Muslim state of Pakistan, led to a movement of people fearing religious persecution and probable massacre. The size of the exodus was gigantic: between 14 and 16 million people moved between the two nations. However, as the immigration to Pakistan was about 7 million and that into India about 8 million, the net migratory movements did little to distort the population dynamics of either country. More serious socially was the migration to India of over 10 million Hindu peasants from Bangladesh following the suppression of the independence movement in 1971 by the Pakistani Government. The addition of 10 million people to India's population negated the effect of about three years' effort in population control. Their return to Bangladesh after the intervention of India and the establishment of the new nation of Bangladesh relieved India but has imposed considerable strains on the new nation.

Apart from the Indian subcontinent, migratory flow between developing nations largely has ceased since 1960, because of legal restriction on movement. In 1965–71, for example, only five countries had a net migration (immigrants less emigrants) of 100,000 or more. These nations were the U.S.A., Canada, Australia, Argentina and Brazil.

Most of these migrants are Caucasian, under the age of 40, who bring to the recipient country a number of dependants under the age of 16. For example, in the 1961–65 period, 24 per cent of the 1·4 million migrants to the U.S.A. were under the age of 16, and only 12 per cent over the age of 40. There is increasing doubt of the economic value of migration in a modern technological society and increasing awareness of its adverse effects on the population dynamics of a nation.

Australia may be used as an example to demonstrate this new concept. Australia is large and relatively under-populated. Up to 1940 a slow net immigration occurred, mainly of people from the British Isles, but the Japanese war stopped this. Suddenly, Australia was physically and psychologically alone—a Caucasian outpost in an Asian sea. The Japanese bombed Darwin and invaded New Guinea. Time, courage and the U.S. Navy saved Australia from an alien occupation. The lesson was learned. In the war years Australia had changed from being a wool-shed, a wheat store and a dried fruit warehouse for Britain, into an embryo industrial nation. And she was short of manpower. In addition, humanitarian impulses induced her to accept many European refugees, dispossessed of their homes and goods by the redrawn political map. On three grounds Australia sought immigrants, who were to be almost exclusively Caucasian so that they would assimilate more readily. The first was defence. Populate or perish was the cry! More people meant more strength, and God was known to be on the side of the big battalions. The Yellow Peril was in the forefront of people's minds. And even if Japan had been defeated, there were others. China, perhaps; or Indonesia; or even, in the wildest fantasy of some leaders, India. The second reason was economic. Low birth rates during the late 1920s and 1930s, together with the wartime casualties, had reduced the work force available. Workers were needed for the burgeoning factories and the migrant workers were prepared to take any job. The third was humanitarian. Australia took her share of Europeans displaced from their homes by the ravages of war and by unacceptable political regimes.

The policy was encouraged by setting up centres in Britain and other European nations, and by offering subsidized passages to the migrants and their families. The scheme worked.

By 1971 net migration was boosting Australia's population growth rate to 2·0 per cent, one of the highest in the developed world. And questions began to be asked. Most immigrants had settled in the main cities, adding to the social congestion. Many were employed in labour-intensive jobs and, because of high wage rates, many industries sought tariff protection against more cheaply produced equivalent imports. These two factors led people to question the economic basis for immigration, which was that 'immigration contributed to the economic and technological base on which national security today depends so heavily'. It was pointed out that a community of 25 million led to no greater economies in production than a population of 12·5 million, and immigrants were being used by manufacturers as cheap labour, which reduced the need of the industrialist to develop innovatory technological methods to offset labour shortages. The real question was what was the real cost to the community of an immigrant worker. An accepted and much quoted figure was $650 per migrant family; but the real cost was claimed to be much higher, as houses, roads, electricity, water supplies, sewage disposal, education for the immigrant's children and health care for his family had to be provided by the community. Against these costs opposing economists set the addition to the economy provided by the work of the immigrant (and often his wife), and the addition to the variety and quality of life in Australia provided by the presence of people from many parts of Europe.

Despite these gains, the actual and hidden costs of immigration have to be taken out of the pool of capital available for national development, for educating existing Australians and for improving social services. Immigrants were needed, but to service the needs of the immigrants more immigrants were needed. In other words, the labour shortages which inspired the immigration programme were partly caused by the programme itself.

There is no relationship between the conditions in North America in the late nineteenth century and that in the late twentieth century in Australia. In the first place, the migration to North America was proportionately far smaller (to size of the population). Second, most migrants to America went to open new lands. They were frontier men, requiring little capital and demanding few amenities. And later, when the immigrants did go to the cities, they congregated, in squalor, in the slums and no social welfare expenditure was made to help them improve their lot, so that they contributed more to economic capital than they received in social capital in the form of schools, houses, health care, sewerage and a pleasant environment.

Most of Australia's immigrants have chosen to live in the larger, industrial cities, and over 76 per cent of male immigrants to Australia between 1945 and 1971 have brought families with them. But in contrast with America in the late nineteenth century, in Australia in the late twentieth century, the immigrant families have expected, and have received, a very large expenditure on social welfare measures, as I have mentioned already.

Moreover, for maximum efficiency modern technology requires large amounts of capital and only relatively small infusions of labour. Encouraged immigration, therefore, seems to be less advantageous for economic growth and for defence than previously thought; in fact, it may be a dis-economy, since the migrants are often under-educated. A place will remain for limited immigration of those bringing in exceptional skills and attitudes, and those who replace Australians with such skills who emigrate. But increasingly it appears that the main reason for immigration will be a humanitarian one, so that families may be reunited.

The available evidence shows that in recent years the net effect of migration on the population dynamics of most nations has been minimal, with the exceptions of the U.S.A., Canada, Australia and Brazil which have registered net gains. The fact is that forced massive migration to under-populated countries, were this politically possible, would be logistically impossible. Not only are there insufficient ships to carry the migrants and their household goods, but potential recipient countries have neither the facilities nor the money to make ready the areas for their reception, to construct the roads, to build the houses, to organize schools and extend social services, and to make available jobs for more than a very few. Even those developed countries which have continued to seek migrants in the past decade are currently reviewing their policies, and tending to reduce quotas because of the ecological, industrial and psychological problems involved.

It is clear, therefore, that emigration can do nothing to relieve the population pressures in Asia, or in Latin America, although it may be possible to redistribute some of a single nation's population within its own boundaries.

5

International migration in recent years is having a diminishing effect on the population dynamics of a nation, although it appears inevitable that some permanent movement of people, either voluntary or involuntary, will continue.

In place of international migration, internal migration within a nation is increasing, particularly from the rural areas to the larger towns, the cities and the megalopoli of the nations.

Urbanization is occurring in all nations at an alarming rate, and is compounding the problems facing man in the last years of this century. At present in the affluent developed nations of the world, between 55 and 65 per cent of the people live in urban aggregations of 20,000 people or more. By the year 2000, if the present trend continues, it is anticipated that over 80 per cent will be urban dwellers. In the hungry, expectant, developing world 25 per cent of people live in urban areas today; by the year 2000 the percentage is likely to be nearly 50 per cent (Fig. 5/1). The Conference on the Human Environment held in

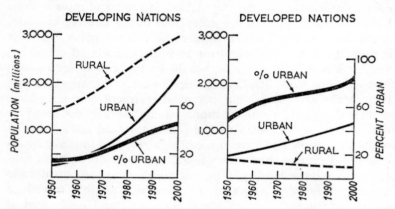

FIG. 5/1. The increasing rate of urbanization in the world. Source: *Growth of the World's Urban and Rural Population*, U.N., New York, 1969.

Stockholm in 1972 commented, 'the problems that this trend are giving rise to are likely to become unmanageable. It could lead to a major collapse in many of the larger cities of the world, which are functioning under conditions of great hardship, and will further endanger the precarious existence of human settlements in many parts of the world.'

The change from rural to urban living has been particularly rapid in Europe and the U.S.A. In America at the beginning of the century, 60 per cent of people lived in farms, in villages or small country towns. Today, 70 per cent of Americans live in, or near to, cities of 50,000 or more and by A.D. 2000 the ratio will be over 85 per cent. The impact of urbanization in the U.S.A. is even more graphically shown when the decade

1960 to 1970 is studied. Between 1960 and 1970 the population of the U.S.A. increased by 13 per cent. In the same decade the urban population rose by 23 per cent. Within the cities a further change is occurring; the more affluent are fleeing from the inner city areas to live in the endless, mindless, uniform suburbs which are connected to the city by poor public transport and by the umbilical cords of superb motorways. And because of the poor transport, people have to have automobiles so that they can travel to and from work, travel to shops and offices, and to and from schools. Automobiles add considerably to urban environmental pollution.

In the decaying centres of the cities, urban slums house the poorest of the people, in conditions of overcrowding and squalor. Whilst the conditions of the poorest section of the affluent nations might seem good, when compared to those of the poor of Calcutta, Bombay, Manila, Lima or Rio de Janeiro, they are deplorable in the context of an affluent society.

In all nations the housing shortage in the urban areas is worsening. In affluent England, London is short of between 150,000 and 200,000 family homes. In India the housing shortage, on the most modest standards, has risen from nearly 3 million units in 1950 to over 12 million in 1972. In Latin America, one third of the rapidly increasing urban population lives in slum conditions, and each year the congestion, the noise, the disposal of waste, the unemployment and the health hazards rise. The Malthusian corrective of pestilence becomes a more likely, and inhuman, reality. Even the most affluent of the affluent nations, the U.S.A., is fighting a losing battle against urbanization and against the housing shortage.

If urban living poses such a hazard to the dignity of man, why is it occurring? In the first place, those who detect the dangers are largely middle-class people with middle-class values. To them, the insanitary slums, the open fetid sewers, the mass of half-starved humanity represent a threat to their conscience and to their way of life. In Manila, the rich have solved this by creating enclaves surrounded by walls, guarded by dogs and by armed police, in which they live, isolated from the degradation in the slums outside the walls.

To the poor, urban life offers a hope of work. In the next 25 years, at the current annual rate of population growth, 170 million new jobs will have to be found. The population explosion has resulted in there being more people than can be usefully employed on the land, and this tendency is aggravated by the introduction of labour-saving agricultural machinery. But small-scale agriculture does not permit the accumulation of sufficient capital to buy the machinery, or the other capital intensive consumer goods, which man appears to want. This in turn leads to consolidation of land holdings, and to an increase in landless peasants, who see no future in the country, and flock to the towns in the hope of finding jobs. They have the hope that by doing this, they, too, can save to buy the consumer goods so persuasively advertised. The cities act as a magnet in which, even if the streets are not paved with gold, there is hope of work, and of excitement. For most, the magnetic city is a mirage, and life is even more degrading than it was in the rural area. But because of the bustle, the congestion and the constant movement, it seems more exciting.

In many of the cities, migrants from specific areas create urban villages. But they are villages with a difference. The dominant rigid social structure of the village is not introduced: instead, authority rests with the strongest or the most knowledgeable man, who controls all his fellows. In this hostile, aggressive environment, leaders who offer the dispossessed tangible rewards obtain an extraordinary loyalty from their followers. To obtain the goods, and to provide psychological security for the disadvantaged, societies and gangs are formed which add to the dangers of the decaying cities. In the U.S.A. crimes of violence per 100,000 population in cities of more than 250,000 people are nearly five times as frequent as in communities of 10,000 or less (Table 5/1). Cities are causing social disruption.

The current exponential growth of cities follows different patterns in the affluent and in the hungry nations. In the rich nations, the growth of cities is largely determined by the automobile. In the middle ages the size of the city was limited by the distance a man could easily walk, and by the need for defence against marauders. In the twentieth century, in the industrialized nations, the size of the urban plot is determined by the automobile, the motorway and the sewage line. Transport has been called the life blood of the city. If it ceases the

city dies. If it becomes malignant, as does the blood in leukae-
mia, the city, or the patient, dies. At this moment, in the cities
of the developed world, and in many cities in the developing
world, transport is malignant. Take a taxi in Bangkok or New
York, Jakarta or Detroit, Bombay or Paris, and the sickness of
transport is evident.

TABLE 5/1

The relationship between city size and crime rate in the U.S.A., 1960

Population size of Cities in 1960	Average number of people per square mile	Number of Crimes per 100,000 people per year			
		Murder	*Rape*	*Robbery*	*Assault*
Over 250,000	7,100	6·8	15·2	117·6	154·1
100,000 to 250,000	4,271	5·6	7·6	56·5	83·3
50,000 to 100,000	3,190	3·3	5·5	36·6	58·9
25,000 to 50,000	2,810	2·9	4·7	22·6	39·9
10,000 to 25,000	2,530	2·4	4·0	15·7	35·2
Under 10,000	1,700	2·7	3·3	12·8	28·9

The idol of the late twentieth century—the automobile—is
not only determining the shape of the cities, but may be determining whether cities will persist. Mobility is clogging the
arteries of the city.

The cost of land in the desirable ring of suburbs within easy
reach of the city is so high, and the decay in the centre of the
city so marked, that most young couples seek to buy their first
'home' in distant suburbs where land is relatively cheap and
developers particularly active. If the supreme salesmen are
those who dispose of secondhand cars they are closely followed
in persuasiveness, in the purveying of half truths and in the
psychology of the soft sell, by the real estate developers. And to
the developers, the construction or improvement of a major
road, or hopefully announced plans for a motorway or freeway,
is a signal for bigger and better profits. The congestion of the
new suburban development creates the need for a motorway.
The motorway is built to ease the congestion. Because of the
motorway the population increases, which increases the congestion, which leads to more motorways being built. The feed-
back loop is in operation. Congestion, crime, increased health
hazards all increase as the size of the city grows.

In the developing nations the city acts as a magnet, but because the automobile has not yet replaced the human leg as a mean of locomotion, the congestion tends to be central. Again, the good land is too expensive, so the poor have to make do with land which no one thinks worth developing. Shanty towns of shacks crawl up the hillsides, perching precariously between sky and earth, ready to be dislodged by a major rainstorm. Water is obtained from infrequent standpipes; the open drain is the sewer, the washing place and the play area for thousands. Garbage collection and scavenging are non-existent except for the ubiquitous activities of the pigs and carrion crows.

In both the developing and in the developed nations the cause of increasing urbanization, and the mounting urban decay, is us. We, the people, are the culprits. To reverse the decaying trend we must devote a considerable quantity of our resources to correcting the most glaring damage done in the past; and we must limit our population growth rate. It is not possible in the urban type of life, which is increasingly favoured by more and more people, to have as many children as we want and to live with human dignity. Louis Mumford, who studied cities throughout his life, in 1938 quoted Aristotle: 'Men came together in cities in order to live: they remain together in order to live the good life.' In the cities of today the good life is becoming increasingly hard to find. The description of the life of the Irish, who migrated to New York after the great famine, applies all too often to urban conditions today, especially in the cities in the developing world. 'To reach these tumbling and squalid rookeries', the Committee on Tenant Houses wrote in 1848, 'the visitor must penetrate a labyrinth of alleys behind horse stables, blacksmiths' forges and inevitably beside cheap groggeries. Rubbish lies in piles of decaying matter which gives off a nauseous smell, and round the buildings are filthy pools of standing water. . . . Vagrant pigs wander through the streets acting as scavengers and are dangerous as hyaenas.' This description applies today to Bombay or Calcutta, to Bogota or Rio, to Manila or Lagos. And it is getting worse, as more and more people crowd into the cities, and as the population growth rate continues to increase. Most thinking people believe that change is urgently required. The most appropriate methods remain under discussion, but it is generally agreed that urban renewal will have little lasting effect unless, concurrently, the rate of population growth is reduced to zero. Man created the messes which are today's cities; man can reverse the trend, but only if he reduces his profligate fertility.

CHAPTER SIX

The Hungry World

'Now here, you see it takes all the running you can do, to keep in the same place. If you want to get somewhere else you must run at least twice as fast.'

The Red Queen
in 'Alice Through the Looking-Glass' by
LEWIS CARROLL.

I

In Bangladesh Ismail Zulkifli went to bed hungry last night. He had gone to bed hungry the night before, and the night before that, and he will go to bed hungry tomorrow and the day after. He is five years old. And he represents one of the 500 million people in the hungry, expectant, developing world who are undernourished, which means that they obtain insufficient calories each day to supply their energy needs. He also represents one of the 1,800 million people who are malnourished, which means that they eat insufficient protein, minerals or vitamins each day to restore fully the tissues of their bodies.

It is important that every individual obtains the necessary calories and the amount of protein appropriate for his needs. The interrelationship between calories and protein has only been properly appreciated recently. The three main components of the diet—carbohydrate, fat and protein—can all supply energy, but most people obtain most of their calories from carbohydrate. In the hungry nations, where unrefined cereals are the staple, these also supply most of their protein needs. But if the person eats insufficient calories for his needs, the protein he eats is used to provide energy, rather than being used for its proper function which is to restore body tissues.

The daily energy needs of an individual depend on his body-size, his age and his activity, but it is possible to find the daily per head needs of a population by referring to tables developed by the United Nations Food and Agriculture Organization. These show that the average per capita needs are 2,400 calories per day for every man, woman and child in the world. But this is a fairly crude figure.

It is possible to make a more accurate calculation from tables of the size of age groups in a population, and from data obtained by two British nutritional experts, Drs. Payne and Waterlow, who have calculated an individual's energy requirements by a so-called factorial method. Energy is mainly supplied by carbohydrates and fats, and is expressed as calories. At every minute of the day, or night, energy is being expended. Calories are being used up in sleeping and in waking, in sitting and in walking. The calories needed to keep the body in order at rest are maintenance calories and the quantity needed is related to body size. In addition, until a person is an adult, energy is required for growth. This can also be calculated. From these calculations the average calories required for essential maintenance and growth can be computed, and the calories needed for activity can be added to find the total calorie requirements of an individual or of a population. The figure for the average person in the developing nations works out at 1,900 to 2,300 calories, and in the developed nations at 2,400 to 2,600 calories a day (Fig. 6/1). In the developing world the fact that average calorie needs are only just reached implies that many people obtain too few calories each day. They are undernourished.

Proteins are essential for life. Without adequate protein intake man cannot survive, as he is unable to repair his tissues and replace the protein he has burned up. Proteins are especially important in infancy and early childhood, for protein deficiency is known to reduce resistance to disease and may be associated with mental slowness. The World Health Organization recommends a daily average intake of 0·52 to 1·5 g of

The Hungry World

protein per kilogram body weight depending on the age of the person. For example, pregnant women, infants and children under the age of 6 need more than 1 g of protein a day per

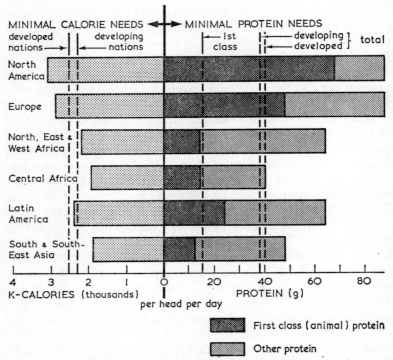

Fig. 6/1. Calorie and protein intake per head in various regions of the world related to calorie and protein needs. Calorie and protein needs are related to body size and weight, as well as to the proportion of each age group in the population. The exact per head need is unknown so a range is given. Source: *Provisional Indicative World Plan for Agricultural Development*, U.N.F.A.O., Rome, 1970; Llewellyn-Jones, D., *Human Reproduction and Society*, Faber & Faber, London, 1974 (Table 9/8).

kilogram body weight, whilst non-pregnant adult women only need 0·52 g per kilogram a day. The W.H.O. calculations are based on the assumption that the proteins eaten are high-class proteins. High-class proteins contain the eight essential amino-acids and are found primarily in milk and milk products, eggs, fish, poultry and meat. They are also found, less plentifully, in soya beans and nuts. Most people living in the world are unable to afford a diet providing the needed protein from animal products, and rely mainly on the protein found in grains and cereals. Grains and cereals contain between 5 and 13 per cent protein, but this is not high-class protein. Different grains are deficient in one or two of the essential amino-acids, so that to obtain all the essential amino-acids a variety of grains and vegetables must be eaten. As well as this, the cereal protein is less well utilized, so that more needs to be eaten to provide the same quantity of protein as animal products. Calculations show that compared with egg or milk protein only 60 per cent of rice protein, 50 per cent of wheat protein and 36 per cent of maize protein is utilized. When the diet consists mostly of cereals and vegetables, the amount of protein needed per kilogram body weight increases by about 50 per cent, so that an adult man needs an intake of about 50 g per day. Of this, ideally about 20 per cent should be first-class animal protein, so that all the essential amino-acids are provided easily.

Taking all the facts into account, and recognizing the different age structures of populations in the developing and the developed nations, calculations can be made to obtain a figure which gives the average protein requirements per head per day. These calculations show that in the developing nations an average protein intake of 38 g per head per day is required to provide safely for minimum needs; and in the developed nations the average minimum daily requirement is 40 g (Fig. 6/1).

The F.A.O. has made calculations which show that sufficient protein is produced in each region of the world to enable every individual to reach the minimal average daily intake required for health. Unfortunately, average daily protein requirements presuppose equitable distribution of protein-containing foods. This does not occur, and since proteins are relatively expensive, the poorer section of the community is protein deprived. Investigations in India, for example, by the Indian Council of Medical Research, showed that over 90 per cent of pre-school children of the 'lower socio-economic group' had an insufficient calorie intake, 35 per cent ate insufficient proteins each day, and 30 per cent were deficient in iron or in vitamin A. The scientists pointed out that in India protein deficiency always occurred in association with carbohydrate deficiency, and if the latter was corrected, the children obtained sufficient protein for their needs. Amongst the Indian children surveyed two to three per cent had such severe calorie-protein deficiency that they were either emaciated with wrinkled skin or bloated with retained water. This condition is called kwashiorkor. The word is West African and means 'the sickness that comes to a baby when another baby is born'. In Africa it is the result of protein starvation, and can occur even if the calorie intake is supposedly sufficient. In India this was not so, both calories and protein being inadequate.

Kwashiorkor usually follows weaning, when the infant is replaced at the breast by the next baby—hence the African name. In mild cases growth is retarded, the child's hair develops a reddish tinge, and it gets a pot belly. In severe cases the child's legs become swollen with fluid, its hair falls out, it becomes whining and apathetic, and usually dies. The growth-retarded child, if it survives the disease, remains physically less well developed throughout life; and worse, its brain may have been damaged by the calorie-protein malnutrition.

The effect of calorie-protein malnutrition on the subsequent mental development of the child was assessed in India by administering tests to the children 7 years after the disease had been diagnosed. The tests were also given to normal children matched for age and background. The results showed that the malnourished children were retarded mentally, particularly in perceptual and abstract abilities. The malnutrition had affected their brain cells and hindered brain growth. Information obtained from 26 nations and reported by the F.A.O. in 1966 shows that about 3 per cent of children under the age of 5 in the hungry, developing world have severe calorie-protein malnutrition and about 25 per cent have moderate malnutrition. Additional evidence collected by the F.A.O. and published in 1969 found 'a widespread incidence of calorie-protein malnutrition which affects one quarter to one third of children under the age of 5 in many of the developing countries for which data are available'. This is happening at a time when the majority of people in the affluent acquisitive, developed world are overfed. Is any further comment needed?

In the 20-year period between 1951 and 1971 the total food

production of the world has increased by nearly 60 per cent. The annual increase has been just under three per cent per year. This exceptional agricultural performance has only been achieved by opening up new land (mainly in the developing nations), by selectively breeding new high-yielding strains of seed and by massive inputs of fertilizer, pesticides and agricultural machinery. Over the 20-year period farmers have increased their use of fertilizer from 15 million metric tons per year to 68 million metric tons per year, an increase of 350 per cent. Over the same period they have bought more and more tractors, so that 15 million were in use in 1971 compared with 6 million twenty years before. Using fertilizer and machines the world's farmers have obtained higher yields from the traditional seeds, and more particularly from the new hybrid seeds. But the higher yielding plants are fragile. They are relished by insects and attacked by viruses. To protect them farmers have had to use increasing amounts of pesticides, and the quantity used in the 20-year period has increased by 350 per cent (Table 6/1).

TABLE 6/1

The percentage increase in certain aspects of human activity in relation to food production between 1950 and 1970.
Source: *The state of food and agriculture*, 1972. F.A.O., Rome.

Commodity	Percentage increase (rates in constant dollars)
Fertilizer	350
Pesticides	350
Tractors	156
Food production, total	60
Food production per head: developed nations	32
developing nations	6

These inputs have led to the spectacular increase in food supplies, but because of the rapidly increasing population growth rate the increase in food per person has not been so

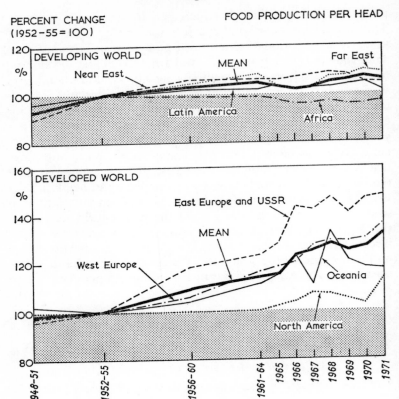

PERCENT CHANGE
(1952-55 = 100)

FOOD PRODUCTION PER HEAD

FIG. 6/2. Food production per head in the regions of the world since 1948. Note: *Far East* includes the nations of South Asia, i.e. Bangladesh, India, Nepal, Pakistan, Sri Lanka and the nations of East and South-East Asia, excluding China and Japan. *Near East* comprises the remaining countries of West Asia (excluding Israel), and the African nations of Egypt, Libya and Sudan. Source: F.A.O. Monthly Bulletins.

spectacular. In the 20-year period between 1951 and 1971, food per head of population has increased in West Asia (the Near East) by 5 per cent, in East Asia (the Far East) by 9 per cent, in Latin America by 2 per cent, but in Africa there is less food per person available today than there was 20 years ago (Fig. 6/2). Under-nutrition and malnutrition remain a problem in the hungry, developing world, and the increased food production has been swallowed up by the concurrent population increase. Only the affluent, capital-rich nations of the developed world have made marked increases in food production per head. The average increase in food production per head in Europe, the U.S.S.R., North America and Australia has been 32 per cent. And it must be noted that the population growth rate of the developed nations is only 1·2 per cent per annum, whilst that of the hungry, developing nations is 2·5 per cent per annum.

Even in the affluent, technologically advanced nations the cost of increased food production has been considerable. The well-documented experience of two technologically developed nations illustrates this. Between 1949 and 1968, United States total agricultural production increased by 45 per cent. This was achieved by increasing agricultural mechanization by 75 per cent, at a cost of reducing the number of people working on the land from 30 million to 10 million, so that today only 5 per cent of Americans work the land. Nitrogen fertilizer use increased in the 20 years by 650 per cent, and the use of pesticides increased by nearly 275 per cent. With all this effort total food crop yield per head of population increased by only 6 per cent.

In Britain a similar story is told. Britain has one of the most intensive and efficient farming systems in the world. Between 1945 and 1970 'very large sums have been invested in technological developments aimed at increasing output and reducing the requirement for labour. Nevertheless, when the effect of inflation on farm prices is taken into account, the productivity of British agriculture has increased by only 35 per cent and there is good reason to suppose that in most major products, yields have now levelled off and in some they are declining.' So write the authors of *A Blueprint for Survival*, after examining the comprehensive data available.

More food is needed. As long as one child in one country goes to bed hungry, as long as one child in one country dies from calorie-protein malnutrition, more food is needed.

What can be done to reduce, and finally to eliminate, undernutrition and malnutrition, so that all people have equal opportunity for a healthy growth? In addition to curbing the population growth it is essential to increase food production, in whatever way possible. Since man is a land mammal the increased use of land offers hope, as does harvesting the sea. But what are the limits to the growth of food?

2

Food from the land . . .

The first need is soil. You cannot grow crops on concrete. But land which has been leached over the ages, and which lacks essential nutrients and minerals, is concrete as far as growing food is concerned. Soil requires to be cared for, to be conserved and to be nourished. This is turn implies the importation of huge quantities of fertilizers and of trace minerals to restore the fertility of the soil. Above all, it requires people who understand soil, and are prepared to maintain it rather than exploit it. Even that is not enough, for plants require water, and if the water is inappropriately applied, it will flow off the soil, leaching it further. The plants also need fertilizer. The best is organic, the faeces of animals or accumulated humus, but because of the shortage of organic fertilizer, increasing use is being made of inorganic materials. The unlimited supply of nitrogen in the air can be fixed chemically, but phosphate, sulphates and potassium compounds are in limited supply. Fertilizers also need to be used properly. They are agrochemicals, and if used inappropriately interfere with the balance between living organisms. Excess fertilizers, if used with excessive, or improper, irrigation, run off with the excess water and can lead to eutrophication problems in rivers and lakes. Eutrophication means over-fertilization, with overgrowth of algae and the death of all fish.

In 1967 President Johnson's Science Advisory Panel made estimates of the area of the earth's surface which is currently cultivated, and the area which is potentially suitable for cultivation. They calculated that about 41 per cent of the total land mass is currently under cultivation. About 33 per cent can never be cultivated because it is too mountainous, permanently frozen, or too cold for any crops to grow, or for livestock to obtain food. That leaves 26 per cent, which the President's Commission considered could be cultivated. Already the richest, most accessible, best-watered land has been occupied by man. The remainder, which amounts to 3,200 million hectares, is mostly forested, or dry grassland. Over half of it is in the tropics lying under thick rainforest. The soil is thin, often lateritic and of very low fertility. Probably only one quarter

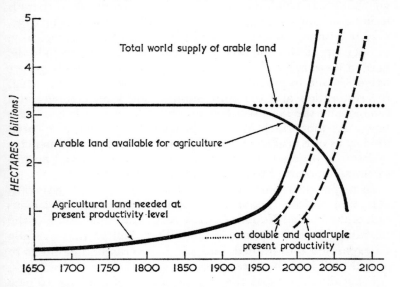

Fig. 6/3. The limits of the available land for agriculture. Total world supply of arable land is about 3·2 U.S. billion hectares. About 0·4 hectares per person of arable land are needed at present productivity. The curve of land needed thus reflects the population growth curve. The light line after 1970 shows the projected need for land, assuming that world population continues to grow at its present rate. Arable land available decreases because arable land is removed for urban and industrial use as population grows. The dotted curves show land needed if present productivity is doubled or quadrupled. Note: a U.S. billion = a thousand million. Source: Meadows, D., *Limits to Growth*, by permission.

of it, at the most, that is 750 million hectares, is economically worth developing and even this will require great care in development, if its rapid conversion into desert is to be avoided. Most of this land is in Latin America or sub-Saharan Africa. It will cost about $1,250 per hectare to clear and to restore the soil, and one hectare will only just keep a man and his wife, at subsistence level. Most of the non-tropical, potentially arable land is of marginal use, as man has found and cultivated the best land in the past centuries. Meadows' computer study, which I mentioned in Chapter 1, suggests that even if it were possible to cultivate all the potentially arable land in the next 30 years there would be no more food per capita than there is today if the current population growth rates continue (Fig. 6/3). And it is impossible, economically, physically and ecologically, to open up all the potentially cultivatable land, to provide the needed trace minerals, to fertilize the soil, to ensure its proper irrigation and to provide adequate crop growth. If the clearing, the restoration and the cultivation is not done precisely and ecologically the land will become eroded, or turn into a dust-bowl, like that which Mr. Krushchev created when he cleared the forests of Kazakhstan in 1954—and turned 30 million acres of forest into desert. It has taken nearly 20 years, and an undisclosed amount of roubles, to restore its fertility.

In a gloomy report, made after careful study of the available, and projected, data, the Food and Agriculture Organization of the United Nations foresaw very little exploitation of the remaining potentially arable land. They believe that by 1985 all expansion into unused land will have ceased. The limits to growth will have been reached.

From this it appears that the possibility of opening up new land to feed the increasing numbers of people on earth is limited. Even so, it should be possible to increase yields on existing land by better agricultural practices; by conserving, and using water properly; by providing proper fertilizer, and necessary trace minerals; and by using high-yielding seed; to produce, in fact, a green revolution.

3

In winter the climate in the great plain of the Ganges, which stretches from the Himalayan foothills, is nearly perfect. The days are warm and sunny, the nights cold. The air sparkles, even under the dust haze which hovers above the plain. In the mud-walled villages of the Punjab, of Haryana and of Uttar Pradesh, the peacocks roost on the walls, and the fields are green, rippling seas of growing wheat. The camels still plod interminably around the Persian wheels, drawing up water to irrigate the growing crops, but more and more they are being replaced by tube-wells—10 cm metal pipes driven through the earth to reach the water-table. Electric motors, or kerosene generators, pump the water from the tube-wells, and permit the farmer to irrigate his growing plants with greater ease and efficiency than did the slow-turning, 2,000-year-old, Persian wheels.

Bagwan Singh had reason to be pleased. He and his family had been landowners for generations. Although the government had ordered holdings to be reduced in size to help the landless peasants he had kept his land intact by the simple expedient of redistributing it to his family, whom he controlled. He was a progressive farmer with a feel for land. He had been one of the first to try the new foreign seed developed in Mexico by the American, Norman Borlaug. He had met the American expert when Borlaug had visited India in 1963 and had been very impressed. Two years later he had been one of the first in his area to use the miracle S64 seed which the Minister of Agriculture, Mr. C. Subramaniam, had imported from Mexico in 1965. He had followed the complicated watering and fertilizing required and had raised a bumper crop of wheat. It was true the hybrid wheat didn't taste as good as the varieties he had grown before, but that didn't matter. Bagwan Singh had sold it to the cities, keeping the native wheat for his own family. Moreover, the whole experiment had been highly profitable and Bagwan Singh had grown fat. After two years the yield of S64 had dropped, but by now he was using a newer hybrid seed; and the yields had risen. He had put some of his capital into sinking tube-wells, he had applied fertilizer and his reward had been a bigger crop. He had rebuilt his house, and installed electric light and a concrete floor. Now, as he looked across the swaying young wheat, and thought of his sons who were in University, of his daughters who had married well, of his docile labour force and of his high status in his village, he was a satisfied man. He thanked God, Subramaniam and Borlaug for the Green Revolution. He had become wealthy and he had produced more food for his hungry fellow Indians. It was good that self-interest and the public good should so readily coincide.

4

The current excitement about the green revolution in Asia must be tempered. Ecologically, it is suspect as it is based on the monoculture of a single crop, either wheat, rice or millet, which makes for a very fragile ecosystem. The less complex an ecosystem the greater is the chance of unexpected disaster. The more complex and diverse the ecosystem the better can it tolerate stresses. When monocultures replace the diversity of natural species the ecosystem becomes increasingly unstable. Economically, the objective of the green revolution is an im-

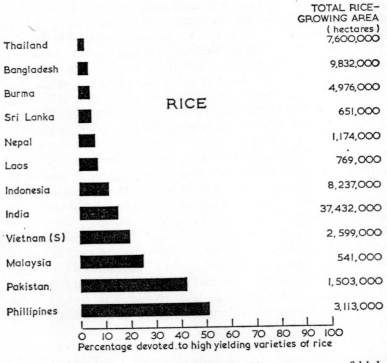

FIG. 6/4. How green is the revolution? The percentage of high-yielding varieties of rice and wheat to total growing area in nations involved in the 'green revolution' (based on information provided by the F.A.O.).

mediate maximization of cereal yield by means of hybrid seed, heavy fertilization and irrigation, with only a sidelong glance at the future ecological impact of this maximization.

The main areas of hybrid Mexican wheat and millet development are in the Gangetic plain, from Uttar Pradesh to the Punjab, and in Turkey; whilst hybrid rice, developed in the International Rice Research Institute in the Philippines, is being grown in South India, the Philippines, Indonesia, Bangladesh, Thailand, Burma and Malaysia (Fig. 6/4). The hybrid high-yielding seeds require a complex package of agricultural practice if they are to reach their expected performance. The package consists of irrigation, fertilizer and plant protection

		TOTAL WHEAT–GROWING AREA (hectares)
Jordan		220,000
Iran		4,200,000
Algeria	WHEAT	2,995,000
Morocco		498,000
Lebanon		61,000
Turkey		8,208,000
Iraq		2,033,000
Bangladesh		126,000
Afghanistan		2,966,000
Syria		376,000
Tunisia		735,000
Nepal		388,000
India		17,892,000
Pakistan		6,061,000

Percentage devoted to high yielding varieties of wheat

FIG. 6/4 *(continued)*.

by pesticides, each element of which has to be applied to the young plants in a precise sequence at a precise time.

Irrigation is the key, for the exotic strains of wheat and paddy are thirsty. The water, which is mainly obtained from tube-wells, needs to be applied precisely, six or more irrigations being recommended during the growing cycle. The narrowest bore tube-well (6·25–7·5 cm diameter) discharges 7 to 10 times the water obtained by the traditional Persian wheel, and the newer 10·0 cm bore tube-wells discharge 10 to 15 times the amount. Whilst this is of great benefit to the thirsty plants it is depleting a limited water resource. The number of tube-wells in India has risen from just over 1·0 million in 1965 to 3·3 million in 1971. Ground water accumulates from precipitation during the monsoon. Although the use of water is increasing rapidly the input from rain remains constant, with a result that the water stocks and water-tables are beginning to fall. Already, in one area of Uttar Pradesh, the water table has fallen from 2 feet below the surface in 1960 to 20 feet today. This in turn could lead to the accumulation of salt and alkali in the root growth zone of the plants, as the chemicals are drawn up by surface evaporation and capillary action. Additional water in North India can be obtained from the canal systems developed by the British 100 years ago. These are filled from the great rivers and again depend on the monsoon. They are not inexhaustible. In 1969 there was not enough water for all users to irrigate their crops and water thefts were reported.

The next year, 1970, was a much better year, but in 1971 the increase in food production slowed to only 1 per cent, so that the amount of food available per person fell. In 1972 adverse weather conditions, and the partial failure of the monsoon, meant that there was not enough water for the young wheat and the crop was poor.

Even when the rains are good, and fill the rivers and canals, excess water can cause environmental damage. Seepage from the canals (and over 50 per cent of the water is lost between source and seed) leads to salinization and alkalinization.

Plants will not grow unless they can obtain sufficient nutrients from the soil. The two main requirements are nitrates and potassium. The nitrates are obtained by bacterial action in the plant roots which fixes nitrogen from the humus of the soil. If there is insufficient nitrogen the plants fail to thrive. The new hybrids are particularly greedy and there is insufficient nitrogen in the overused land of the Ganges plain to meet their demands. For high yields and for double cropping, heavy applications of fertilizer are necessary. Currently, the recommended application during the growing period is 120 lb. of nitrogenous fertilizer, 80 lb. of superphosphate and 80 lb. of potassium (120 : 80 : 80 NPK) per acre. However, many farmers work on the principle that if some fertilizer produces bigger yields more fertilizer will produce still bigger yields.

The heavy applications of fertilizer and water lead to a flow-off of nitrogen. This is carried to swamp lakes and slow-moving streams, with resulting eutrophication and the eventual death of all aquatic life.

There is a further potential danger which may arise from the overuse of nitrogenous fertilizer. This affects human infants, and has been investigated most extensively in the U.S.A., although it might also occur in India. If excessive nitrogenous fertilizer is applied to crops the run-off may contaminate the water supply of neighbouring towns or the wells supplying villages. In the farmlands around Decatur, in Southern Illinois in the U.S.A., farmers have almost doubled the yield of corn per hectare in the past 20 years by using large amounts of fertilizer. Fertilizer is cheap, and the higher yield has enabled them to survive economically in a period of rising costs. But the nitrate run-off has produced an unacceptably high level in Decatur's water supply.

In Israel, too, heavy repeated applications of fertilizer have aided the nation's agricultural expansion. As might be expected, the run-off has increased the nitrate concentration in many wells in the rural areas.

In most cases raised nitrate concentrations in drinking water appear to do no harm to human health. The exceptions are infants under six months of age. If infants drink nitrate-contaminated water micro-organisms in their stomachs convert the innocuous nitrate into dangerous nitrites. If the nitrite is then absorbed into the bloodstream of the child it affects the ability of the red blood cells to carry oxygen. The result, termed methhaemoglobinaemia, is that the infant becomes blue, finds difficulty in breathing and may die. Several hundred deaths from methhaemoglobinaemia have been reported in the U.S.A. Oddly, no infants have been affected in Israel. Dr. Shuval, the energetic head of the Department of Medical Ecology of the Hebrew University in Jerusalem, has investigated this. The reason appears to be that Israeli babies, in the susceptible age, either are breast fed or are fed on whole cows' milk, and in addition are given free orange or tomato juice, which is rich in ascorbic acid. Ascorbic acid is an antidote to methhaemoglobinaemia. By contrast, babies in the U.S.A. are largely not breast fed, and are put on to 'formula' feeds made up from milk powder, which is made liquid by adding tap water.

At present, the pattern of feeding infants in India's rural areas resembles that of Israel rather than the United States, but persuasive salesmen are extolling the value of dried milk powders, and tins are found in many village stores. The disease could occur unless action is taken.

A further disturbing piece of information about nitrates is that they may combine with other chemical substances, obtained from the diet, to form compounds called nitrosamines (DMN), which have caused cancer in laboratory animals.

Excessive demand for water and the misuse of fertilizer do not tell the whole story. It has been found that the hybrid strains of cereals are particularly susceptible to diseases, although most can be controlled by repeated, heavy spraying with insecticides, pesticides and fungicides. The effect of the accumulation of these on the ecology is not yet fully known.

The widespread application of DDT in the control of malaria in the years just after World War II is one of the outstanding examples of preventive medicine. Used for this purpose the trade-off between eliminating the anopheles mosquito and the effect of DDT on other forms of wild life clearly was in favour of malaria control. To quote the World Health Organization who reported in 1971, 'More than 1,000 million people have been freed from the risk of malaria in the past 25 years, mostly thanks to DDT. This is an achievement unparalleled in the annals of public health. The improvement in health resulting from malaria campaigns has broken the vicious circle of poverty and disease resulting in ample economic benefits: increased production of rice (and wheat) because the labour force is able to work; opening of vast areas for agricultural production and augmented land value where only subsistence agriculture was possible before.' To this one might add that the control of malaria has permitted the increased rate of growth of population. When the trade-off is calculated, and the balance between benefit and damage is evaluated, the increased population due to DDT control of malaria must be included. Population control, which is currently accepted as being an urgent need, is expensive. DDT is a persistent organo-chemical, and as one moves up through the food chain its concentration increases. There is also the anxiety that it may be harmful to man. The Report of the Secretary's Commission on Pesticides and Their Relationship to Environmental Health was published in the U.S.A. by the Department of Health Education and Welfare in 1969. It stated, '. . . DDT can be regarded neither as a proven danger as a carcinogen for man, nor as an assuredly safe pesticide, suspicion has been aroused and it should be confirmed or dispelled'.

If the use of DDT, and other persistent organo-chlorides had been confined to malaria control, there could be no real argument, although increasing numbers of malarial mosquitoes are now resistant to DDT, and in Central America the use of synthetic organic chemicals has failed to stop malaria. But DDT, aldrin and dieldrin have been widely used as controls of agricultural pests, where they are less than perfect, and by reducing non-target species may, in fact, create new pests. They have been widely used in the green revolution, and their use has been defended vigorously by Dr. Borlaug who initiated that revolution. In a lecture to the Governing Conference of the Food and Agriculture Organization in November, 1971, he spent a considerable portion of his time defending the use of DDT, which he claimed was harmless to man. He added, 'I have dedicated myself to find better methods of feeding the world's starving population. Without DDT, and other important agricultural chemicals, our goals are simply unattainable.'

This is the opinion of one expert. Others have different views and feel that the uncontrolled, inappropriate use of the organo-chlorine chemicals has potential long-term dangers. Jean

Dorst, who is a professor at the Paris Museum of Natural History, is not sanguine. In an article in 1972 he stated, 'The long-acting insecticides therefore produce grave consequences to individuals and populations. They are also capable of disrupting equilibriums within biological systems. Since they are non-selective they destroy all insects, those we want to destroy as well as the harmless and useful species. . . . Thus we should observe the greatest prudence in using pesticides precisely because of our ignorance of their long-term effects. . . . This applies especially to tropical regions where pesticides, sometimes useful, can be extremely pernicious because of ecological conditions.'

There is clearly a difference of opinion. In this situation it does not mean that all pesticides should be banned: it means that they should be used with caution, and when possible DDT and the other persistent organo-chlorides should be replaced by non-persistent insecticides. In the areas of the green revolution pest control is essential, for the hybrid plants are particularly relished by pests. And DDT is cheap. There is no other cheap, simple pesticide. The nearest substitute, malathion, is eight times more expensive.

Once again a trade-off has to be evaluated. Should mankind persist in using a cheap, but potentially dangerous method of pest control so that more food may be produced cheaply, or are there other methods? At this moment in time the answer is clear. DDT should be used: more food is needed. But the use of persistent organo-chlorines could be limited, if the rich nations subsidized the use, by the poor nations, of the more expensive, short lasting, substitutes. In return, the farmers of all nations would be educated to use pesticides as only one weapon against unwanted agricultural predators. They should be used as auxiliaries to help the environment's natural defences, not as the only weapons of agricultural warfare. Simultaneously, even more intensive research should proceed to seek biological weapons rather than chemical ones.

Even with precise irrigation, fertilization and plant protection, the yield of each new hybrid decreases in successive seasons. In the first season the yield is two or three times that of the indigenous varieties. In the second year, with high inputs, this yield may be maintained, but is more likely to fall. By the third year the plants are reverting to their dwarf characteristics, and the yield declines to little more than that of the native seeds (90 lb. per acre compared with 85 lb. per acre using indigenous strains). As one agriculturalist remarked, 'No one mentions S64 any more'. Yet S64 was the original wonder wheat of Borlaug's programme. It has been eclipsed because of its high susceptibility to disease and because of falling yields. Today's wonder, the Triple Gene Dwarf, may be tomorrow's discard. The economic balance fluctuates. Costs of development of new strains, of providing stocks of new seed, of fertilizer, pesticides and water, only make the project viable if the yields are high, and remain high.

This applies to 'miracle-rice' and to the hybrid millets as much as to 'wonder-wheat'. Disaster can strike unexpectedly, despite precautions, as might be expected in ecologically fragile monoculture (single crop) systems. In 1969 the Tungru virus decimated much of the rice crop in eastern Uttar Pradesh, 400,000 acres (162,000 hectares) being affected and 60 to 100 per cent of the crop being lost. Even in the U.S.A. with all its technological expertise, and apparently limitless finance, 15 per cent of the hybrid corn crop was devastated by a new mutant strain of leaf blight in 1970.

The heavy water requirements, the complex regimens of precisely timed irrigation and fertilizer application, and the meticulous attention to detail, means that the best results are obtained by the more progressive farmers, working in co-operatives, or on farms of reasonable size. It is only rarely that a peasant farmer can achieve the potential yields. From the point of view of increased food grain production it is perhaps fortunate that in India, particularly, most of the land reforms have been directed more to the redefinition than to the redistribution of land. There are many Bagwan Singhs in India who have bent the laws of land reform, so that the larger holdings needed for maximal yield of food grains do, in fact, exist. It was feared that increased mechanization, both by the use of tractors and by electrification of tube-wells, would increase unemployment, and lead to a further drift from the land, with serious social consequences. However, water and fertilizer nourish weeds as well as the cereal plants, and labour is required for this purpose, so that the impact on internal migration has been limited. In fact, in the Ganges plain the expected drift of unemployed, landless peasants has not increased in volume since the introduction of the new hybrid cereals.

The green revolution has had a further consequence. It has led to turbulence in the villages. In the past, when everyone was poor, the landless and near landless peasant, who compose almost 45 per cent of India's rural population of 450 million, could relate to the landowner. Both had been through hard times together. But since 1967 the high-yielding cereals have enriched the few, whilst leaving the masses untouched. The Bagwan Singhs of India form only 10 per cent of the rural population, and they have thrived. Their houses are finer, and made of brick and concrete; their children are well clothed; their wives bejewelled. Inside the houses furniture has appeared and beds have replaced traditional charpoys. Electricity has given the rich, electric light, refrigerators and electric fans. The landless poor, by contrast, continue to live in earth-floored, mud huts, with insufficient food, insufficient work for most of the year, and insufficient cash-income to buy the goods they see conspicuously displayed in the homes of the rich and the shops of the merchants.

The problem is, what is to be done? Should it be radical land reform with the development of communes on the Chinese model; or would it be better to concentrate, not on land reform, but on an expansion of the revolution so that more can share? This in turn means that larger areas of land will have to be supplied with water, and water, even in India, is a limited commodity.

The dilemma remains and is one which will increase as the population grows. In 1971, in the whole of India, there were 15 million unemployed and 40 million under-employed people, a three-fold increase since 1961. The estimate for 1981 anticipates a four-fold increase over the 1971 figure, to 60 million unemployed, and 160 million under-employed.

Even if food production, thanks to the green revolution, is keeping up with the population increase, the latter is likely to continue to grow more rapidly in the next decade, and the social effects of the revolution have yet to be determined.

There is also the question of whether the green revolution will continue.

5

It is not the first green revolution in India, as Elizabeth Whitcombe has pointed out. She also commented, wryly, that the lessons of the earlier revolutions have been ignored in the organization of this new green revolution. Dr. Whitcombe, who is an historian, an economist and a classicist, believes that Northern India 'offers a "natural laboratory" for the detailed examination . . . of successive innovations introduced piecemeal, in accordance with a policy of maximization, into the world of monsoon agriculture'. She is able to make this statement after studying detailed records kept by the British of their agricultural activities in India. The records started following the appointment of Allan Octavian Hunt as Secretary of the Department of Agriculture in about 1870. Hunt had a great love for India and Indians, and spent much of his time in determining the reasons for the poor yield of food obtained in India. He was convinced that it was not due to the ignorance nor the indolence of the Indian farmer, who did surprisingly well despite lack of capital, and under extremely difficult conditions of work. Hunt believed the main cause was that the land had been over-exploited, and agriculture in India had become 'and becomes daily, more and more . . . a system of spoliation'. He held that yields 'of every kind of crop' could be increased by 30, 50 or even 70 per cent with proper manuring and proper tillage. He proposed a co-ordinated agricultural campaign, in which all the elements were linked and which followed a scientific sequential pattern. He devoted all his efforts to an ecological approach, and he failed. The other longer-established departments and the government wanted to maximize food production, much of it to be exported to Britain, and they proposed to do this by irrigating the dry soil in the winter growing season.

In the second half of the nineteenth century, the most extensive system of irrigation schemes the world had ever seen was developed in Northern India. Water was drawn from the great rivers and fed through a system of canals. The water permitted the cultivation of cotton, sugar cane, wheat and indigo, which produced quick returns at the expense of soil exhaustion. And no co-ordinated system of manuring, or use of inorganic fertilizer, was initiated. The objective was maximization of production, more to benefit the British raj than the Indian agriculturalist.

The irrigation schemes were successful in that the objective of larger yields was attained, but they led to a marked eco-agricultural distortion. The older polycrop, small-scale, well-irrigated agriculture was replaced by large-scale block cropping of monocultures. In the autumn indigo and cotton were harvested, and in the spring, on the same land, wheat was cropped. In the far north-west the disturbance was least, although by the 1860s the soil was becoming worn out. However, further to the south-east problems mounted. The canal embankments prevented proper drainage; water seeped laterally through the unlined canal walls; heavy, uncontrolled, flushing surface irrigation flooded the soil with more water than could be drained. In addition, forests were cleared to provide land and to provide wood for the railways. The ecological balance was upset. Stagnant water accumulated in low-lying lands, forming swamps. In the cleared land, increased evaporation rates drew up subsoil water, which was heavily loaded with alkali salts. These salts accumulated in the root zones, or appeared on the surface as a crystalline deposit. Hunt wrote, perhaps dramatically, of the result: 'At first the result may be good, and marvellous are the crops that have been raised in the Doab on the first introduction of canal irrigation, owing to the first slender doses of potash and chloride of sodium. . . . Time passes on, some crops begin to be unprofitable; in the hottest time of the year, a glimmer as though of a hoar frost over-spreads the land. The land grows worse and worse, but every night and day nature works slowly on, and the time comes when, abandoned by the cultivator, the land glitters white and waste as though thickly strewn with crisp, new-fallen snow; never alas! to melt away, except under the rays of science.

'Along the little old Western Jumna Canal, thousands of fields are to be seen thus sterilized. Along the course of the mighty Ganges Canal—a work as it were but of yesterday

144

(opened, 1854)—the dreary, wintry-looking rime is already in
many places creeping over the soil.

'Come it quickly or come it slowly, the ultimate result here
is also certain; and, unless a radical change is effected in
existing arrangements, we know, as definitely as we know that
the sun will rise tomorrow, that the time must come when some
of the richest arable tracts in Northern India will become howl-
ing saline deserts.'

By 1891 there were 3 million acres of saline soil in north-
west India, and 75 years later, in 1964, with increased canal
development, the desolate wasted land was conservatively
estimated at 7 million acres.

The first Indian green revolution had failed. After an initial
success the land had become increasingly impoverished, and
finally large tracts lay waste, glistening with accumulated
alkali.

6

It is true that in the new green revolution compared with the
previous ones, there are two additional elements. These are the
heavy applications of inorganic fertilizer and the heavy use of
pesticides. Yet this will not delay the spoliation of the soil.
Indeed it may increase it. Monsoonal tropical soils only store
nitrogen poorly; to retain fertility they need organic manure,
which the peasants use for fuel, not for fertilizer. Pesticides have
disadvantages; resistance by insects, and moulds, develop
rapidly.

The new green revolution is following the exploitation path
of the old: maximize output even if it is only for a short time;
technological innovations will solve any problems which arise.
The soil is being raped rather than being gently seduced to give
more. The agricultural ecosystems are being distorted in
multiple ways. Elizabeth Whitcombe believes that: 'The recent
agricultural history of northern India is characterized by the
pursuit of maximum yields per acre—a policy of highest economic return at lowest economic cost: in short, maximization
through major technological innovation of the productive
potential of the most promising alluvial areas. In tracing the

intensification of agriculture from the early nineteenth century the liabilities as well as the assets are clearly evident;
arising in the first instance from the introduction of irrigation, in
the context of public works development, without accompanying measures to provide the necessary supply of fertilizer and
alkaline amendments to the soil, and in the second, from the
introduction of exotic strains of cereals and chemical treatments
together with intensive exploitation of new irrigation sources,
chiefly groundwater, in an ecosystem already distorted through
the cumulative effects of an earlier green revolution.'

Even Norman Borlaug, the father of the green revolution,
who in October, 1970, was awarded the Nobel Prize for his
work, is cautious. He considers his programme of constantly
developing new genetic strains of high-yielding seed 'only a
stop-gap, not a solution to the world's food problem'. The
Mexican dwarf wheats, and the Philippine dwarf rices, have
obtained a 30-year respite from the potential world famine.

When Borlaug accepted the Nobel Peace Prize he delivered
a lecture. In this he said: 'The green revolution has won a
temporary success in man's war against hunger and deprivation;
it has given man a breathing space. If fully implemented the
revolution can provide sufficient food for sustenance during the
next three decades. But the frightening power of human reproduction must also be curbed; otherwise, the success of the green
revolution will be ephemeral only.'

7

. . . and fish from the sea

The growth of cereals provides carbohydrate, but only a
minimal quantity of urgently needed protein. And since
protein deficiency is not only widespread, but in childhood
has serious effects on mental development, increase in protein
for the people of the world is urgently needed. Carnivorous
man obtains his high-class protein by eating herbivorous animals
or fowls, or by eating fish from the sea. The cultivation of
grazing animals is expensive, and the meat obtained is beyond
the price that many people can afford. But the sea, which
covers two-thirds of the surface of the world, should have an

inexhaustible supply of protein in the form of fish. The question is: has it?

The fertility of the sea is even more variable than that of the land, and depends on the density of plant plankton in the upper sunlit waters, and on the presence of nutrient minerals.

The oceans have three food-producing regions. The first, and largest, is the deep ocean which comprises 90 per cent of the seas, and which is almost a 'biological desert' according to the eminent American marine biologist, John Ryther. The second is the coastal region. These coastal waters form 9·9 per cent of the oceans, or 36 million sq. kilometres, and are fairly productive. The third and very productive regions are the upwelling areas which exist off the coasts of Peru, California, Arabia, Somalia and Southwest Africa. Here, richly nutrient waters are forced up from the deep ocean into the plankton zone. Given sunlight, minerals and plankton, photosynthesis leads to a rapid or a slow plant growth, the abundance depending on the quantity of upwelling, the water temperature, the quantity of sunlight and the absence of pollutants. One calculation suggests that 130,000 million metric tons of plankton are produced each year. These plants are eaten, or die, and are decomposed by bacteria and become mineralized, so that the ingredients enter a new cycle of production. About 10 per cent of the total plankton production becomes incorporated in the next step of the food chain (Fig. 6/5). Tiny crustaceans, oysters, clams and mussels, filter plankton from the water and grow, as do some small fish, particularly the anchovy family, in the rich upwelling off the coast of Peru; whilst in the colder, antarctic waters, the small shrimp, the krill, lives on plankton. The smaller fish are eaten by larger fish, and they in their turn are eaten by still larger fish. Man eats some smaller fish and some larger fish.

It has been calculated that about 0·25 per cent of the primary plankton production per year would be available to man for food—that is a total of about 300 million metric tons. But this potential food supply is widely distributed. In shallow seas about 70 per cent of the fish can be harvested, in deep waters only 40 per cent. This gives an average of 50 per cent, or 150 million metric tons per annum. What such a heavy harvesting would do to the marine ecosystems, and how it would distort the complex food chain, is presently unknown, for at present 70 million metric tons are being harvested annually, and over-fishing has resulted in a diminishing catch of some species. In 1971, for the first time since 1930, the world's total fisheries production did not increase, owing to poor catches. This was

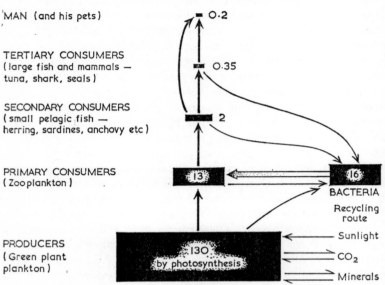

F IG . 6/5. The aquatic food pyramid, showing the direct and re-cycling routes for conversion of plant material into animal tissue. The figures in the proportional rectangles show the estimated animal production in U.S. billions of metric tons per year of organic matter. From *Resources and Man: A Study and Recommendations* by the Com-mittee on Resources and Man of the Division of Earth Sciences, National Academy of Sciences, National Research Council, with the co-operation of the Division of Biology and Agriculture. W. H. Freeman and Company. Copyright © 1969.

despite the fact that the waters of the southern Pacific were being fished, and that larger, better equipped fishing vessels were being used.

As well as deep-sea harvesting, it should be possible to farm the coastal waters. Hectare for hectare, the sea is probably as productive as the land, and the very rich areas, those with up-wellings and the coastal waters, are more fertile than land.

Fertile, that is, if the correct sea animals are cultivated—and they are few. The most successful are oysters, mussels, eels, mullet, yellowtails and milkfish. The larger ocean predators, tuna, herring, mackerel and shark, require too much food and too much water. The cultivated varieties tend to be highly priced, and shellfish are the most favoured. At present fish culture yields about 4 million tons a year. Experts such as Clarence Idyll believe that it is theoretically possible to harvest 40 million tons annually, but that this amount will never be achieved. The coastal waters are prized by fishermen, swimmers, water-skiers, and those whose relaxation is to drive noisy motor boats at high speed. Even more, they are prized as a free dump into which ships, cities, and industry can discharge their waste. The coastal waters of the developed nations are being polluted at an exponential rate, with a doubling time of 5 years, or ten times that of the population growth rate. Sewage, industrial wastes, fertilizer, pesticides, silt, garbage and oil all go into the sink of the estuaries and the sea, into the very areas where fish culture could take place. With the tragedy of Minamata Bay fresh in people's minds, with increasing bacterial contamination from sewage, the areas of potential fish culture are diminishing. Canada has closed 25 per cent of her potential shellfish grounds and the U.S.A. 10 per cent because of pollution. Unless the developed nations take action quickly to stem the surge of pollution, the hope of fish culture will remain largely a hope.

It would seem that the estimate of a fish harvest of 150 million tons a year is over-optimistic, particularly as the sea is becoming increasingly polluted. Ryther has calculated the maximum annual fish crop possible, without upsetting the marine ecosystem, as 120 million tons, or less than twice today's catch of 70 million tons. The capital investment to achieve this would be considerable and fishing would have to cease being predatory. Because of this it is unlikely that the target will be reached within the next 30 years. By that time the world's population will have doubled so that the fish available per capita will at best have remained static, and, more likely, will have declined.

Just as with the soil and the grain crops on land, the sea and the fish need to be cared for, cultivated and culled, rather than raped and exploited for today's immediate gain, with tomorrow's possible disaster ignored. If not, the tragedy of the wild whales will be repeated.

In 1968 Roger Payne wrote in *The New York Zoological Newsletter* about the largest of mammals, the whales. For years Dr. Payne has studied whales. He knows them, and their habits, better perhaps than he knows the habits of the Esquimaux or the Australians. He has lived amongst wild whales, and by attaching minute radio transmitters to their backs has found where they live, where they feed and where they go. And he is sad because man is killing off the whales, merely to exploit quickly their blubber. They are being pack hunted, not harvested, just as the bison was hunted on the American prairies in the nineteenth century. A century ago, a whaling ship killed an average of one whale a month. Today, the technologically efficient whaling ship, hunting the whale by radar, and using explosive harpoons, kills between one and three whales a day. Between 1930 and 1940, the hunters went after the largest of the whales, the blue whale, and killed off about 20,000 a year, until only about 500 were left. To preserve the survivors, they are now fully protected, as are the humpback whales. After 1945 the whalers switched to the next largest, the fin whale. By 1965 they had almost eliminated them. In the same period, 1930 to 1965, twice as many whales had to be killed each year to produce half as much oil. As the fin whales became scarce, the whalers turned to the seis whale, and more particularly to the sperm whale which is being hunted with ignorant enthusiasm, and without limit on numbers (Fig. 6/6).

Although an International Whaling Commission had been established after World War II to regulate the harvest, and to protect whale species from extinction, the whaling nations could not agree, and the slaughter continued although it was agreed that only male sperm whales of a minimum length of 10 metres (35 feet) should be taken. Helicopters are used to find the whales, which are then pinpointed by radar, and they are killed with explosive harpoons. The carcase is filled with compressed air, and a radio beacon is attached to its skin so that it can be located and towed to the factory ship to be turned into oil.

The oil is used as the raw material for margarine, lipstick, transmission oil and shoe polish. And for all of these products there are alternative cheaper substitutes. In Stockholm in 1972, the Conference on the Human Environment recommended a

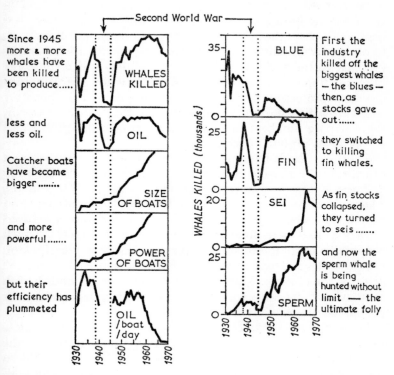

FIG. 6/6. Hunting the whale. As the larger, more easily hunted whales have been killed off, smaller species have been chased and killed to keep the industry alive. Source: Roger Payne, 'Among Wild Whales', New York Zoological Society Newsletter, by kind permission. (The original has more detail.)

total ban on whaling to last for 10 years. As yet the whaling nations have failed to ratify the ban, and whaling continues. Japan and the U.S.S.R., capitalist and communist, have placed short-term self-interest over the long-term interests of ecology. Soon there may be no wild whales. Man, who has the most complicated mammalian brain, is unable to learn.

And what he is doing to the whales, he is trying to do to other fish species.

There once was a man who had a goose which laid golden eggs, and being greedy for gold, he killed it. That was a fairy story, but the slaughter of the wild whales continues. And in his arrogant ignorance, man, in this case Russian man, has begun to harvest the krill, which is the baleen whales' main food, to obtain its protein and oil now that the whales are becoming less easy to hunt. Baleen whales are toothless and include the blue, the fin, and the seis whales, which are now scarce. Given absolute protection and good food supplies, their numbers could grow over the next decades. It is, in Roger Payne's words, 'Like wiping out beef cattle in order to have the pleasure of eating grass-protein concentrate.'

There is a limit to what can be taken from the sea without disturbing the marine ecosystems. Hunt the fish too furiously and the system is distorted. Use the sea as a sewer and the system is distorted. Thor Heyerdahl found oil patches, and polythene packs, in mid-Atlantic. Wurster has produced evidence that persistent pesticides, such as DDT, which eventually accumulate in the oceans, reduce phytoplankton photosynthesis. Toxic waste from industry poured into the sea disturbs the ecology. Man needs to cherish the sea and the fish that swim in its deep waters. If he doesn't he can produce a marine desert. Already the yield is dropping.

Even if man harvests the sea in a responsible, ecological manner, he is still irrational. In the late 1950s the fertility of the waters of the upwelling Humboldt current off the coast of Peru was appreciated. The rich, nutrient-laden waters, heavy with plankton, encouraged the growth of millions of protein-rich anchovetas. This fishery had been exploited since 1957 and until 1972 gave a high yield, when mysteriously (perhaps due in part to over-exploitation) the anchovetas virtually disappeared. Trawlers from Peru, and the U.S.A., have drawn thousands of metric tons of anchovies, most of which have been exported to the U.S.A. There they have been ground up to make chicken feed for mid-west chicken farmers, at a time when protein malnutrition is widespread in Latin America. Even more appalling, much of the fish meal has been canned so that affluent Americans can feed their pet cats.

8

One night Ununbu died. He was four. He had been hungry ever since he had been weaned. He had survived the terrors and the starvation of the Biafran war, he had survived cholera. One night he died in Ibadan Hospital from protein malnutrition—from kwashiorkor. But perhaps a black Nigerian boy is less deserving of a protein meal, than Mrs. Babbit's Persian pussy.

The morality of feeding protein to Mrs. Babbit's cat is questionable. Even in the richest, the most technologically advanced nation in the world, which has, to quote President Nixon's address in accepting nomination in 1972, 'the best-fed people in the world with the lowest percentage of the family budget going to food of any country in the world'—even in that nation people are hungry. Dr. Mayer headed a White House Conference on Food, Nutrition and Health. In 1972, the same year as President Nixon's speech, he reported that between 20 and 30 million Americans, or 10 to 15 per cent of the population, were malnourished. That this can occur in a nation which 'has more freedom, more prosperity than any people in the world', and 'the highest rate of growth of any industrial nation' (again to quote President Nixon) is a sad commentary on the values of mankind.

The old dilemma of Malthus of population pressing on food supplies has only become a reality 200 years after his birth, but today it is a real problem. Mankind must put investment into agricultural technology so that maximal yields of food can be obtained, and maintained, without disturbing the ecosystems unduly. It is a damning indictment of human nature that the advanced nations have used funds to orbit Mars, to put men on the moon, and to develop a fearsome collection of destructive weapons, whilst at the same time over one-third of the people of the world are undernourished or malnourished. It is a damning indictment of human values that the developed nations restricted food production because they found it economically inadvisable to grow more food. It is a damning indictment of Western civilization that napalm and herbicides have been used to destroy food crops in Vietnam, rather than that large sums of money are given to intensify research into the methods of increasing food production in an ecologically balanced manner. Two quotations should give guide lines. The first was made in 1721 by Jonathan Swift. He wrote: 'Whoever could make two ears of corn or two blades of grass to grow upon a spot of ground where only one grew before would deserve better of mankind, and do more essential service to his country than the whole race of politicians put together.' The second is an old Chinese proverb. It states: 'If you give a man a fish you feed him for one day, if you teach a man to fish you feed him for life.'

Today, there is an urgent need to provide food reserves by establishing a world food bank, and to feed men for life by teaching them new agricultural practices. And at the same time there is an even more urgent need to restrict the exponential population growth, so that all men, women and children may go to bed with full bellies, tonight and every night.

CHAPTER SEVEN

A Precarious Ecological Balance

. . . the risk is very great that we shall overshoot in our environmental demands (as some ecologists claim we have already done), leading to cumulative collapse of our civilization.

It seems obvious that before the end of the century we must accomplish basic changes in our relations with ourselves and with nature. If this is to be done we must begin now. A change system with a time lag of ten years can be disastrously ineffectual in a growth system that doubles in less than fifteen years.

'Man's Impact on the Global Environment', Report of the Study of Critical Environmental Problems, p. 126. M.I.T. Press, 1970.

I

Sydney harbour is one of the most beautiful harbours in the world. If you arrive by sea, early on a spring morning, the sun rises directly behind you out of the Pacific Ocean. As your ship slips in between the two headlands guarding the entrance the harbour opens out in front of you. Sparkling water stretches between the low hills, some covered with houses, some still covered with the bush which was there when Captain Phillip, aboard *Sirius*, let down his sails and went ashore at Sydney Cove in 1788. Just inside the Heads the liner turns slightly south, and there, four miles away, are the towers of the modern city of Sydney. Tall buildings glisten in the morning sun. The air is clear, sparkling. Slowly the liner moves down the harbour past the sandy beaches, each with its shark-proof net, so that

Sydneysiders can swim in safety. Soon you see the great grey structure of the Harbour Bridge, which joins the north and south parts of the city like a giant coat-hanger. The liner comes near Sydney Cove, and is towed into the terminal at Circular Quay in the centre of the city, and just below the bridge. You may now look around and think how delightful it must be to live in Sydney.

It is. Particularly if you live in the Eastern Suburbs. You are within six miles of the city centre, you overlook the harbour, and facing north you catch the sun. You may swim at your leisure in the enclosures of Camp Cove, or Parsley Bay or Neilson Park. The water is warm, the sand firm. Or by driving three miles you can surf on one of the ocean beaches where the long Pacific breakers sweep in, having gathered their momentum across one thousand miles of open ocean. In winter the days are crisp, the nights cool; in autumn and spring the weather is perfect. In summer it does become hot and humid for two months, but the water is cool and clear.

Unfortunately, it will not be like that much longer. The effects of ecologically unbalanced productive technology are spoiling Sydney.

Like Los Angeles, Sydney lies in a basin with hills in the distance. Like the inhabitants of Los Angeles, Sydneysiders enjoy owning their own individual houses, so that the city has spread twenty miles west, and south and north. Like the people of Los Angeles, Sydneysiders travel by automobile. The car is worshipped. There are today in the Sydney area nearly one million motor cars, most of which are ritually and religiously washed and waxed on Sunday mornings. Modern automobiles have high-compression, high-performance engines. They burn large quantities of petrol, particularly when in heavy traffic, and the waste gases emerge from the exhaust at high temperature. Amongst these gases are carbon monoxide, hydrocarbons and nitrogen oxides. In the industrial area of Sydney, factory smoke-stacks push waste gases into the air from burning coal and fuel oil. The waste gases contain sulphur dioxide.

Sulphur dioxide is a component of smog. So are nitrogen oxides. If they are activated by sunlight, of which Sydney has plenty, they combine with organic compounds, such as waste petrol, to produce photochemical smog. On many days of the year the towers of the city of Sydney, when viewed from the Eastern Suburbs, stick up out of a dirty brown haze. It looks as if a child has smudged a light brown crayon over a photograph of the city, just so that he could spoil it.

In recent years it has become less safe to swim in the harbour. Pollutants from factories along the Parramatta River, the seepage of sewage and the discharge from ships, have increased the bacterial content of the water. As yet it isn't too bad and it's safer than the Mediterranean, but the warning is there.

Just north of Bondi Beach, that symbol of sunburned, athletic, Australian youth, where the bikinied girls parade, and where the surfies ride the long Pacific rollers, the sewage treatment plant and its submarine outlet is situated. The load on the plant has increased, in recent years, and sewage not fully treated is frequently discharged. It's fun to swim with faeces!

Sydney is not unique. In fact, compared with Tokyo, Chicago, New York or Los Angeles, Sydney is relatively free from pollution. Almost every industrial city in the developed world has air pollution problems. In some, where the amount of sunlight is low, such as London, the pollutants are mainly hydrocarbons, sulphur dioxide and dust. In those cities which have abundant sunshine, the pollution is due to a mixture of sulphur dioxide and photochemical smog.

Man, through his activities, has made this mess. Man, in chasing the phantom of unlimited economic growth, has created the problem. Efficiency in industry means higher productivity and high profits. Higher profits are the gods of industrialization, and the lower the cost of production the bigger are the profits likely to be. At present, environmental damage is not added by industrialists to the costs of production. But we, the people, pay for it in deteriorating health, in reduced pleasure and in a decaying environment.

2

Alone of all the mammals, man is fouling his own nest. Lake Erie, in the U.S.A., is sick. Few fish swim in its waters, except coarse fish such as catfish, carp and perch. Industrial pollutants discharged without control by factories; raw, or partially treated, sewage disposed of cheaply by cities; and nitrogenous fertilizer excessively applied to farmland, have been carried into the sink of the lake. Each has contributed to Lake Erie's ill-health. The chemical agents carried into the lake have encouraged the overgrowth of algae, which sink as they die and are decomposed by bacteria, so that bacterial over-growth has followed. The excess bacteria have used up the oxygen in the water until there is too little for the fish, which die, and then too little for the bacteria, which also die. In the mud at the bottom of the lake, nitrogen and phosphorus salts, contained in the dead algae, collect. This process is termed eutrophication, or overfertilization of the lake. In Commoner's graphic words, Lake Erie has become 'a kind of huge, underwater cesspool'. Dead fish, decaying piles of algae, oil from ships and plastic containers discarded by humans litter the shores in summer. The cost to restore Lake Erie to health has been estimated at more than $1500 million. And if we want to do that, we, the people, will pay for it; not those whose unecological activities have caused the lake to sicken and nearly die. Except that they are also us.

In Europe, the Rhine is now a sewer for the waste of the unecological manufacturing processes and for the sewage of the expanding towns along its banks. The Lorelei sings to polluted waters in which only coarse fish swim and where even the eels are finding it increasingly hard to survive. In the Mediterranean excessive loads of industrial and domestic sewage have injured the health of its coastal waters. In Italy, in 1971, every one of the 6,000 registered beaches was reported to be dangerously polluted. In Switzerland, with her tradition of order and cleanliness, three lakes, Leman (Geneva), Constance and Neuchâtel, have become polluted with industrial and domestic effluent, and the numbers of lake trout are declining.

And that is not all. Before Europeans criticize America's air and water pollution too strenuously they will have to examine their own territory. A recent study by Gunter Weichart concludes that the North Sea is one of the most heavily polluted sea areas in the world, particularly in its southern part. The North Sea is the catchment area for large rivers from seven highly industrialized countries. At least 60,000 metric tons of phosphate and 600,000 metric tons of nitrogenous compounds are discharged into it each year. As I mentioned earlier, the Rhine is now a sewer which discharges large quantities of heavy metals into the North Sea. The sewage from Greater London, alone, adds 800 metric tons of zinc, 200 metric tons of copper, 50 metric tons of nickel and 10 metric tons of cadmium to the North Sea each year. Ships are dumping industrial waste materials in increasing quantities each year. In addition, ships discharge their waste material and waste water into the sea, usually without any treatment so that oil, faeces, kitchen waste, plastic bottles and packing materials, and cans are thrown into the sea. In 1973 it was estimated that at least 100,000 metric tons of crude oil was discharged from ships. As a result light to middle oil pollution was detected on north German bathing beaches on 50 per cent of all days during the summer, and the pollution was recorded as heavy on 34 per cent of all days.

Unlike Lake Erie, the North Sea is cleansed at least in part each year by an exchange with the relatively clean Atlantic waters which flow in along the east coast of Scotland, so that although the pollution is high, the problems of Lake Erie have not arisen.

Problems of water pollution even affect the relatively under-populated and only moderately industrialized nations of Australia and New Zealand. In these countries in 1972 fish and chip shops could no longer sell flake—which is really shark meat—because samples have been found to contain over 0·5 parts per million of mercury, a level above that permissible for safety.

The most obscene story of mercury pollution comes from Japan. In 1953 a strange disease broke out amongst the people of Minamata Bay. At first it was noted that a number of people were becoming dizzy, and had difficulty in focusing their eyes. Later, some lost control of their limbs, and eventually 36 became insane and died. Autopsy showed that they had died of mercury poisoning. Their bodies contained more than 100 parts per million of mercury. The outbreak was traced to a chemical plant which discharged waste mercury into the waters of the bay. Settling in the mud it was converted by bacterial action into the deadly methylmercury, which accumulated in tiny crustaceans. These in turn were eaten by crabs and larger fish. The people of Minimata ate the 'sea food', and a deadly, painful disease resulted.

Even when man's intentions have been good the results have been unexpected, because he acted without thought of the eco-systems he was distorting.

The Aswan high dam was created to irrigate and so open up more land to meet the needs of Egypt's expanding population. During the time it has taken to construct the dam, and to fill the lake, Egypt's population has increased by so much that all the advantages of the dam have been lost already. More than that has been lost. The dam was built without considering its ecological consequences. Already, waterweeds are clogging the shore of Lake Nasser behind the dam. The lake is also beginning to silt up, a process which will increase over the years. But it is doing more than that. The richly nutrient silt was previously carried down in the floodwaters of the Nile, and deposited as a rich layer over the worn, eroded soil of the Nile delta. This no longer happens. The dam is robbing the soil of the silt, which made it one of the most fertile lands in the world. The irrigation canals have carried water to the newly irrigated areas, but the high evaporation rate in Egypt is threatening to draw up subsoil alkali and salt, producing alkali-salinization, and a blighted land. Meanwhile the canals have become the habitat of schistosomiasis-carrying snails, and of hookworm. Both the diseases are increasing amongst the Egyptian pea-sants.

No longer does the Nile carry the rich nutrients out into the eastern Mediterranean. Without the nutrients, the sardines which feed on them, and the fish which feed on the sardines, are diminishing in numbers. The Egyptian sardine catch fell from 18,000 tons in 1965 to 500 tons in 1968, and has continued to fall since then.

The Aswan dam, and Lake Nasser above it, were created to improve the economic and social lot of the people of Egypt. I appears that because it was designed by technologists who didn' care, or didn't understand ecology, it has failed. In the long run it is more likely to add to the disease, the suffering and the hunger of the Egyptian people, than to improve their condition of living.

A Precarious Ecological Balance

These four examples have been selected to show how man has had an adverse impact on the ecological systems. The significant factor is that the various factors interact with each other and the total effect may cause considerable environmental stress. When ecological stress occurs, predators, that is animals and fish which eat other animals and fish, are affected earlier, and more severely, than herbivores which eat plants. The experience of Erie, Leman and Aswan show that in aquatic systems top level predators, which eat other predators, are the most sensitive of all. This is the reason why Lake Erie has lost nearly all its lake sturgeon, most of its blue pike and only coarse fish remain. It is the reason for the concern about lake trout in Switzerland's lakes, and for the collapse of the Egyptian sardine catch.

The examples can be multiplied, but with each one the realization comes that the base cause is man's inability to live in harmony with the environment. In his arrogance he has obeyed the biblical instruction to 'Be fruitful, and multiply, and replenish the earth and subdue it: and have dominion over the fish of the sea, and over the birds of the air and over every living thing that moves on the earth.'

Man began to become ecologically insane during the industrial revolution of the early nineteenth century, when he created Blake's 'dark satanic mills'. But the insanity was limited, because the numbers of people involved were limited. That the people who lived in the industrial towns of North England developed lung diseases from the pollutants discharged into the air they breathed did not matter. Bronchitis and emphysema were normal—elderly men and women who did not cough and wheeze were rarities. That children in Glasgow, Liverpool, Hamburg, Hull and Huddersfield developed rickets because their diet was deficient in calcium and vitamin D, and because the sun was hidden by dust and sulphur dioxide discharged from factory chimneys, didn't matter. They were expendable. The Yorkshire slogan of 'where there's muck, there's brass' motivated the manufacturers. Economic progress had to be increased: there was money to be made.

The exponential growth rate of ecological insanity became evident after World War II. Science had made far-reaching discoveries in the years before and during the war. Technology would now take over and would convert the scientific theories into practical applications. Mankind would benefit. This was the creed of the technologists. Profits would increase. This was the creed of the industrialists. Nature would be tamed and would yield to man's technological ingenuity. Man would subdue the earth.

Man, modern technological man, dreamed his insane dreams and came up with a new technology. If production rose profits rose, provided people bought the product. The industrialist told the technologists to find out ways of increasing productivity, preferably without increasing costs. He told the advertising man to mount campaigns to convince the consumer that the new product was in every way superior to the old.

And he produced:

- detergents instead of soap
- high-compression, high-powered automobiles instead of low-powered cars
- man-made fibres in place of wool, cotton and jute
- plastics instead of metals, wood and leather
- aluminium and steel instead of iron or timber
- inorganic fertilizer instead of manure
- misleading packaging instead of simple, protective containers, which could be used again
- non-returnable bottles and 'one-trip' metal (usually steel) containers instead of 'recycling' bottles.

The driving force in the changes has been relative prices and profits. Technology has been asked to replace expensive materials with cheaper ones, and expensive fuels with cheaper fuels to reduce costs of production. If these changes added to the cost of the environmental decay, it was too bad. The cost of causing pollution was not included in the cost of production.

The technological innovations have met their objective. They have increased profitability. But the private profit has been increased at the public expense, through environmental pollution and its cost to health and happiness; and in the costs of its correction.

A Precarious Ecological Balance

Many of man's technological innovations have been made without thought of the consequences. Unecological productive technology has produced the ecological insanity which at present affects Western man. Western industrial man makes up one-third of the population of the world but consumes 80 per cent of the world's natural resources which are extracted each year. The degree of madness varies. It is at its peak in the U.S.A. and Japan, but the other industrialized nations are not far behind. It is a contagious madness.

It has resulted because man, in his unthinking arrogance, has ceased to keep his place in the terrestrial ecosystem. He has ceased eating food which was produced by organic methods. He has ceased returning his organic wastes to the soil, preferring instead to use chemical fertilizer whilst his faeces contaminate the rivers and the sea. He has ceased husbanding the natural resources of field, forest and ocean, and has replaced husbandry with rape. He has failed to limit his consumption to real needs and has altered his needs in response to mind-manipulation by acquisitive producers, and seductive advertisers.

In all these ways he has insanely altered the ecological balance and in doing so has started an ever-accelerating juggernaut, by which the ecological laws have been distorted or broken. He has failed to understand the complex web of nature. He has failed to understand that any man-made alteration in the ecosystem inevitably has far-reaching consequences and these are more likely to be detrimental than beneficial. This applies particularly to the introduction of man-made materials not found in nature, as they are unlikely to be degraded by bacterial or enzymatic decay. He has failed to understand that the world litter of waste he has created in his economic 'progress' has to go somewhere—for matter is neither created nor destroyed but only changes in form. He has failed to recognize that nothing is for nothing, and that every game is won at some cost. He has ignored the old Spanish proverb which states, 'Take what you want, says God, take it—and pay for it.' And he has failed to compute the cost to himself and his descendants.

That the crisis is real and immediate is accepted. The question which is unresolved is what to do about it all.

3

Barry Commoner, writing particularly of conditions in the U.S.A., and by implication in other American dominated, or imitating, industrialized nations, has analysed this ecological insanity. He concludes that the increased environmental pollution since 1946 is largely due to the adoption of un-ecological productive technology, allied to anti-social advertising and amoral salesmanship. The creed has been to extract the maximum profit, even if it injured the environment. He instances the change from an ecologically balanced agriculture to agro-business. This has enabled the U.S.A. to produce more food cereals and more meat protein on smaller areas of land. It has been possible only by using inorganic fertilizer (instead of manure) and by confining the animals to feed lots instead of allowing them to range freely. The run-off of fertilizer from the fields and the decay of dung in the limited area of the feed lots, has led to eutrophication of water. He instances the use of man-made fibres instead of wool and cotton. The former rely on chemicals and fossil fuels. These base materials are transformed at the cost of environmental pollution and after expending at least three times the energy needed to produce natural fibres. He instances the automobile industry, which by making bigger cars with increased engine power and compression, has increased exhaust chemicals, and has produced photochemical smog. And he quotes Henry Ford III who said, 'Minicars make miniprofits.'

Commoner, instancing one particularly offensive example of ecologically faulty productive technology, writes about non-returnable, 'single-trip' beer and soft-drink containers. When soft-drink manufacturers and breweries found it was cheaper to put their product in single-trip containers, they mounted a campaign to convince the public that they were doing them a favour. Between 1950 and 1967 the growth of the population of the U.S. increased by 37 per cent, and the consumption of beer increased proportionately. Currently, it is 37 gallons per head per annum, fifth in the world beer-drinking league! But non-returnable beer bottles produced per gallon of beer increased by 408 per cent.

A Precarious Ecological Balance

In parts of the U.S.A. and in Australia it is becoming increasingly difficult to buy beer in anything but non-returnable bottles, or steel or aluminium cans, and soft drinks are usually sold in cans. It requires a courageous shopper to demand his drink in returnable bottles.

This has had a detrimental effect on the environment. The stereotype Australian is a lanky, rangy man with a sunburnt, wrinkled, craggy face and penetrating blue eyes fixed on the far, hazy, brown horizon. He peers from under his wide-brimmed hat, and breathes the clear air. In fact, he is more likely today to be a short, squat man with an impending belly who takes 'the wife and kiddies out of a Sunday' in the sedan, to have a barbecue at a picnic spot. As they drive they throw out of the car wrappings from cigarette and sweet packets, and parts of the Sunday tabloid. At the picnic spot they leave a litter. The ground glistens with the fragments of non-returnable beer bottles and soft-drink cans of indestructible steel or aluminium.

According to Commoner's evidence only the American is more of a polluter. With 6 per cent of the world's population, he consumes 40 per cent of the world's natural resources and produces half of the world's industrial pollution.

Commoner calculates that over 75 per cent of environmental pollution in the U.S.A. is due to the adoption of ecologically faulty productive technology and excessive consumption of goods, and only 25 per cent to population growth. There is much doubt about the validity of his calculations, and a critical analysis of his book by Ehrlich and Holdren points out possible errors. They conclude that in the U.S.A. the increasing, and increasingly demanding, population accounts for at least half of the environmental pollution. In their view, and mine, the urgent control of population growth is as imperative as is the change from unecological productive technology and the greedy acquisition of consumer goods. Commoner, by contrast, argues that the major aim should be to change the attitudes and activities of the manufacturer and the advertiser, by coercion if necessary, rather than to coerce people to limit population growth. But he adds, appearing to realize the importance of population growth, 'Clearly there are logical grounds for supporting both ecological reform of productive technology and the reduction of population growth as a basis for environmental improvement.' We are not so far apart in our views.

4

The extreme condemnation of technology for all modern man's ills is ridiculous. Technology has enhanced living conditions for many humans, particularly in the last 50 years. It is only ecologically faulty technology which should be condemned and, here, as in all socio-economic matters, there are trade-offs.

To take the example of aluminium, which I mentioned earlier. It is true that aluminium beer and soft-drink cans are ecologically wasteful. The energy required to make the can is three times that required to make a glass container, and unlike glass the can makes permanent litter, as aluminium does not fragment or rust. But only 10 per cent of the aluminium produced each year goes to make beer and soft drink containers. Thirteen per cent is used in electrical services where it replaces the increasingly valuable copper. Over half of the annual production of aluminium is used in the building or the transport industries. It is in these, particularly, that trade-offs must be considered.

In building, aluminium is rapidly replacing wood and galvanized iron for window and door frames, and in some cases for roofing. For these purposes aluminium is superior to wood, or galvanized iron, although it costs three times as much. Aluminium is nearly maintenance free, it does not rot or require painting, and it lasts at least six times as long as most wooden frames. If wood is used trees have to be cut, and the wood has to be painted. Both of these have potentially damaging effects on the environment. In assessing the trade-off this has to be taken into account.

The use of aluminium in the transport industry permits lighter automobiles, lighter trucks and lighter trains. The cost of production is admittedly greater than that of steel, and more energy is used, but the vehicles last longer, and being lighter require less fuel for propulsion. And fossil fuels are becoming increasingly scarce.

Trade-offs also have to be assessed when the use of plastics and man-made fibres are considered. In the building industry plastics are replacing wood and iron in many instances. Plastics require little maintenance, and are comparatively cheap. Man-made fibres, which originally replaced cotton, wool and silk in making fabrics, because of their advantages of resistance to crushing and to dirt, are now being mixed with natural fibres. In the past 20 years the demand for fabrics has risen by 100 per cent, largely because of the increasing numbers of people on the earth who require clothes. If man-made fibres had not been developed, the demand would have had to be met by increased cotton and wool production. Wool production is ecologically sound, as sheep are largely in harmony with the environment, but cotton production is complex. It is true that the manufacture of man-made fibres is wasteful in energy, and is polluting, unless care is taken. But the large-scale production of cotton can be just as damaging if care is not taken. The cotton plants require heavy fertilization, repeated applications of pesticide and frequent irrigation. These processes consume energy. Fertilizer and pesticides have to be manufactured and are potential ecological hazards. Water is lifted by electric pumps, which consume energy, and tend to lower the water-table. Energy is also used in harvesting cotton and in converting the raw material into fabrics. Again, one process has to be traded off against the other before the true impact of each on the environment can be assessed.

What is clear, however, is that the more people there are, the more fabrics will be required, and whatever the trade-off, the factor of population adds considerably to the environmental hazard.

Other examples could be given, but these two suffice to point out that the problem is not as simple as it seems. The common factor in all the processes outlined is that they require energy. It is true that natural products use energy they trap from the sun, whilst manufactured products require the use of limited energy stocks found in fossil fuels. Currently, there is considerable concern that energy supplies will become increasingly scarce if the current exponential use of them continues. Even this hazard may be exaggerated.

There is no doubt that the known and potential reserves of oil are likely to be exhausted within 30 years, and it will be necessary for man to turn to solar, water or nuclear sources, for energy. Indeed there is a cogent argument that man should do this without delay so that the fossil fuel supplies can be kept for more useful purposes, such as the production of man-made fibres and plastics.

But in the half-century since oil became the preferred fuel there is no doubt that air pollution diminished, at least until the last decade. The change from burning wood and coal to that of using diesel oil, and particularly electricity, in factories and homes, considerably reduced environmental pollution. It is only due to the automobile, the god of modern industrial man, that it has increased once again.

In the case of the automobile the damage to the environment is obvious. In part this is due to the anti-social action of the automobile manufacturers who have stressed the need to change models frequently; who have stressed speed as a desirable trait in automobiles and who have built rapid obsolescence into their products. In part it is due to the increase in the numbers of people who want to travel and expect to do so in their personal vehicle. Ecologically faulty productive technology and increased numbers and affluence of the population are equal culprits. Even Commoner, who tends to deny population pressures as an element in pollution, accepts this. An ecologically faulty technology has been allowed to develop; but Commoner omits to say that the possession of an automobile has a social status value which has become distorted due to persuasive advertising and man's tendency to imitate.

In any case fossil fuel propelled vehicles will only persist for a relatively short time. The exhaustion of fossil fuels, which is inevitable, presages their doom.

The change from fossil fuel to solar or nuclear energy will be environmentally beneficial rather than damaging. Both solar and nuclear energy eliminate the unsightly aspects of strip mining and the health hazards of deep-pit mining. Both eliminate the air pollution resultant on burning coal or oil, and the water pollution consequent on oil spills during transport.

At present the ancient dream of unlimited power from solar energy is still a dream, although solar energy has been used for heating water and cooling homes on a very limited scale. The technological problems of harnessing solar energy on a large scale to produce power are immense, but it is an aspect of technology which is environmentally beneficial, and research is continuing. Until the technological breakthrough comes and man is able to produce cheap photovoltaic cells, or new highly efficient absorbent surfaces, solar energy is unlikely to replace nuclear energy as the main source to meet man's needs.

Admittedly, nuclear energy adds to the problem of heat emission and dispersal, but even with existing technology this is no greater than that released from existing sources of thermal energy. And nuclear energy supplies are almost inexhaustible, as well as being relatively clean in an ecological sense. The major problem is the potential hazard of a nuclear accident, which is luckily very remote if proper controls are instituted and if the plants work properly. The other ecological problem is the disposal of nuclear wastes which it is estimated will reach 27,000 megacuries in the U.S.A. by the year 2000. Nuclear scientists acknowledge this problem and propose three solutions. The first is to store the wastes in selected isolated spots on earth in concrete vaults. The second solution is to collect the wastes and send them, by rocket, to some inaccessible part of outer space. The danger of this approach is that the launch may fail, and the cost is enormous. The third approach is to bury the wastes in deep, dry (bedded) salt mines in which the salt beds are at least 100 metres thick. The fact that the salt is dry is evidence that it has not been in contact with water, at least in the last 200 million years, and the radioactive waste will therefore be isolated. The waste is first calcined to form a dry solid which is then enclosed in metal containers. These are placed in the salt mine and surrounded by packed salt. When the mine is full it is sealed, and the waste is permanently isolated. There are dangers, of course, which the Director of Oak Ridge National Laboratory, Dr. Alvin Weinberg, admits. In 1971 he gave the Rutherford centenary lecture in which he outlined the problems and concluded: 'We nuclear people have made a Faustian bargain with society. On the one hand, we offer—in the catalytic nuclear burner—an inexhaustible source of energy. Even in the short range, when we use ordinary reactors, we offer energy that is cheaper than energy from fossil fuel. Moreover, this source of energy, when properly handled, is almost non-polluting. Whereas fossil fuel burners must emit oxides of carbon and nitrogen, and probably will always emit some sulphur dioxide, there is no intrinsic reason why nuclear systems must emit any pollutant—except heat and traces of radioactivity. But the price that we demand of society for this magical energy source is both a vigilance and a longevity of our social institutions that we are quite unaccustomed to. The society must then make the choice, and this is a choice that we nuclear people cannot dictate. We can only participate in making it. Is mankind prepared to exert the eternal vigilance needed to ensure proper and safe operation of its nuclear energy system? This admittedly is a significant commitment that we ask of society. What we offer in return, an all but infinite source of relatively cheap and clean energy, seems to me to be well worth the price.'

One particular major advance in techology in the past 50 years also requires to be accounted in the form of trade-offs. This is the advance in medical technology, which, by the production of effective vaccines, antibiotics and other pharmaceuticals, has enabled more people to survive to adult life and has helped in prolonging life for many. It has been, also, a factor in producing the current population problem. In most developed nations better nutrition and better health have altered the patterns of disease. Diphtheria, tetanus, poliomyelitis and smallpox are now rare. Tuberculosis is uncommon, and infection is controlled. The modern man-made pharmaceuticals have radically altered diseases. With the example of the developed nations, the leaders and the people of the developing nations are determined to effect the same changes in their territories, with the certain result that the deaths of infants and children will be reduced, and more people will survive to add to the population problem.

Technology, in many aspects of life, has improved man's lot, particularly in the developed world. It has produced for most people in the industrialized nations, a more leisured life in better surroundings, with better conditions of work and the opportunity to live for longer and in better health than was possible 50 years ago.

But once again the trade-offs have to be computed. The technology used for manufacturing has, by and large, added to environmental decay, and the costs of this have not been included in the cost of the product. Technology has produced many frivolous and unnecessary goods, and the manufacturer, believing in a growth economy, has induced people to purchase these goods in increasing quantities, portraying them as necessities. Technology, in the medical and health fields, has reduced the death rate, particularly in early life, which has given a stimulus to the rate of population growth. The combination of an increasing number of people living in an environment in which the greed for material possessions is artificially stimulated by seductive advertising to sustain a growth economy, has led to two problems facing man today: the problem of unlimited economic growth by ecologically faulty productive technologies, and the problem of the exponential growth rate of human populations. I believe the latter to be the more serious, and since people have desires it stimulates the growth of the former. But, since both are serious, unlimited economic growth requires consideration.

5

In the developed industrialized world two competing groups of people have polarized. The first group believe that the past years of unlimited economic growth, and the recent surge in population growth, will inevitably lead to disastrous famines, intolerable environmental pollution and the rapid exhaustion of limited minerals and fossil fuels. Mankind will fail to survive, they say, whatever he does. Their opponents believe that technology will provide the answers and will enable industrialized man to continue populating as he wishes, to continue on the mad, accelerating misuse of non-renewable minerals, to continue increasing environmental pollution and to persist with the unecological industrial processes currently adopted. The first group call the second, environmental ostriches; the second group call the first, doomsday-men.

What I have been trying to point out in this book is that both extremists are wrong. There is a third group, whom I call the

Noahs. This group is aware of the problems of unlimited economic and population growth, but believes that once the problems have been identified there are sufficient rational people in the world to seek urgently solutions to both problems. The modern Noahs are like the biblical Noah who listened to the word of God: 'The end of all flesh is before me, for the earth is filled with violence through man, and I will destroy man and the earth. Make an ark of gopher wood . . .' And Noah did all that God had commanded him. The Noah's men of today see the problems facing man, and neither climb to the mountain top to pray and await the inevitable end of man, nor do they bury their heads in the sands of technology, believing that technology will cure all the world's ills. They believe that action now, urgently taken by all concerned people, will permit our survival. But to survive we will have to limit population growth, and control economic growth.

To the two-thirds of the world which is non-industrialized, these arguments are remote and the polarization is sterile. Most of their leaders have been trained in the nations of the developed world. Those who now lead the nations which were previously British or French colonies have adopted the economic attitudes of the 1940s and 1950s that growth is all-important, at whatever cost. Those who lead Latin American nations have been strongly, subtly influenced by visits to the U.S.A. where they have seen America's industrial might and her vast array of consumer goods. And from Africa, Asia and to a lesser extent, Latin America, potential leaders have travelled to Russia to see the economic progress of state capitalism.

There is a good, but a wrong, reason why the leaders of the Third World should want a growth economy. In states which are often merely aggregations of disparate societies, each with its own ethos, its own language and its own traditional lands, it is hard to develop a national consciousness. Many African states were created by the colonial powers merely by drawing lines on an inaccurate map. In such an environment a leader can only keep his place, if he suppresses all dissent ruthlessly, or if he acts charismatically by articulating the aspirations of his followers, by concentrating their frustrations on a real or imagined enemy, and by giving them the goods they want.

To the relatively unsophisticated villager or townsman in the

developing nations, the real or rumoured affluence of the European, and the observed or reported behaviour of many of their
own leaders who adopt, quite effortlessly, European styles and
values, and become what Tarzie Vittachi calls 'Brown Sahibs',
induces frustration, and a desire to obtain the goods apparently
reserved for the elite.

In their expectations many people in the developing nations
have been influenced by comparing the standard of living enjoyed by the Europeans in their community, by seeing the
goods introduced by the traders and mercantile houses, and by
the impact of radio, television and the cinema. The influence
of the mass media on the wants of people in the developing
nations has been commented on by Elisabeth Kirkby, who
worked for some years for Radio Malaya and who has studied
the impact of television in a developing nation. In an address
to the International Association of Women in Radio and
Television in 1970, she said:

'Too often, the very worst aspects of Western civilization are
being presented to the people of Asia in the sugar-coated pill of
the TV series. Children in Thailand, Malaysia and Korea now
watch *Star Trek*, *Gunsmoke*, *The Flintstones*, *Gilligan's Island* and
Hogan's Heroes, and all the programmes that have been described by one English TV critic as the "bilious mid-Atlantic
adventure series. . . ."

'A hundred years ago, some of our forebears believed it was
their Christian duty to take Christianity to people they believed heathen. They even had the temerity to believe that it
was their duty to convert Buddhists and Hindus, whose religion
gave a far greater cohesion to peasant peoples than Christianity
has ever given the West.

'In this day and age we can preach much more successfully
and speedily an even more divisive doctrine. The doctrine that
progress and civilization means more consumer goods, that
men who live in cities use graft, blackmail and violence as their
weapons; that development as a nation means more cities and
more armaments, more power.

'Whilst we struggle in America and Europe to combat pollution and the decay in the quality of life, we are still selling to
Asia and Africa, through the medium of TV, the very ideas
that have led to our present dilemma. . . .

'In 1968, at your last meeting, Mr. Hahr mentioned the political significance of communication satellites, particularly direct-broadcast satellites. I feel that the cultural significance of such satellites is equally alarming. Do we want 2,000 years of western civilization to be presented to Asia and Africa in terms of the consumer society? As Europeans, do we want a thousand years of creative endeavour, philosophical thought and political change appear to result only in megalopolis?

'The achievements of Europe, the richness and diversity of our way of life can surely be portrayed in better ways. We live with protest and dissent, we are still divided by religion and by class, but there is far more vitality and meaning to our lives than is suggested by *Peyton Place*. . . .

'I believe most sincerely that we have to attempt in every form of programme we do, to make people think—that possibly no longer can this be done by governmental agencies, by nations or blocks of nations, but only by small personal revolutions. And perhaps as women in radio and television we have a duty to instigate small personal revolutions. The sort of revolution that would put dignity in place of deceit, good in place of goods, thought in place of things, and above all people in place of profit.'

Is it not excellent that women should feel this way, for their voice has been heard too little? Yet, in matters of population, they are more important than men. It is they who carry the unborn child in the womb, it is they who obtain abortions, it is they who die as the result of childbirth, it is they who care for, and cherish, the child. It is they who have been dominated politically, economically and socially by men for many generations, rather in the same way that the Europeans have dominated the rest of the world in the past century, and have sought to impose their values, their beliefs and their greed on the peoples of other nations.

6

The desire for European consumer goods is most stylized in the Melanesian myths of cargo, and in similar separatist cults in Africa.

A Precarious Ecological Balance

Until 1871, when Baron Nikolai Mikhoulo-Maclay visited the north coast of New Guinea, the villages had a static unspecialized society. They were primarily agriculturalists, but hunted wild pigs, or fished when they needed extra food. They had no knowledge of metallurgy or of weaving, but made artefacts from clay, stone and shells, and they had domesticated dogs, pigs, fowls and cassowaries. It is doubtful if it was an idyllic society, but it was a stable society. Each individual was self-sufficient for survival. He knew how to grow food, he could build a house and he could make the tools and weapons he needed. There was no profit motive: the economy was designed to produce only enough wealth, mainly food, to keep people alive, with a small surplus for ritual. Trade, which did occur on a small scale, was by barter and was performed without rancour. Each item had a traditionally agreed value, and exchange was made on this basis. There was no desire for economic growth, for additional possessions and there was no accumulation of capital. The social structure was built up on kinship, locality and on trade. It was undifferentiated and egalitarian. The social relationships were achieved by the exchange of goods and services and by the performance of specific obligations which had to be undertaken even if they injured a man's personal reputation. Each kinship group exchanged these obligations, and they had to be reciprocated in some way at some future time. Population growth was slow because of a high mortality from disease and intertribal warfare, which was undertaken, not for economic motives, but for revenge, to repay homicide, or because of adultery. When population growth threatened the stability of the people, they resorted to abortion or infanticide.

Life was slow and traditional, and was regulated by the gods and spirits, who were conceived as invisible, powerful beings, and who could take on human, animal or insect shapes at will. As the gods and spirits had human emotions, they had to be recognized, and special rituals had to be performed to appease them. If the right ritual was known, their co-operation was guaranteed. If a venture failed, it was not due to the caprice of the gods, but to the incompetence of the ritual operator, who had not remembered the exact words in the exact order, or performed the right ceremony.

The world existed for man, and the physical environmen
had been given to man by the gods. God, who had variou
names, had created nature. One day, about five generation
back, time had started when God had emerged from a cav
and had seen a bare planet. He didn't like it, and so ha
created nature. Then he had created two gods, Kilibob an
Manup, either by magic or by creating a woman and by im
pregnating her. Kilibob and Manup then started inventin
things. Kilibob invented wood carving and canoe building
Manup invented love-sorcery, magic and warfare. One da
one of the two brothers was induced by the wife of the other t
'tattoo a design on her pudenda'. This incensed the othe
brother, and they agreed to separate, one going north, th
other south.

Kilibob and Manup were the big gods, but other gods an
spirits lived in all natural objects. These gods and spirits ha
to be respected, by performing ritual and observing taboo:
If these duties were done, the gods were obliged to help man
They lived with man, and appeared in dreams. In dreams the
had taught man how to plant crops and how to make artefact:
and they had taught man the ritual dances.

Then the white men came. First Baron Mikhoulo-Maclay
then the traders and missionaries. They came in big ships an
had many novel goods. All the white men did was sit in offices
and make the black men work. The missionaries introduce
the concept of a big all-powerful god, but the people merel
integrated him into the person of their god. It didn't alter thei
way of thinking.

As the Europeans had so many goods, and came from a lon
way, it was obvious that they had a special ritual which gav
them the cargo denied to the native people. If the people coul
learn the ritual secret they, too, would be given cargo by th
gods. And as the traders had taken land from the tribes and ha
expected the people to provide labour, the reciprocal obligatio
of the European was to give the secret of cargo to the native:
If they didn't get it they would always be subordinate an
treated with contempt.

When Kilibob and Manup had sailed away, in the begin
ning, five generations back, one of them, it wasn't clear which
had sailed to Sydney, and had created white men, to whom h

had given the cargo secret. Once the natives could learn the secret, Kilibob or Manup would return from Sydney bringing all the cargo that would be needed. He would give the native people building materials and trade goods. Then they would be socially equal to the Europeans.

The possession of the cargo of the gods, which the Europeans had, would enhance the status of the islanders and make them equal. Cargo would also make life easier, so cargo was essential.

7

It is not clear to what extent the spiritual aspect of cargo, or to give it its proper modern name, economic growth, is important to the peoples of the developing nations, but it does have an impact. Only the leaders can identify with national aims; the majority of the people are bound by the small area in which they live.

Whatever the reason, the leaders of the Third World want economic growth. They have learned growth economics well. They also know that to retain power they have to offer their people some of the cargo of the developed nations. To reduce turbulence they have to find jobs for the inevitably increasing 'work force' consequent on a population growth rate of over 2·5 per cent per annum. They have learnt from history that economic growth, judged by increased per capita income and increased capital accumulation from savings, only occurred in the developed nations when they became industrialized. They believe that for the next century it is their turn to have part of the action. They have also learnt, in their reading, and during their visits to the developed nations, that industrialization inevitably leads to reduced poverty, to increased health care, to better education, to a better diet, to increased opportunities for leisure and to a longer life.

Yet now, when the Third World has achieved independence, and is on the threshold of economic expansion, the developed nations are telling them that they must reduce both population growth and economic growth. The question which must cross their minds is, is this just another trick to keep their nation perpetually the plantation, the fibre shed and the quarry of the affluent nations? Is it just another device to exploit them and their people? Is it just another way of keeping them from obtaining their rightful cargo—industrialization?

To the leaders of the developing nations the current stress by the developed nations on environmental conservation sounds hypocritical. The exponential environmental pollution, the excessive use of energy and exploitation of finite mineral resources is due to the economic activities of the industrialized nations. They caused it, and they should cure it. The Third World questions if it is reasonable that they should be forced to participate in preventing a possible collapse of society, due to the twin evils of exponential population growth and ecologically faulty productive technology, when they have played no part in its causation. They resent the suggestion that they should help the rich nations to clear up the mess they have made. They are suspicious that the call to environmental conservation is merely another device by which the rich nations will keep their wealth, and will prevent the expectant, hungry nations from getting their share of prosperity. They fear that the concern with the environment by the rich nations may merely be a pretext for discriminating trade practices which will limit still further the access of the poor nations to the markets of the developed world. They believe that only economic growth and the transition of their nations into developed nations can meet the aspirations of their people and ensure that they have a fair share in the prosperity of the world.

If in achieving this aim they add to environmental pollution, if they use more of the limited mineral resources, if they adopt unecological productive technology, if they further damage the very small planet on which we live, should not the rich nations accept this? The poor nations have had to accept the damage done by the affluent nations for generations. The developing nations, only recently emergent from colonialism, have been exploited for so long that they are suspicious of any action or suggestion made by the developed nations. The ugly American, European, Russian, Japanese and Australian businessmen, traders and tourists are perpetually within their territories offering supposed bargains, and, it seems, making large profits. Their reading of history, and their cultural inheritance, equates national strength with a big population and with an expanding economy. To convince them otherwise is like an affluent middle-class citizen, who has his own house, well-equipped with labour saving devices—washing machine, refrigerator, washing-up machine, oil central heating, television, solid-state record player, constant hot water service, deep freeze unit and telephone, and who has a country retreat to which he goes in his high-powered car, saying to a slum dweller that he must not seek the same amenities because environmental pollution, the overuse of minerals and the excessive use of energy is threatening us all. It is the 'I'm all right, Jack' syndrome applied to international relationships. And it is small wonder that the leaders of the Third World are suspicious and hostile to the arguments of the conservationists.

But the example of the mess the developed nations have made should be a warning. The demonstration of how man is destroying his own environment is obvious in the polluted skies over the industrial cities of the developed nations, in their contaminated rivers, lakes and estuaries, in their decaying urban congestions in which automobiles clog the roads, and wheeze to a halt. The observation that man is rapacious and selfish is clear, and it is disturbing, though not surprising, that the Third World appears to be rejecting the call to limit population growth and restrict economic growth.

The trouble is that they are applying an outmoded demographic and economic theory to a unique situation in man's history.

Modern economic theory shows that decreasing fertility, given the same labour force and the same total national income, will increase savings, and will lead to a higher level of net investment than current or increased fertility patterns. Fewer children are beneficial economically. This is because in nations with high fertility a large proportion of the national income is needed for immediate consumption by dependants, fewer women are able to work outside the home, and taxation exemptions are increased. Thus there are smaller savings. And smaller savings means there is less capital to invest in economic growth.

It has also been shown that if fertility decreased by 50 per cent over 25 years, there would only be a 10 per cent decrease in the total work force in 30 years, after which a further percentage decline would occur, although the total work force would remain high. Without decreased fertility the potential work force increases. A larger labour force requires a larger stock of capital (i.e. facilities for production and services) in order to obtain the same *per capita* productivity. This factor has been analysed by the American economist, A. J. Coale, who has calculated that the percentage of the national income which must be invested merely to keep productivity from declining, is three times the annual rate of growth of the labour force. Currently the average annual increase in the labour force in the Third World is about 3 per cent, implying a 9 per cent growth required in the national income. Few, if any, developing nations can achieve this economic growth rate.

Whilst many leaders of the developing world are beginning to accept that the rate of population growth must be reduced, they are less likely to accept that the rate of economic growth in their nation should also be reduced.

The stress, until the last five years, on unlimited economic growth, has distorted their views. They have learned the lesson of growth economics too well from their tutors in the industrialized nations. They have seen how the gap between the industrialized nations and the hungry nations has increased in the past two decades. They have seen how the rich have got richer, and how the value of primary agricultural and mineral products has dropped on world markets. They suspect that the current campaign in the industrialized world to reduce economic growth, so that pollution is reduced and non-renewable minerals are conserved, is merely a stratagem to prevent the hungry, expectant nations from industrializing, a plot which would permit the rich countries to grow still richer, at their expense.

They have also misread history. In the nineteenth century, economic growth took place in an expanding world, which still had empty spaces. These are filled today. Nineteenth-century economic growth took place when mortality was high, so that population growth was slow. It took place using relatively unsophisticated technologies which did not markedly damage ecosystems.

The leaders of the Third World have failed to explore the consequences of rapid industrialization. If the labour patterns in the history of all industrialized nations are examined, the general trend has been to a steadily decreasing proportion of workers in agriculture, and to increasing urbanization. In the early phases the number of workers in agriculture remained constant, so that the non-agricultural labour force had to absorb all the increases of the working force population. Later, even in countries where agriculture is an industry, such as Denmark, there has been a decline in the absolute number of workers in agriculture. Increasing economic growth demands better technology, or an increasingly larger work force, and it demands increased markets. If all developing nations industrialize, even to a mean 50 per cent of that of the U.S. today, there will be a rapid depletion of non-renewable resources, a huge demand for energy and, as a result, an exponential growth of pollution will occur.

The problems are real and are incompletely understood. One main problem in the developing world is the widespread poverty and a high level of under-employment. Economic growth may increase, rather than reduce, these two social evils unless it has been carefully thought out and properly planned. The current accelerating trend to urbanization in the developed nations, which was discussed in Chapter 5, is so great that even massive industrialization is unlikely to provide sufficient jobs; and the idea that industrialization can eliminate poverty is probably untrue. Even in the U.S.A., the most affluent of the affluent nations, which has a *per capita* gross national productivity nearly 40 times that of India and 56 times that of Nigeria, 10 per cent of the population live in poverty. It is possible for excessive consumption and abject poverty to co-exist. And if this occurs in the richest nation in the world, what hope has ecologically faulty economic growth of eradicating poverty and unemployment in the poor nations?

A disturbing report from the United Nations Committee for Development Planning, published in 1972, shows that both unemployment and mass poverty are increasing in many developing nations. Industrialization has not been the expected panacea. Although economic growth rates have risen, the new industries have provided only a few additional jobs, and the prosperity from the increased productivity has gone into the bank accounts of a relatively few families. The great mass of the population has been untouched. By 1980 there could be 300 million people in the developing countries looking for work.

In chasing the mirage of industrial growth, national leaders have neglected the rural areas and ignored agriculture. Instead of stressing developments in the rural areas, governments have tended to allow them to deteriorate, with the result that the migration to the towns has accelerated. The slums and shanty towns which ring the cities like the scum on the edge of a stagnant, polluted pond bear testimony to this neglect.

The conclusions of the United Nations Committee are sombre. If disaster is to be avoided, conscious policies must be implemented which make a more equitable distribution of income and check the surge of people from the rural areas to the towns. 'Employment and mass poverty', they report, 'must be moved from the periphery to the centre of all development planning.'

To do this means that the leaders of the Third World will have to re-think their economic objectives and must re-examine if ecologically faulty productive technology is the goal. It is obvious that they will have to increase their development, but it must be a development 'in which there is a mutually re-inforcing relationship between social objectives and economic growth', between improvements in employment, income distribution, education (in which the emphasis is on vocational and technical training) and health, as well as an increase in the capital accumulation.

The leaders of the developed nations have to do more than mouth warnings of disaster. They have to take what may be unpalatable actions. They have to convince their friends in the developing world that they are genuinely concerned, and that their actions in seeking that all nations adopt the twin goals of population growth restriction and economic growth restriction is not just self-interest masquerading as interest in the survival of mankind.

Today, both the developed and the developing nations are in the same overcrowded ark. For different reasons all of us must change our foolish ways. The hungry, expectant developing nations need to increase their economic growth so that their peoples may lead a more fulfilling life; they also need to reduce their rate of population growth so that they can achieve economic growth.

The developed nations also need to change their foolish ways. The gap between the rich and the poor nations is widening. In the interest of humanity, and in the interest of the affluent nations, the gap must be reduced, if only because the increasing disparity is likely to 'generate urges and pressures which cannot be contained for any length of time'. The rich nations will have to increase development aid, not only for economic growth, but to reduce the mass poverty and unemployment. And they will have to increase trade with the developing nations.

In their own nations they will have to abandon ecologically damaging productive technology, spurious advertising and super-salesmanship. The costs of environmental pollution—the biological costs—incurred in production, must be added to production costs to give the real costs of the product. No longer should society support profit-hungry free enterprise, which, of course, is not really free since it uses the public's complaisance to commit its polluting activities.

The industrialists and manufacturers must voluntarily change to ecologically balanced productivity, and if they will not must be coerced to do so. This means that the industrialized, developed world must rely less on synthetically produced goods and more on goods produced from natural products. These products in many instances are more efficiently produced in the Third World.

Leaders in all three worlds will have to do some hard thinking. The ostrich attitude that technology will solve all is proved wrong. If mankind is to have any reasonable future, if we are to 'survive economically as well as biologically, industry, agriculture and transportation will have to meet the inescapable demands of the ecosystem'.

It will mean that the standard of living of the affluent nations will have to fall so that that of the hungry nations can rise.

It will mean that all nations will have consciously to reduce their rates of population growth, so that stationary populations are reached in as short a time as possible.

It will mean that the rich nations will have to alter their

terms of trade with the Third World, so that the terms of trade are favourable to the latter, and the current high tariffs against their products are eliminated. This could also be ecologically beneficial. If the rich nations made manufacturers carry the ecologically damaging costs of the pollution they make, the prices of their goods would rise. If, at the same time, West Africa and South East Asia grew the palm oil, made and exported the soap, it could largely replace detergents in the affluent world. If Indonesia and Malaysia grew the rubber and made the tyres, these could replace tyres manufactured in the rich nations. If India, China and Thailand were encouraged to export more cotton and silk, these fibres could largely replace the man-made fibres of the industrialized nations. If all nations expended money on research to replace chemical pesticides with biological ones, environmental pollution would diminish, and the quantities of inorganic pesticides reaching the oceans would fall. If the industrialized nations learned from China how to return sewage and garbage to the soil, the rivers and waters would be cleaner, and the use of chemical fertilizer would be reduced. If all chemicals were reclaimed from combustion processes, and all re-usable metal, glass and paper were recycled, pollution would be reduced and the availability of non-renewable resources would be extended. If nations sought to discourage power-hungry, labour-sparing industries and replaced them with power-sparing, labour-intensive industries, unemployment would drop and energy supplies would be conserved.

It will mean that the rich nations will have to increase considerably their aid—and aid without strings—to the developing nations, particularly for social projects such as education, health care, housing, and birth control. For ultimately, in addition to changing our outmoded, socially destructive, belief in self-acquisitive affluence, and our pursuit of an expanding ecologically faulty technology, which is making the ecological balance precarious, mankind must deal effectively with the major threat to our survival, that of over-population. Above all, surmounting all other needs, is the need for population control. Increasing numbers of people are making the ecological balance on Earth still more precarious.

CHAPTER EIGHT

A Plethora of People

The growth of world population during the next twenty-five years, therefore, has an importance which transcends economic and social considerations. It is at the very heart of the problem of our existence.

'The Future Growth of World Population', United Nations Publication, 1958 (Population Studies Series No. 28).

I

The grim warning given by the United Nations fifteen years ago seems to have been largely ignored. We are over half-way through the period and the rate of growth of the population of the world continues to increase. Truly, there is a plethora of people.

The study of various societies, both primitive and sophisticated (for it would be difficult to call many modern societies 'civilized'), indicates that population has always been regulated to some extent, and that it is only in the past 25 years that the rate of growth has finally escaped control.

Since the population growth rate is merely a way of expressing collective family size, it must be assumed that individual families make decisions about the number of children they wish to have, and only a few leave the matter to fate or to 'God's will'. Following an investigation in Latin America, where the predominant religion is Roman Catholic and where the biblical injunction to 'multiply and replenish the earth' might be expected, Stycos says: '. . . . the surveys demonstrate that couples want a moderate number of children, that they are convinced of the economic disadvantages of a large family, and that they are eager for information on what to do about it'. The encouraging point about this statement is that it is the opposite of the opinion of political, intellectual and religious leaders in Latin America who claim that to 'oppose population is to oppose civilization'.

However, it appears that decisions about family size consciously made after rational discussion occur in only a minority of families. Most decisions are made on the basis of convention, or with respect to prevalent cultural attitudes towards fertility, or in deference to collective behavioural norms. If all the families in the community have many children, the individual family also tends to have many children, particularly if this is culturally accepted as evidence of a man's virility. In other instances, in supposedly sophisticated societies, individual families have additional children in imitation of a respected leader, or a folk hero.

Since these psychological attitudes are rarely verbalized, the social scientist is at a considerable disadvantage when he attempts to analyse the population dynamics of past times.

The inadequate evidence available suggests that until this century societies as a whole sought to create populations in which births just exceeded deaths. When a disaster struck, during which the death rate rose, it was followed 9 to 20 months later by a sudden spurt in the birth rate. Over the centuries, the near balance of vital rates led to a slow growth of population. The actual growth or decline depended on the availability of food supplies, the avoidance of famine, flood, war and epidemics, and the cultural need of the society for children either as extra labour or for ritual purposes.

Investigations into population growth, from historical information (which is often anecdotal) and from data collected from European parish records, have led to the theory of demographic transition. In essence, this theory is that most societies seek to improve the welfare of their members, usually by keeping their bellies full and by providing commonly used goods. Such an end is best achieved if there is a relative balance between deaths and births. It is obvious that this state can be attained by having high death and high birth rates as occurs in many African nations today. It can also be attained by having low death and low birth rates. In many modern industrialized, or post-industrialized societies, a considerable measure of death control has been obtained, and the nations are striving to obtain birth control. Examples today include the majority of developed nations, and a few developing nations. The process of moving from high death and birth rates to low ones is called the demographic transition of a country. A very few nations have completed the demographic transition and have obtained populations which have low birth rates and low death rates so

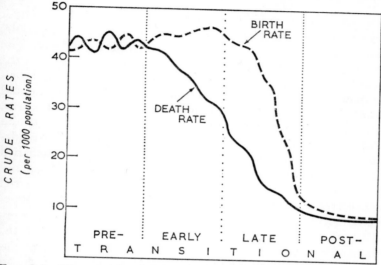

FIG. 8/1. The process of demographic transition from high fertility and mortality to low fertility and mortality.

that population growth is slow, and becomes in balance demographically once again. The process of demographic transition is shown diagrammatically in Fig. 8/1.

It is impossible to study demographic transition in most countries over a long period, which is the only valid way, because the vital statistics needed are either unavailable or very inaccurate. Two European nations, Britain and Sweden, have reasonably accurate data stretching back for two centuries. Both are now near the end of transition, and in fact Sweden has entered post-transitional equilibrium.

In all nations, the pre-transitional period is long, and

stretches back to the beginnings of societies. In pre-transitional societies, death rates were high and fluctuated widely, as a result of epidemics, famines or wars. Nobody actively tried to delay death, which was thought a supernatural event. But as the birth rates were also high, and like the death rates fluctuated widely, population growth was slow.

2

In A.D. 1086 the Norman overlords of England thought it was time that they had a census of the numbers of people, houses and resources of their newly acquired property. The resulting Doomsday Book was the first census conducted in the country and showed that population was about one and a half million. Over the next three hundred years the birth rate and death rate fluctuated, but on the whole, births exceeded deaths, and in 1348 it was estimated that the population of England and Wales was about 3·5 million. Then the most severe epidemic of bubonic plague ever known—the Black Death—reached England, and in 22 years reduced the population to 2·5 million. For three hundred years, epidemics of the plague recurred which reduced the population, but in the intervening plague-free years it rose, so that by 1670 it had doubled to 5·0 million.

Then, inexplicably, the frequency of the epidemics fell, the plague-free years increased, and with the agricultural revolution which began about 1720, food supplies increased. Between 1720 and 1780, the face of the English countryside changed as the Enclosure Acts enabled farmers to consolidate their holdings and to experiment with new agricultural techniques. Before, with much land held in common and divided amongst tenants in narrow, often scattered strips, improvement had been nearly impossible. With consolidation of land and soil improvement, new strains of wheat were developed and food supplies increased. The introduction of marling the soil, of clover cropping (instead of having to let the land lie fallow) and the development of winter grasses, permitted the farmer to keep his livestock alive all winter, instead of having to kill and salt the beasts in autumn. With this agricultural development new types of sheep were bred which had thicker fleeces and a higher

meat content. These changes led to an increase in the food
supply and the cessation of gross food shortages, so that the
population began to increase, although slowly at first, with a
slight rise in the birth rate and a slight fall in the death rate
after 1720. By 1770, the population had risen to 7 million, an
increase of 5·5 million since 1086 (Fig. 8/2).

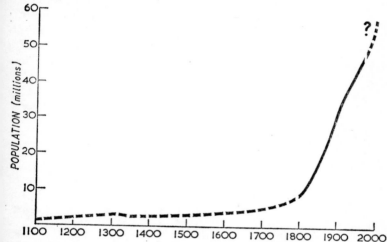

Fig. 8/2. The growth of the population of England and Wales
since 1066.

The effect of these changes, and the accelerated rate of
population growth from about 1750 are shown in Fig. 8/3.
Similar accelerated population growth rates occurred in other
North-West European nations.

England and Wales were emerging from the pre-transitional
stage, and entering the transitional stage. This has been
divided into an early transitional period and a late transitional
period. In the early period of demographic transition the death
rate falls, with a particular reduction in the numbers of infant
and childhood deaths. Because of this, in the early part of the
transitional stage, the high birth rate may be increased still
more as more children reach the reproductive years. Population growth occurs at an increasing rate, but with considerable
fluctuations, as control of the environment is inadequate, and
food supplies are uncertain.

The early period of transition took place in England and Wales between 1770 and 1870. From 1770 the death rate began to drop, whilst the birth rate remained at its high level. For the first 40 years the birth rate rose, as more children reached marriageable age, and because more women married at a younger age. The fall in the death rate persisted throughout the century. In 1770 it was 32 per 1,000, and by 1870 it had fallen to 20 per 1,000. This decline was not due to advances in curative medicine, or to the provision of hospitals. Curative medicine was still in the pre-scientific phase: the number of drugs, and compounds of drugs, was enormous, but only a very few

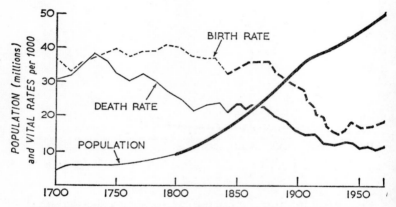

FIG. 8/3. The accelerated growth of the population of England and Wales since 1750.

had more than a placebo effect. Of all the drugs available in 1850, fewer than ten had a specific action. These included laudanum and other opiates which relieved pain; digitalis obtained from the foxglove, which was used to treat 'dropsy'; purgatives which were effective in emptying the bowels, even if they didn't cure the disease; and perhaps mercury, which was used to treat syphilis. Since patients believed in medicines and physicians needed to feel that they had done something, the doctors prescribed drugs, which, if they did no good, at least did little harm. But placebos cannot have much effect on the death rate.

In surgery the scene was just as uninspiring. Until the last years of the century, anaesthesia was unavailable and operative surgery, although often heroic, was frequently followed by the comment that the operation was successful but the patient died. Surgeons amputated limbs, 'cut for bladder stone', and incised abscesses. The mortality after the first two operations was very high and even after inhalational anaesthesia had enabled surgeons to operate slowly, and to invade the peritoneal cavity, deaths following surgery were common. In 1874 a London surgeon wrote about his colleagues that 'skill in the performance has far outstripped the success in the result'.

The results in midwifery were little better. Maternity hospitals had been established in Dublin in 1747 and in London in 1749 and were followed by many others in provincial cities. But most women were confined at home and their babies were delivered by midwives, who were usually untrained.

In none of the three main divisions of medical practice could medical treatment, or the hospitals, claim to have been the cause of the declining death rate. It was even said, perhaps unfairly, that most patients survived an illness in spite of, not because of, the doctors.

What led to the lowered mortality was not medicine but sanitary engineering, and better nutrition. The years between 1770 and 1870 were the years of the Industrial Revolution in Britain. It led to the rise of the manufacturing industrial towns, and the drift of people from the country. In 1770 only three towns in England had more than 50,000 people. These were London, which had 500,000, Bristol and Norwich which had 50,000 each. By 1820 eleven towns had more than 50,000 people, and apart from London, Bristol and Plymouth, all were in the industrial north. The factory owners, as much for profit as from humanitarian motives, soon realized that the efficiency of the labour force was reduced unless a certain amount of sanitation was provided in the festering slums they had created. With the provision of piped water, and of protected wells, and with better personal and domestic cleanliness, the incidence of the diarrhoeal diseases, and of typhus, fell.

Important as sanitary engineering was, it had less impact on the death rate than the better nutrition of the people which occurred over the period. There has been considerable argument amongst historians whether the diet of the average person improved after 1770, when an increasing number of people left the rural areas for the greater economic opportunities offered in the towns and factories. It has been stated that in the rural areas a man could always grow his own potatoes and cabbages and keep hens, both of which were denied the townsman. This over-states the position for, in the early years, the towns were fairly small, and many factories were built in rural areas, where water power and coal could be obtained easily.

It is likely, too, that the attractions of rural England were more apparent to middle-class travellers than to the inhabitants. Arthur Young, who travelled extensively in rural England, reported that food consisted principally of bread and cheese, washed down with water or beer. Meat was eaten very rarely. Wages were minimal, often paid in kind, and working hours were long. Life in the factories and in the burgeoning towns was not much better, but there was a greater opportunity for employment and a larger disposable income, so that food could be bought more plentifully. It is probable that the townspeople did obtain a better diet than the countrymen, and the rise in the nutritional levels of the population was a factor in the fall in the death rate.

Investigations in the developing nations today show that there is a close positive correlation between infant nutrition and infant mortality: the better the nutrition, the lower the infant and childhood death rate. Between 1770 and 1870, infant mortality in England fell from over 200 per 1,000, to just over 100 per 1,000. The evidence is suggestive that nutrition improved over the period.

A further factor contributed to the fall in the death rate between 1770 and 1870. This was that the virulence of the common infectious diseases diminished. The reason for this is not clear. It is possible that it was also a consequence of better nutrition of the people, but there is no evidence either way. The facts are that scarlet fever, which had been very common in the eighteenth century and which had carried a high mortality, began to decline in frequency and in intensity. Some time between 1830 and 1870, the death rate from scarlet fever began to fall and it has continued to do so throughout the rest of the century and a half, so that today it is an uncommon and mild disease.

Pulmonary tuberculosis is another, and significant, example of the diminution of virulence which occurred in the nineteenth century. Tuberculosis is spread by droplet infection, coughed or blown out of the victim's lungs so that the infection spreads by close contact with an infected person. This obviously occurs in conditions of overcrowding, either at home or at work. In the English industrial towns in the period from 1820 to 1870, congestion in dwellings was increasing, hours and conditions of work were deplorable. Both of these should have increased the incidence of tuberculosis and should have raised the mortality of those people infected. They did not. In fact, from about 1850, the mortality from tuberculosis began to fall. This occurred at a time when nutritional standards were rising. The relationship between nutrition and tuberculosis was made clear in World War II. In the concentration camps, established by the Germans, food was very scarce, overcrowding considerable and tuberculosis affected over 90 per cent of the inmates. In mid-nineteenth century England, despite marked overcrowding, better nutrition led to a fall in the severity of the disease.

By 1870 England was in the middle of the period of demographic transition. The death rate was falling, but the birth rate remained high, with a consequent high rate of population growth. This is what is happening in many developing nations today.

After 1870 the improvement in mortality from infectious disease control and improved hygiene continued, but now other measures began to play a part in the process of demographic transition.

In the period 1871–1971, medical science began to play its part in reducing the death rate. The doctor changed from merely being able to offer reassurance and comfort, to being able to offer potent, specifically effective drugs. From about 1906 increasing attention was paid to maternity and child welfare, and to school health. These measures, together with increasing advice about health and hygiene, reduced the death rate still further.

In the second half of the period preventive inoculations became available against more and more of the common infectious diseases, and increasing numbers of children were protected. The treatment of infection became possible in 1938.

when the sulphonamides were discovered, and gained an impetus ten years later with the discovery of penicillin. In the years from 1900, the main reduction has been in infant and childhood mortality. By 1971 infant mortality was one-sixth the 1841 rate and childhood mortality was one-thirtieth that of 1841.

From about 1870, too, the birth rate began to drop. The start of this decline coincided with, and was possibly the result of, the widespread publicity which attended the trial of Charles Bradlaugh and Annie Besant. These two social reformers, who had been publishing articles about contraception for over 10 years, invited prosecution by publishing a book which gave contraceptive advice. After two protracted trials, which received wide publicity, both of the accused were acquitted. The publicity occasioned by the trial spread the knowledge of contraception widely, and may have played a part in the fall of the birth rate.

By 1971 the birth rate in England and Wales had fallen to 17 per 1,000, and the death rate to 12 per 1,000. The gap between the two was closing. England and Wales were nearing the end of the demographic transition. If birth rate trends continue, England will have completed the demographic transition by 1990. However, because of the age structure of the society, the population will continue to grow, as the 'bulge' of young people reaches the reproductive years. It has been estimated that it will take between 35 and 50 more years for the population of England and Wales to become stationary (i.e. neither declining nor growing). At that time it will be between 63 and 68 million.

3

Unfortunately, only a very few nations have entered the post-transitional phase. The majority of the developed industrialized nations are in the late transitional phase, and the majority of the hungry, developing nations are in the early transitional phase.

The demographic characteristics of the two types of nations have been analysed, and the essential data are shown in Fig. 8/4. The characteristics of the developing nations today are

STATISTICS	DEVELOPING NATIONS Early Transitional	DEVELOPED NATIONS Late Transitional
Total population (millions)	2510	1082
Average birth rate	30—50	15—25
Average death rate	15—25	5—15
Rate of reproductive change	35—15	20—0
Dependency ratio	YOUTH 42.1 AGE 2.9 TOTAL 45	YOUTH 26.4 AGE 8.6 TOTAL 35

CHARACTERISTICS		
Economic :—	Generally poor	Generally affluent
Per capita income	Low	High
Industrialisation	Low	High
Energy consumption	Low	High
Communications	Poor	Good
Transport facilities	Poor	Good
Unemployment	High	Low
Environmental :—	Mostly rural	Mostly urban
Pollution	Low	High
Mobility of people	Low	High
Most usual occupation :—	Farming	White collar
Labour	Unskilled	Skilled
Social and medical :—		
Literacy	Low	High
Education	Poor	Good
Social services	Poor	Good
Calorie & protein intake	Low	High
Death rate	Falling	Low

FIG. 8/4. The demographic and socio-economic characteristics of developing and developed nations.

remarkably similar to those of late eighteenth-century England, with one exception. This is that the death rate is being reduced at an increasing velocity, whilst the birth rate remains high, and in Africa, at least, is tending to rise.

This has the effect of distorting the population structure, and has led to an increasing youth dependency burden on the economy of the developing nations. In these nations the high proportion of young people imposes a need to find the capital to finance the health and educational needs of an economically dependent group. This limits the amount a family is able to save, it limits the amount of taxes a government can impose, and both limit the amount of capital available for investment in agriculture and selected industry. The effect of the population's age structure on the population growth rate is quite obvious: a large youth dependency will tend to produce a high birth rate as increasing numbers of young people become active, reproductively. It also creates the need to produce a large number of jobs so that the young people can find employment.

The population of the world in 1971 was estimated to be about 3,634 million. In 1971, an additional 73 million people were added, and in 1972 an additional 74 million. In 1973 the increase was 75·5 million. This means that the population of the world is increasing at over 207,000 people per day, over 8,600 per hour and over 140 persons a minute. Each month a new Ecuador, each three months a new Tanzania, and each year a new Bangladesh is created.

These crude statistics hide the difference between the population growth rates of the developing and of the developed nations. Amongst the 1,100 million people living in the affluent developed world of Europe, the U.S.S.R., North America, Japan, Australia and New Zealand, and Israel, the annual growth rate is between 0·6 and 1·5 per cent. Amongst the 2,500 million people living in the hungry, developing nations of Asia, Latin America and Africa, the annual rate of population growth is between 2·0 and 3·0 per cent. The differences are shown in Table 8/1.

A nation cannot plan ahead unless there is reasonably reliable information about the probable population, its age structure and its distribution at any given time in the future. One of the main objectives of demographers is to provide this

TABLE 8/I

*The annual reproductive growth rate (per cent) and population
doubling times for the various regions of the world*

Area	Population in mid-1971 (millions)	Annual growth rate (per cent)	Number of years to double population
WORLD	3,709	2·0	35
AFRICA			
Northern Africa	354	2·7	26
Western Africa	89	3·1	23
Eastern Africa	104	2·6	27
Middle Africa	100	2·6	27
Southern Africa	37	2·2	32
	23	2·4	29
ASIA			
Southwest Asia	2,104	2·3	31
Middle South Asia	79	2·9	24
Southeast Asia	783	2·7	26
East Asia	295	2·8	25
	946	1·6	40
NORTH AMERICA	229	1·2	58
LATIN AMERICA			
Middle America	291	2·9	24
Caribbean	70	3·4	21
Tropical South America	26	2·2	32
Temperate South America	155	3·0	24
	40	1·8	39
EUROPE			
Northern Europe	466	0·8	88
Western Europe	81	0·6	117
Eastern Europe	150	0·6	117
Southern Europe	105	0·8	88
	130	0·9	78
U.S.S.R.	245	1·0	70
OCEANIA			
Australia and New Zealand	20	2·0	35
Other nations	16	1·2	58
	4	2·8	25

information. But since any projections must be based on the trends of current death (or mortality) rates and birth (or fertility) rates the population forecasts are not what *will* happen, but what *would* happen if existing birth and death rates continued, or if the observed trends in the rates persisted. In this regard it is easier to forecast the future trends in mortality rates than in fertility rates, for the latter are so much more subject to the vagaries of human behaviour, to the influence of fashion and to multiple factors which lead to the decision to have another child.

For these reasons, demographers, being cautious, try to make as much allowance as possible for unexpected changes in fertility and mortality rates by making three estimates of population. These are a high estimate, an intermediate estimate and a low estimate. The assumption is that the population projected for a given year will fall somewhere below the high estimate and somewhere above the low estimate. In 1968, after very careful study, the United Nations made three estimates, all of which assumed that some degree of family planning would take place in most nations of the world. But to show what was likely if no birth control occurred, the demographers added a fourth estimate which assumed that existing birth rates would continue. The population projections only extended to the year 2000. Beyond that date the projected populations became increasingly difficult to determine, and it was hoped that the startling information would be sufficient to induce national leaders to act now.

The United Nations Population Projections, using the medium variant, are shown in Table 8/2.

The publication of the population projections has occasioned a fierce argument amongst demographers and economists. They tend to polarize into the optimists, who are called ostriches by the pessimists, and the pessimists who are called doomsday men by the optimists.

The optimists point out that although the death rates are falling in most developing nations, mainly due to reduction in infant mortality, the rate of this reduction may become slower in the next 30 years. This is because the effect of better sanitation and environmental health is now probably nearing its maximum; and preventive inoculations against infectious

TABLE 8/2

The projected world and regional populations in the year A.D. 2000
(U.N. medium estimate)

Area	Actual mid-1971 (millions)	Estimate, 2000 (millions)	Percentage increase
World	3,709	6,500	75
Africa	354	800	126
Asia	2,104	3,718	77
North America	229	350	53
Latin America	291	720	147
Europe	466	527	13
U.S.S.R.	245	353	44
Oceania	20	32	60

disease are now readily available. These two measures can effectively reduce the crude death rate to between 15 and 20. Any reduction beyond this will be expensive. It demands an educated and motivated population, it is difficult to organize and it requires considerable numbers of health workers. In addition, since good infant nutrition is a factor in reducing mortality, the possibility of recurring food shortages may hinder any further reduction of infant deaths. The optimists also point out that the United Nations projections may have underestimated the rapidity with the family planning programmes progress. In other words, the projections fail to make allowance for an acceleration in birth control, and hence in fertility decline as family planning measures are more readily accepted. These, they argue, should have a cumulative effect on birth rates by the year 2000, so there is little need to worry, and technology will solve any remaining problems.

The pessimists take the opposite view. The expectations of the leaders, and the people, of the developing nations will not be met if the death rate does not continue to be reduced, so that levels approaching those of the developed nations are achieved by the year 2000. They hold that all the evidence so far indicates that, except in a few nations, family planning programmes have had a low cost benefit and that neither the leaders (particularly if military), nor the people, have really accepted the need to limit fertility.

They also point out that the demographic transition which took place in the developed nations may not be reproduced exactly in the developing nations, and that the optimists fail to recognize that the population of a nation continues to grow after the transition is completed because of the age structure of the country. Even if population control were miraculously obtained in the developing nations by the year 2000, and the two-child family was the norm, the size of a typical developing nation would increase by between 2·5 and 3·0 times its present size. This means that the giants, China, India, Indonesia, Brazil, Bangladesh and Pakistan would have stationary populations of 1,900 million, 1,800 million, 330 million, 290 million, 235 million and 190 million respectively, a total of nearly 5,000 million people!

There is not enough reliable information to support either the optimistic or the pessimistic position, but the pessimists seem to have the greatest chance of being right. The only rational course is to accept the medium estimate of the United Nations as being likely, and to determine if any solutions exist to the problem that the current annual growth rate in too many nations exceeds 2·0 per cent, and that by the year 2000 the world will have more than 6,500 million people who will require food, housing, education, health care and jobs. Failure to provide these necessities will lead to an increased death rate, turbulence and possibly to the Malthusian correctives of famine, pestilence and war.

4

Earlier in this book it was argued that two main problems posed grave dangers to the survival of man. The first, and major problem, was exponential population growth, and the need to produce sufficient food for the increasing numbers of people. The second, and interlinked, problem was that of exponential economic growth, which is rapidly depleting known finite mineral resources and causing increased environmental pollution. An inventory of the remaining supplies of many mineral resources, even allowing for the discovery of unexpected hidden wealth, shows that the current rate of economic growth cannot be supported for much longer. The current, rapid depletion of unrenewable mineral resources, by consumption and wastage, could be limited by improved technology which involved the search for less scarce substitutes, and by improving recycling processes. But this will only buy time, and will add considerably to the increasing pollution of land, water and air, which in turn threatens to reduce food supplies and to increase disease. This has led to the belief that ecologically faulty industrialization and 'unlimited' economic growth must be rapidly reduced. It is noticeable that the majority of people supporting this thesis are members of the affluent third of humanity. To the people of the developing nations, this reversal of a long-held opinion of the primacy of continued economic growth seems cynical. For nearly two centuries the developing nations have been the quarry, the farm, the plantation and the fibre shed of the industrialized nations. The latter bought their agricultural products and their minerals cheaply, turned them into manufactured goods and sold them back expensively. The Third World has seen this process continue until today, and now, when the potential for industrialization is theirs, the United Nations, and informed opinion, have suggested that economic growth must cease. It is little wonder that cynicism and suspicion of the motives of the developed nations are voiced. Yet the evidence that economic growth must decline is so strong, so persuasive and so urgent (as is the belief that accumulated capital must be diverted from consumer goods to social ends), that it would be unwise to ignore it.

Many leaders in the developing world believe that a larger population means a larger market, a stronger nation and cheaper industrialization. That this is a mirage is difficult to explain, and hard to make convincing. Yet it is so.

One way in which developing nations might accept the honesty of the affluent world is if the rich nations at once reduced considerably their own economic development, instituted favourable terms of trade for developing nations by massive aid, encouraged specific social and industrial progress in the developing world (ensuring bilaterally that *total* economic growth was reduced), and instituted a world food bank. Simultaneously, all nations would be seen to reduce the rate of population growth, for this is the greatest of our problems.

5

The optimist-ostriches, who argue that there is no need to be concerned over the rate of population growth, for it will resolve itself, are supported by the professional pronatalists. These people, either on religious or mystical grounds, are convinced that population control is either unnecessary or counterproductive.

Their first argument is that every increase in population is beneficial as more people make for a stronger nation, better able to defend itself, better able to attack, and with a bigger voice in international affairs. It is the argument that God is on the side of the big battalions! A bigger population also means a bigger market for consumer goods, and with a bigger market a nation will be able to produce a wider diversity of goods at a lower cost. God is on the side of big business!

The fallacy of this argument is that it is not an increase in total population that adds to a nation's wealth, but an increase in the proportion of healthy, educated, thrifty, motivated people. And even if the argument is accepted that population growth is beneficial, the *rate* of growth is crucial. Too fast a growth rate is the opposite of beneficial. The World Bank in a recent report says that the 'most immediate and measurable effect of slowing population growth is the increase in *per capita* income'. In a thrifty nation this permits higher savings and the accumulation of capital. This capital can then be used for investment in human resources, such as improving the quality of education, enhancing social welfare services and for financing technological research. If it is used wisely it will increase economic growth.

The second argument by the professional pronatalists is that increases in population can always be matched by increases in agriculture and industry. They point out that the gloomy prophecies of Malthus were found to be false. But they ignore that the situation in the last quarter of the twentieth century is quite different from that in the first quarter of the nineteenth century. The M.I.T. scientists have clearly demonstrated what may happen. Malthus' prophecies are likely to be fulfilled, unless man acts sensibly and soon. When millions of people are hungry it is obvious that agricultural production must be increased, and that a large investment in agriculture is needed. It is also evident that a large investment in social welfare and in socially desirable industrialization is needed in the developing nations, but this must be balanced by reduced industrial activity in the developed nations, or the limits to growth will be reached, and soon. The question which you should ask the professional pronatalists is not 'how many human beings can be kept alive on a minimal diet', but 'how many human beings can be given a life which is not taken up by the effort merely to survive'.

The third argument is an historical one. It is that urbanization and industrialization automatically reduce the birth rate, and as nations become industrialized they pass through demographic transition. Electricity cuts conceptions! It is true that the nineteenth-century experience of Western Europe shows that industrialization did lead, after a time lag, to a reduction in the birth rate, but the evidence is that much of this was due to voluntary contraceptive measures. It also occurred at a time when the industrialized nations depended for their economic growth on a supply of cheap materials from their colonies, and had a colonial, captive market for their manufactured goods. The population of the world in 1850 was only 1,240 million. It was growing at a rate of 0·6 per cent per annum, so that in the year 1850–51, 7·4 million people were added and subsequent exponential growth additions were not excessive. Today with the world's population over 3,856 million and a growth rate of 2·0 per cent, 77 million people will be added in 1974, and the subsequent exponential growth rate is impressive. Demographic transition, with the fewer problems of the nineteenth century, took time. As I will show, even if all nations attain a birth rate equal to the death rate by the year 2000, the size of the populations will continue to grow for a further 35 to 50 years. Today we haven't time for the nineteenth-century type of demographic transition to be effective, although with better communication techniques and contraceptive measures, the fall in the birth rate is likely to be faster than it was 100 years ago.

The fourth argument is that if births are reduced, the population will grow old, and there will be a disproportionate number of old people to support. No rational person suggests a moratorium on childbirth. What is sought is to reduce births so that they just replace deaths. Temporarily it is true that as the youth dependency falls, the aged dependency will rise, but this is only temporary. Once a stationary population is obtained, there will be a balance. Economically, the reduced youth dependency will give savings, since the resources needed to feed, care for, and educate a child for 15 years are greater than those expended on the feeding and care of an old person whose life expectancy at 65 is ten years or less.

6

To reduce the plethora of people, which threatens to overwhelm us, our objective must be to change the present pronatalist attitude into an antinatalist attitude with the least delay. This would mean that the majority (preferably all) of mankind accepted that it was in their own best interest that the rate of population growth was reduced to zero as soon as possible, and that a society developed in which births equalled deaths. This situation would be obtained if most families had no more than two children. The two-child family would become the socially desirable objective. Since about 15 per cent of the married couples in a nation are unable to have children, and 5 to 15 per cent of women never marry, there would be a margin for those married couples who could not, or would not, contain their urge for procreation.

If most couples limited their families to two children or less, population replacement level would be achieved. (The number of children per family is actually between 2·1 and 2·4, depending on some complicated demographic considerations, but 0·1 or 0·4 of a child is a complex concept.) However, even when population replacement (or zero population growth) was achieved, the population of a nation would continue to grow for about 60 years. This is because of the population structure of a nation. At present about 30 per cent of the population in the developed nations and nearly 50 per cent in the developing nations are under the age of 18, and have not yet procreated. As most of these young people will wish to have children, the size of the population will continue to increase before it becomes stationary or stable, and zero population growth is reached.

Calculations made by the U.S. Bureau of the Census show that if the population replacement level, that is the two-child family, is generally achieved by 2000–2005, the population of each of the developing nations will continue to grow for the next 50 to 60 years because of the high proportion of young people in their populations. When stability is reached, that is, when births equal deaths, the population of each developing nation would be about three times as large as it was in 1970. In the affluent, developed nations, who have advanced much further towards the ideal of the two-child family, a stable population would be reached sooner, by about 2045, and the size of each nation would average 1·3 times their population in 1970. Some examples of the calculations are shown in Table 8/3. Assuming the two-child family is the norm by 2005, by the year 2060 the population of the world would be about 9,000 million, two and a half times today's population. It would then fluctuate around that figure. In other words, zero population growth will have been achieved by 2060. Of these 9,000 million people, about 7,500 million would live in today's hungry, developing nations, and 1,500 million in today's affluent, over-fed, developed nations.

Unfortunately, it is unlikely that the two-child family will be the norm, in all the nations of the world, by 2005. It might be, but rather than being unduly optimistic, like the ecological ostriches, or unduly pessimistic, like the doomsday men, it is not unreasonable to legislate for a rather larger final population. Assuming that none of the Malthusian correctives will be permitted and that the world, as a whole, reaches the population replacement level by 2025, 50 years from now, the stable population of the world will not be 9,000 million, but between 15,000 and 18,000 million. Of these, 80 per cent will live in what are today's hungry, developing nations.

The question which should be put to national leaders by concerned citizens today is, 'Can our nation feed, house, keep

TABLE 8/3

The effect of zero population growth (i.e. if all couples had tw
children or fewer) by A.D. 2000–2005 on the size of the final stabl
population of the fifteen largest nations

Source: U.S. Bureau of the Census, *The Two-Child Family and Popula*
tion Growth, U.S. Government Printing Office, Washington D.C.
1971

Country	Population mid-1970 (millions)	Final stable population (millions)	Year in which stable popula-tion reached	Final population as a multiple of the 1970 population
DEVELOPING NATIONS				
China	750	1,963	2065	2·1
India	576	1,763	2060	3·0
Indonesia	120	329	2065	2·7
Brazil	93	292	2060	3·1
Bangladesh	74	235	2065	3·2
Nigeria	63	167	2075	2·7
Pakistan	59	190	2060	3·2
Mexico	50	167	2060	3·3
Philippines	38	130	2060	3·3
Thailand	37	115	2060	3·1
DEVELOPED NATIONS				
U.S.S.R.	243	330	2035	1·3
U.S.A.	204	288	2055	1·4
Japan	104	132	2025	1·3
U.K.	56	71	2065	1·3
France	50	68	2055	1·4

healthy, educate and find employment for the inevitable in
crease in the population, or will the only redress be by th
correctives of famine, pestilence and war?' If the question i
difficult to answer, how much more difficult will it be if curren
birth rates continue, and if the two-child family is not achieve
in the next 25 years?

At this time the world is putting its hope in a voluntar
family planning programme, which seeks to ensure that ever
child is a wanted child, and every family has the freedom t
choose how many children they will have. Analysis of the 2
nations in the developing world which have adopted famil
planning programmes suggests that perhaps more is needed
Only eight countries have achieved their targets in five or mor
years of effort. All are small nations, either islands or penin

sulas. In seven nations, together containing 780 million people, progress has fallen far short of the targets. In eight countries the programmes have been operative for too short a time for analysis, and in three the data are insufficient for analysis.

Effective birth control, or an increased mortality, is essential if the current rate of population growth is to be reduced. No rational person wants to increase the death rate. This means that only birth control is practicable and humane.

But despite the very considerable efforts made in family planning programmes in developing nations, the birth rate was only reduced by 3·3 per cent in 1971, and an excess of 74 million births over deaths occurred in that year.

It may be that family planning measures will have an exponential growth rate. But it may not. Their very limited success raises the question of whether voluntary measures are sufficient, or whether the rewards and sanctions of a heavily motivated persuasion policy should be used. This is discussed in Chapter 15.

The example of China could well be studied now that the People's Republic is a member of the United Nations. The Chinese are very pronatalist. Children are treasured and tended. Big families used to be a sign of success. In China the population growth rate is currently 1·4 per cent per annum, which is no higher than that in some affluent, developed nations. The Chinese government has achieved this by having a socially motivated people; by officially encouraging people to delay marriage; through the widespread dissemination of information about contraceptives; through the education and emancipation of women, and through the ready availability of all birth control measures, including abortion. It is a remarkable success.

The future of man is uncertain. The problems are immense. But of all the problems facing man—unbridled economic growth, the increasing gap between the affluent, rich nations and the hungry, poor nations, the increasing use of non-renewable minerals, and increasing pollution—that of exponential population growth is the most serious.

The plethora of people threatens their own survival. And we are not lemmings, although we are behaving like lemmings at the moment.

CHAPTER NINE

A Child by Choice

Somewhat more than a century ago, men in the Western World asked
the question: 'How can we justify compulsory servitude?' and came up
with the answer, 'By no means whatsoever.' Is the answer any different
to the related question: 'How can we justify compulsory pregnancy?'
Certainly pregnancy is a form of servitude: if continued to term it results
in parenthood, which is also a kind of servitude to be endured for the
best years of a woman's life.

GARRETT HARDIN, 1968

I

Throughout recorded history, mankind has tried to adjust the
number of births to the level accepted by the particular society
in which the woman lived. In general, the aim appears to have
been to replace deaths by a small excess of births, although in
most cases this aim was pursued unconsciously. The availability
of food was for a long time a limiting factor. In societies subjected to the fear of drought and famine too many mouths
to feed meant that all were likely to perish. Surely it was better
to prevent too many mouths being there? The degree of control
varied, and in each society it was determined by current needs.
To prevent unwanted births magic was used. It was not very
effective. Some groups used potions of pounded seeds, herbs and
pulses. In general, they too were rather ineffective. Other
groups relied on abortion and infanticide, or else the man
withdrew his penis from the woman's vagina during sexual
intercourse before he ejaculated. This method is known as

A Child by Choice

withdrawal or coitus interruptus. In other groups a sequence of ritualistic restraints inhibited copulation. The latter methods were fairly effective.

A few societies were more intelligent and understood the elementary physiological concept that the male sperm was a crucial component required for conception. If the sperms were hindered in their journey pregnancy would not occur. This concept was developed by several primitive races. The Batak people who live around Lake Toba in Central Sumatra used a vaginal plug which was impregnated with tannic acid. Tannic acid is an excellent spermicide.

The first written mention of contraception occurred in about 1850 B.C. in Egypt. The Kahun papyrus described a number of magical potions, which from their variety and the nature of their ingredients cannot have been very effective. But it also described a vaginal plug formed from crocodile dung and honey, which the woman inserted into her vagina before sexual intercourse. It is possible that the time required to find the crocodile dung, and the aesthetic disincentive required to fashion the vaginal plug (even if honey reduced the smell) may have acted as a deterrent to frequent copulation. But if the male's sexual urge was so strong that it overcame the aroma, it would have proved an effective contraceptive.

Three hundred years later, the Egyptians had advanced considerably. The Ebers papyrus mentions a vaginal pessary, or plug, made of lint which was soaked in 'the juice from the tips of acacia shrubs, mixed with honey'. Aesthetically and effectively, this was a considerable advance. The honey formed a film in the vagina which was penetrated with difficulty, even by an excited, aggressive spermatozoon. The acacia tips contained gum arabic which released lactic acid, and lactic acid is an efficient spermicide.

In the Eastern nations of India and China, where civilization was advanced at least as far as that of Egypt, there is little information about contraceptives, but such information as is available suggests that sexual restraint and coitus interruptus were practised.

The Jews, too, despite the biblical injunction to 'be fruitful, and multiply, and replenish the earth', used a vaginal sponge made of wadding, and called 'mokh'. Coitus interruptus was not disapproved, at least after the couple had had two children, despite the story of Onan. (This was rather exceptional, the woman was his dead brother's wife and he didn't like her.)

The Greeks, and later the Romans, took over the magical potions of the Egyptians, with as little effect. Aristotle does mention that a woman desiring no more children should use a cedar oil douche prior to coitus. He does not record what the man thought, or mention how efficient his suggestion was. But Soranus, 500 years later, gave specific instructions how to compound a contraceptive ointment made of olive oil, honey and cedar gum. This was mixed with white lead and smeared thickly on soft wood. The mess was then pushed high into the vagina. Its efficiency was undoubted, but the logistics of mixing and fixing would surely have reduced the male's enthusiasm and discouraged his erection.

During the peak of Islamic culture and expansion, which occurred from A.D. 800 to 1500, Muslim theological writers held that as the embryo and early fetus had no identity, abortion was allowed. As an alternative, coitus interruptus was practised, and some Islamic physicians recommended a vaginal plug made from the rennet of a rabbit, or the leaves of a weeping willow.

In Europe, up to 1650, with a pervasive dominant Christianity, there was an ecclesiastical prohibition against birth control. The prohibition was based on Aquinas' view that 'in so far as the generation of offspring is impeded, it is a vice against nature which happens in every carnal act from which generation cannot follow'. Because of this, the only contraceptive measures used were the ineffective ones based on folk remedies, although to some extent coitus interruptus was practised, particularly amongst the nobility and richer merchants. This is the probable explanation for the smaller size of the families of the wealthy and powerful. In North America, the puritan ethic and the emptiness of the land inhibited contraception, as large families seemed desirable for protection and for additional labour. In Latin America, the power of the Roman Catholic Church was supreme, the land was empty or inhabited by hostile, pagan natives, and fertility was lauded.

Mechanical methods of contraception were unknown in Europe until about 1720, although two hundred years earlier a linen cover for the end of the penis had been recommended as a protective against syphilis, which was then rampant throughout Europe. However, it doesn't appear to have been wildly popular except in brothels. In 1720 the condom (as it was called) was introduced. It was made from sheep's gut and the user was instructed, in rather flowery but graphic language, how to draw it over his erect penis. It was advertised widely in London between 1750 and 1820, but again was mainly used as a protection against syphilis rather than as a contraceptive. It was, however, too expensive a method for all but the wealthy classes.

2

By the last decade of the eighteenth century, the cultural climate had become much more enquiring. At the same time ecclesiastically inspired repression of discussion about sexual matters was diminishing; and amongst intellectuals there was an increasing interest in birth control. With the better food available, the infant and childhood mortality fell, and families reared more children to adolescence, so that the urge to reproduce diminished. As more parents moved to the towns and manufactories young children became a liability requiring food, rather than an asset for exploitation as a cheap source of labour. This changed attitude was accelerated after legislation in 1832 in England which restricted child labour very considerably. In this cultural atmosphere the use of coitus interruptus as a contraceptive method appears to have increased amongst all socio-economic groups.

By this time, too, Francis Place had begun to make his impact. Place, in fact, can be called the founder of the birth control movement. Unlike Malthus, who had observed poverty from the comfort of his carriage, and from his discreet clerical observations, Place knew it from experience. His father had been a violent, uncommunicative boor, whose method of discipline was to beat his children and whose respect for his wife was to desert her for long periods. Francis, the eldest son, had experienced the indignity and the misery of poverty. At fourteen he was apprenticed to a leather-breeches maker. With

uncommon courage and persistence he had educated himself, and prospered in his business. But he never lost his social
conscience and became the secret leader of working-men's
associations. He observed that in bargaining with rapacious
employers, the labourers negotiated from weakness. They had no
savings should they be dismissed from work, and they generally
had large families. Place reasoned that they could obtain better
wage justice, and give their children a better opportunity in
life, if they had smaller families. As he had a belief in non-
violence, he felt that the only way to alter the situation was to
change attitudes. As the change was to be by persuasion, he was
prepared to use propaganda. He rejected Malthus' solution of
moral restraint by delaying marriage, as he believed that this
would lead to vice and prostitution. In place of moral restraint
he favoured the more realistic approach of contraceptive
measures. To spread his views, he wrote a book, and more
important, published a series of handbills. His book reached
the affluent, his single sheet handbills were distributed widely
amongst the workers in London and the industrial towns of
Northern England. The handbills of 1823 were addressed to
'The Married of Both Sexes of the Working People', as well as
to other groups. Although Place took the prevalent Victorian
moral tone against vice and debauchery, he suggested that by
limiting the size of their families, the 'misery of the poor
children' and the parents' 'own sickness' might be mitigated.
The handbills recommended that the women use a 'piece of
soft sponge tied by a bobbin or penny ribbon, and inserted
(. . . into the vagina . . .) just before sexual intercourse takes
place'. The sponge was to be 'the size of a green walnut or
small apple and would not diminish the pleasures of married
life'. Only when the sponge was not available did Place recommend coitus interruptus. In addition to the medico-social
advantages of contraception outlined in his handbills Place
also stressed the economic advantages of small families. Small
families would prevent poverty. They would reduce the need
for child labour, and would raise the standard of living. These
attitudes are echoed today by the stress that is given to family
welfare in birth control programmes in many nations.

Although it is not mentioned in his pamphlets, it is likely
that Place knew about the practice of abandoning unwanted

children. Indeed, his term 'the misery of poor children' suggests this. The rich sent their unwanted children to the country to be cared for by peasant women; the poor merely abandoned them in the hope that they would be admitted to a foundling hospital. In either case the child's chances of survival were low. Population control in Victorian England, and in other European nations, was achieved by disguised infanticide. In one foundling hospital in Paris in 1818, over 72 per cent of children died within the first year of their life. In Italy the mortality of orphans was over 80 per cent. In England it was between 60 and 70 per cent. Disraeli, later to be Prime Minister, wrote in 1845, 'Infanticide is practised as extensively and legally in England as it is on the banks of the Ganges.'

Place detested hypocrisy, which was so evident amongst the English middle classes. He must have reasoned that contraception was infinitely superior to an unwanted pregnancy, the product of which was 'legally' disposed of by disguised infanticide.

At the same time in the United States of America, Robert Dale Owen, the son of the Scottish philanthropist and social reformer, published a book *Moral Restraint* in 1830 in which coitus interruptus was recommended in preference to the vaginal sponge, and the condom. He claimed that the vaginal sponge was of doubtful efficacy and 'physically disagreeable', whilst the condom was 'inconvenient'. Although Owen's book had sold 75,000 copies by the time of his death in 1877, it did not have the impact of Dr. Charles Knowlton's *The Fruits of Philosophy: or a private Companion of Young Married People* which was first published in 1832. Knowlton's book had gone through 10 editions by 1877, and was reprinted in Britain in that year. This new edition led directly to the trial of Charles Bradlaugh and Annie Besant, with resulting widespread publicity about 'birth control'. Knowlton's recommended method was douching using an 'astringent vegetable' infusion, or soda bicarbonate, but he was 'quite confident that the liberal use of pretty cold water would be a never-failing preventative'. He did not think coitus interruptus safe, and apparently rejected the vaginal sponge as unaesthetic.

3

By 1860, in England, it was considered safe to write about contraception. Charles Bradlaugh, a liberally minded politician and social reformer, published articles recommending contraception in his journal *The National Reformer*. Early in 1877 a Bristol publisher, Henry Cook, had printed and distributed an edition of Knowlton's *The Fruits of Philosophy* in which it was alleged he had interleaved obscene pictures. For this he was sentenced to two years' imprisonment with hard labour. As the book had been circulating for over twenty years, Bradlaugh, together with his fellow reformer Annie Besant, objected and invited prosecution by publishing another edition of the book (without the pictures). Bradlaugh and Besant were duly prosecuted, and after two trials, which were attended by much publicity, were acquitted, and the right to publish contraceptive information was established. At the same time another reformer, Edward Truelove, then nearly seventy years old, published a new edition of Owen's booklet and was prosecuted as the booklet 'would have an injurious effect on the minds of the young'. Again two trials were needed before Truelove was convicted and sentenced to four months' imprisonment.

The effect of these two trials scandalized intellectual society, many of whom were already using birth control. Not only was intellectual opinion incensed, but the general public now learned that contraceptive methods were available, and information about them might be obtained legally and without hazard.

By this time, too, the condom had come into general use. In 1843, vulcanization of rubber had been discovered, which had lowered the cost of making thinner, stronger sheets of crepe rubber. This new rubber was found suitable for condoms. Using the thin rubber, they were as satisfactory sexually as the more expensive sheep's gut condoms.

Following the Bradlaugh–Besant trial, public interest in contraception increased and sales of books dealing with birth control rose dramatically. For example, the edition of Knowlton's *The Fruits of Philosophy*, published by Bradlaugh and Besant, sold 185,000 copies in the next four years, and other editions were published in industrial towns in the North of England. In 1879 Annie Besant wrote, and published, a book which replaced Knowlton's dated work, and had the effect of further spreading knowledge of contraception. This book, *The Law of Population: Its Consequences, and the Bearing on Conduct and Morals*, was dedicated 'To the poor in the great cities and agricultural districts, dwellers in stifling court or crowded hovel in the hope that it may point out a path from poverty and may make easier the life of British mothers, to them I dedicate this essay'. The sales were large, 175,000 copies having been sold at 6d. a copy. Mrs. Besant condemned abortion and felt the 'safe period' (which had incorrectly been assumed to be from the 5th to the 15th day of the menstrual cycle) was uncertain. She accepted coitus interruptus as 'absolutely certain' and without injurious side-effects, but considered the vaginal douche and the use of the condom to have obvious aesthetic disadvantages 'as a matter of taste and feeling'. She felt that the vaginal sponge was the preferred method, and in later editions also approved soluble vaginal pessaries. By 1885 she added that the sponge should be soaked in a dilute quinine solution, and that the following morning the wife might douche using a quinine solution. She also recommended a rubber cervical cap in place of the vaginal sponge as both were 'absolutely unobtrusive'.

In 1885 a Leeds physician, Dr. Albutt, wrote *The Wife's Handbook* in which one chapter dealt with 'How to Prevent Conception When Advised by the Doctor'. Albutt described in careful, non-sensational detail the methods then available for birth control, including the use of the vaginal diaphragm, which had recently been introduced in Germany. Two years later he was indicted for 'unprofessional conduct' and was examined by the General Medical Council, which is formed from representatives of the doctors to police their own profession. They found him guilty of the 'offence' charged against him; 'that is to say, of having published and publicly caused to be sold, a work entitled *The Wife's Handbook* in London and elsewhere, at so low a price as to bring the work within the reach of the youth of both sexes, to the detriment of public morals'. This act, the Council decided, was 'infamous in a professional respect', and Allbutt's name was removed from the Medical Register, his licence to practise medicine thus being

revoked. As has occurred so frequently, the medical profession
was not in the forefront of social change. The action of the
General Medical Council again led to widespread publicity
and according to a weekly journal, the *Pall Mall Gazette*, was
'one of the most glaring illustrations of professional prejudice
and human folly'. It also led to a large sale of *The Wife's
Handbook*.

The effect of all this publicity from 1877 onwards was to

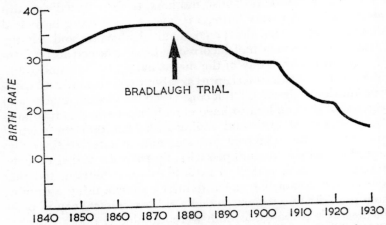

FIG. 9/1. The effect of the Bradlaugh–Besant trial on the birth rate
in England and Wales.

induce people to ask how many children they wanted, and if
they reached the desired number to use one or other of the
contraceptive methods available.

The use of contraceptive measures increased in the forty
years from 1880 to 1920, particularly amongst the upper and
middle classes. That this had a considerable influence on the
birth rate, which began to fall from 1877, is evident in Fig. 9/1.

4

In the U.S.A., the dissemination of birth control information
had been suppressed by the obsessive behaviour of Anthony
Comstock. Comstock was obsessed by sex and was violently
prejudiced against any spread of contraceptive knowledge

which he believed was the devil's work. He believed that infidelity (which he defined as a lack of Christian faith as well as adultery) and obscenity 'occupied the same bed', which inappropriately perhaps was one of his favourite aphorisms. His obsession led him to undertake to persecute and prosecute any doctor who recommended birth control and to attack the sellers of contraceptives, whom he called 'abortionists'. He saw no difference between the prevention of pregnancy and its premature termination. To make his attacks effective, he formed The New York Society for the Suppression of Vice, and held that any method was justified to eradicate the evil he had perceived. In one of his forays, he and four other vice hunters went to a brothel and hired three young women to parade before them naked, for which they charged a mere $14.50. Comstock then arrested them and charged them with indecent exposure! Between 1873 and 1882, his Society was responsible for 700 arrests; 333 sentences, totalling 155 years; fines of over $65,000 and the seizure of 28,000 lb. of 'obscene books' as well as 65,000 'articles for immoral use, of rubber etc'.

Apart from the misery he caused to a large number of honest, respectable people, Comstock induced the U.S. Congress in 1873 to pass the 'Comstock Law' which made it a criminal offence to import, mail or transport in interstate commerce any article of medicine for the prevention of conception or for causing abortion. The Act also made it criminal to import, mail or transport in interstate commerce 'obscene literature'. In Comstock's view, obscene literature not only included such sexually stimulating works as *The Arabian Nights* but also all literature about contraceptive devices and methods.

Although by the second decade of the twentieth century, Comstockery was largely ignored, the Act was used from time to time to prosecute birth control reformers and, in particular, Margaret Sanger, who courageously fought back.

After working amongst the urban poor in New York, Margaret Sanger became convinced that the Comstock Laws were causing great misery, particularly to the many women who needed contraceptive advice for social or economic reasons and who were being refused such advice by physicians. The medical profession in the face of the Comstock Act did little to change the law, but were prepared to advise their private patients, whilst ignoring the needs of those whose need was greatest. I was left to Margaret Sanger, a nurse and mother of three children, to make the challenge. She did.

One stifling hot day in July in 1912, she was called to the slum tenement of a 28-year-old woman who was suffering from the effects of septicaemia following a self-induced abortion. She had three young children, and her husband, a truck driver, earned only a minimal wage. As Margaret Sanger wrote later in her autobiography, she and the doctor 'settled ourselves to the task of fighting the septicaemia. Never had I worked so fast, never so concentratedly. The sultry days and nights melted into a torpid inferno. It did not seem possible there could be such heat, and every bit of food, ice and drugs had to be carried up three flights of stairs.'

Mrs. Sachs' recovery was slow, but recover she did and at the end of three weeks asked Margaret Sanger, who continues:—

' "Another baby will finish me, I suppose."

' "It's too early to talk about that," I temporized.

'But when the doctor came to make his last call, I drew him aside. "Mrs. Sachs is terribly worried about having another baby."

' "She may well be," replied the doctor, and then he stood before her and said, "Any more such capers, young woman and there'll be no need to send for me."

' "I know, doctor," she replied timidly. "But," she hesitated as though it took all her courage to say it, "what can I do to prevent it?"

'The doctor was a kindly man, and he had worked hard to save her, but such incidents had become so familiar to him that he had long since lost whatever delicacy he might once have had. He laughed goodnaturedly. "You want to have your cake and eat it too, do you? Well, it can't be done."

'Then, picking up his hat and bag to depart, he said, "Tell Jake to sleep on the roof." '

This experience led Margaret Sanger to begin to campaign and it culminated with her 'Contraceptive Advice Station' which she opened in Brooklyn in 1916 to help those too poor and too shy to seek the confidential contraceptive services provided by a few physicians. The clinic was rapidly closed by police action. However, the experience she had obtained was influential in securing a decision by the Court of Appeals that it was legal for physicians to give contraceptive advice 'for the cure and prevention of disease' which could be widely interpreted. The movement was encouraged by the formation, in the 1920s, of the National Committee on Maternal Health Incorporated. It will be noted that all the efforts mentioned were made by voluntary organizations, usually in the face of official indifference, or opposition, and without the support of the medical profession. Despite the obvious need for birth control information, the situation in the U.S.A. was hindered by government and institutional policies which made it difficult for health workers to dispense, and for couples to practise, birth control. From 1936 several court decisions moderated the impact of the anti-contraceptive Comstock laws, but twenty-two years elapsed before the ban on prescribing contraceptives in public hospitals in New York was lifted. This started the trend to publicly financed family planning services, but it was not until 1967 that the U.S. Congress adopted any specific legislation on family planning.

Since 1967 the changes have been rapid. Federal and State agencies in the U.S.A. have initiated policies favouring family planning; and increasing numbers of States have liberalized their abortion laws. At the apex of the changes is the Federal Family Planning Agency which was set up after the passage of the Family Planning Services and Population Research Act of 1970. It is now public policy to help American women avoid unwanted, unwelcome pregnancy, and this measure should play a significant part in helping the U.S.A. to achieve population stability.

5

In Britain, the situation was similar. Birth control information and advice was left to voluntary organizations, and was opposed by legislators and doctors. However, changes were occurring and the general emancipation of women led, in the early 1920s, to the formation of The Birth Control League. More important, birth control clinics were established by interested private organizations to give advice, and to provide devices, for those too poor, or too shy, to visit their family doctor. However, no support was received from the Government, although a resolution in 1926 by the House of Lords had called for the removal of 'all obstacles to the introduction of birth control advice in Maternity and Child Welfare centres'. This was not implemented. Six years later the Minister of Health issued a circular permitting the Maternal and Child Health Centres to give contraceptive advice in cases 'where a further pregnancy would be detrimental to health', but in no other cases. The Government was not anxious to be involved politically with birth control. By 1930 it appeared that over 70 per cent of married women of the upper socio-economic groups used contraceptive methods, whilst in the lower socio-economic groups about half of those who were sufficiently motivated to attend a birth control clinic said they had used some form of contraception prior to the visit. It is also clear from other studies that the higher the socio-economic level of the woman, the lower was the failure rate, which stresses the importance of education in family planning programmes.

Between 1935 and 1955, contraceptive advice continued to be given and contraceptives to be obtained either from birth control clinics, pharmacists' shops or other sources on an increasing scale. During this period no political party in the United Kingdom had any policy about population dynamics. This was understandable in the 1930s when demographers foretold a decline of population, but after World War II the policy continued, despite the recommendation in 1949 by the Royal Commission on Population that the population needed to be stabilized and 'control of men and women over the numbers of their children is one of the first conditions of their own and the community's welfare'. Religious and other pressure groups echoed Sir Norman Birkett's 1939 remark that birth control ought not to be made generally available as it would 'tend to lower the traditional and accepted standard of morality' and might often be 'a source of temptation'. Their influence delayed any implementation of a population policy, although the world's rate of population growth was now a matter of grave concern to many.

It was not until 1967 that the Family Planning Act was

placed on the statute book. This Act gave the Minister of Health the power to order any local authority to provide Family Planning Services as a statutory duty. But between 1967 and 1970, few local authorities had taken much action, pleading shortage of funds. The introduction in 1968 of the Abortion Act widened the indications for legal abortion, and in the first three years the rate rose to 120,000 abortions annually. Belatedly, the Government realized that many of the abortions were being performed because pregnancy had resulted from the unavailability, inconvenience or cost of obtaining contraceptive advice, and it was estimated by the Select Committee on Science and Technology that between 200,000 and 300,000 unwelcome, often unwanted, children were born each year in England and Wales alone. The rising rate of legal abortions, together with the evidence of the large number of unwanted pregnancies, has led to a realization that the Abortion Act was introduced prematurely, and was not preceded by a vigorous campaign to provide birth control measures to those most vulnerable—unmarried girls under the age of 25, and married women, largely urban dwellers, whose income was low, and whose social environment was depressed. A further factor was that under the Abortion Act, abortions were provided free in National Health Service hospitals, but contraceptive advice had to be sought privately, and the contraceptive equipment had to be purchased.

These defects aggravated the situation and increased the requests for abortion as a birth control measure. Middle-class women were able to obtain contraceptive advice from their family doctors or from the Family Planning Association clinics. Lower-class women, and particularly unmarried girls, not only found it difficult to seek advice from predominantly middle-class, usually male family doctors, or the mainly middle-class workers in the F.P.A., but tended to be deterred by the complex administrative arrangements, in particular the need to walk into a building which existed solely to give contraceptive advice. This constraint is due to the sexual prudery of many women, and to the lack of adequate sex education in childhood and adolescence. This has had the effect that contraceptive measures have not been sought by many women who are at risk of becoming pregnant. It has been calculated that failure to use contraceptives was the cause of 70 per cent of 120,000 pregnancies terminated in 1971.

Despite this evidence, the British Minister of Health declared in 1971 that free contraceptives would be 'a gratuitous waste of the taxpayers' money', as the vast majority of people in Britain were capable of seeking and paying for contraception. More significantly he rejected the suggestion that maternity hospital and MCH clinics were suitable places to give contraceptive advice, although most experts, including the World Health Organization, consider that family planning is most suitably linked with maternity and child welfare. Linking family welfare and family planning enables easy referral to take place when gynaecological problems are discovered, enhances the service of each, and reduces costs considerably.

Opposition to the dissemination of contraceptive advice by community leaders has had the effect that although local authorities have had the power to provide birth control facilities since 1967, (and have had funds made available by the State for the purpose), by 1972 only one-third offered such a service, and then not all offered a 'consumer oriented' service.

The lack of enthusiasm and co-operation by local municipal and county authorities was, in part, due to the fear that increased contraceptive availability, particularly amongst unmarried women, would lead to increased promiscuity. Unmarried men had always been able to purchase condoms from pharmacists' shops, or more usually from men's hairdressing shops, but the double standard of sexual morality inhibited the thoughts of many community leaders.

There is no evidence that contraceptive availability increased promiscuity. Both have increased in an increasingly sexually permissive atmosphere. Two careful studies, one in Birmingham, the other in London, confirmed that 96 per cent of 1,500 unmarried girls studied were sexually active when they sought contraceptive advice; that only 7 per cent had changed their sexual partner in a follow-up survey made 18 to 24 months after their first visit to the clinic; that the girls attended of their own free will, and 25 per cent had informed their parents; and that using a personality questionnaire the girls were indistinguishable from the population at large.

Sociological studies suggest that a consumer demand for

birth control exists in Britain. Surveys seeking information about birth control get a higher response than those seeking information about income and expenditures. Newspapers and magazines emphasizing sexual exploits have a large circulation. The constraint to accepting birth control seems to be fear of being snubbed by the health worker, and the cost, not a lack of desire.

In 1973 the British Minister of Health had second thoughts about his 1971 statement, and in introducing changes in the National Health Service, to operate from mid-1974, he announced that he would include contraceptives in the health service. The Pill, and contraceptive appliances, would not be free but would carry a prescription charge. He came to this decision despite the obvious concept that prevention of unwanted pregnancies is as much a part of preventive medicine as are immunizations, cancer smear tests, routine chest X-rays, and the provision of pure water—and in England preventive health measures are provided free. He also ignored the remarkably successful experience of those few local authorities who have provided a free contraceptive service to the poor in their area. In 1974, with a new government in office, regulations were passed enabling contraceptives to be supplied free of charge.

Any nation concerned with the rate of population growth, the number of illegal abortions, and the number of births to unmarried mothers, should first institute a well-organized information campaign about family planning. It should start giving sex education (including information about birth control) in primary and secondary schools and it should offer contraceptives which can be obtained easily and at little or no cost. If this sequence is adopted, legal abortion should only be needed as a 'backstop' when contraception fails, and to help the ignorant, the unlucky and the unfortunate woman who becomes pregnant.

Although political hostility, or at least indifference, has hindered the dissemination of contraceptive knowledge and the use of contraceptives, the advances in contraceptive technology between 1935 and 1955 led to a move away from the less effective methods of conception control (the douche and coitus interruptus) to the use of the vaginal diaphragm, whilst the condom continued to be used at the same proportional rate (Fig. 9/2). It will be noted, too, that the 'Safe Period' which

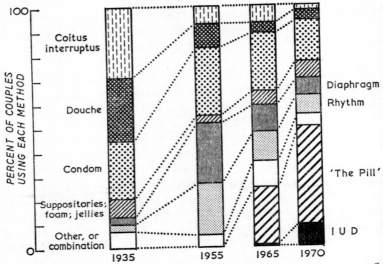

FIG. 9/2. The use of contraceptives in the U.S.A., 1935, 1955, 1965 and 1970, showing the change to the Pill. Source: *Family Planning* **17**, 1, 1967 (for earlier data).

was acceptable to Roman Catholics came to be used increasingly up to 1955 but became less popular after that date. This coincided with the development of oral contraceptives.

6

In 1955 a revolution occurred in birth control technology. In that year Dr. Pincus reported his experience with hormonal oral contraceptives at a meeting in Tokyo, and at the same meeting the Japanese reported their experiences of the reintroduction of the intra-uterine contraceptive device. The latter had been used in the 1920s and 1930s, particularly by Grafenberg in Germany and Oppenheimer in Israel. However, as the IUD was difficult to introduce and was frequently followed by complications, such as pelvic infection, it had been condemned by gynaecologists and had fallen into disuse.

From 1955 on these two methods, 'The Pill' and 'The Loop', became the most frequent methods of contraception recommended. Estimates of the usage of oral contraceptives for the year 1973 showed that over 50 million women were using the Pill for contraception, and 15 million women had intra-uterine contraceptive devices in use. Despite this stress on the Pill and the IUD, a careful randomized survey of sexual habits made in England and Wales in 1970 somewhat surprisingly revealed

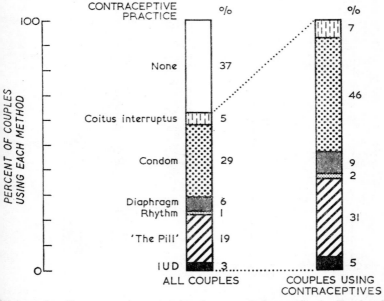

FIG. 9/3. Contraceptive practice by married couples in England and Wales, 1969. Source: Gorer, G., *Sex and Marriage in England and Wales*, Nelson, 1971.

that over one third of married couples used no contraceptive technique, whilst of those using some method, the condom was the most popular, particularly amongst couples of the lower socio-economic group who lived in the north of England (Fig. 9/3).

It is interesting, and instructive, to compare these findings with a study made in Denmark, where sex education is stressed in school and where sex is not considered obscene. Amongst

Danes of all classes there is far less prurience towards sexuality than there is in Britain. In a nation which has a rational attitude towards sex and contraception, preference for the newer, safer methods of birth control is marked. By 1970, 66 per cent of contraceptive users chose oral contraceptives, and the number choosing coitus interruptus or the condom had dropped to less than 10 per cent (Fig. 9/4).

As a final note, it is worthy of comment that since 1960 there has been an increasing awareness by Governments, International

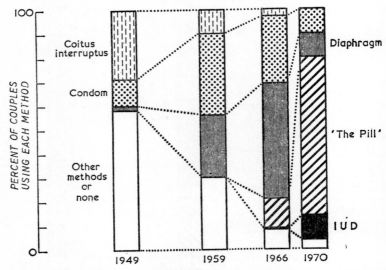

FIG. 9/4. Contraceptive practice in Denmark, 1949–70. Source Oster, M., *Advances in Planned Parenthood* **6**, 35, 1971.

Agencies and individuals that control of population growth essential, and that the most humane and desirable method is by the use of contraceptive techniques. It is ironic that the calumny and derision hurled at the pioneers who suggested that the knowledge of contraception, a desire to use contraceptive measures and the availability of contraceptive devices would improve the human condition, has today been replaced by a awareness that their views were correct, their approach justified and their integrity unquestioned. It would undoubtedly have pleased Francis Place.

CHAPTER TEN

Contraception

I must go down to Golden Lane, Golden Lane,
For Mrs. Brown has popped again, popped again,
That brings her number up to twenty-five,
Fifteen dead and ten alive, ten alive.

Medical students' song, to the
tune of 'A Tavern in the Town'.

I

If the reader accepts that the exponential rate of population growth poses a major threat to the quality of life, that it aggravates the malnutrition in the hungry Third World, and that it is a threat to our very survival, then the question which has to be asked, is, 'Can the rate of population growth be reduced?' The answer to this question is complex. First, the majority of people of all nations must be willing to change their cultural pronatal attitudes, and secondly, contraceptive technology must have advanced sufficiently to have produced birth control measures which are reasonably efficient. It has to be admitted that currently there is no perfect contraceptive, that is, a contraceptive which will consistently prevent pregnancy, which is reversible, is easy to use and which is without side-effects. But modern technology has developed contraceptive methods which are highly effective, and which are available for use by men and women in a variety of cultural, intellectual and environmental circumstances. The concept of a choice of methods, one of which is most suited to a particular person in a particular circumstance, is important. Doctrinaire belief in the superiority of one method, in all places and at all times, is self-defeating. In certain circumstances it may be preferable to recommend a less efficient method, which is more readily available and easier to use than a more efficient method which is complicated to use, and likely to be discontinued by the user after a longer or shorter interval. In this connection, the finding in several surveys in India that nearly half the women studied who chose the Pill, had discontinued its use within 12 months of accepting the method, is, to say the least, disconcerting.

In any examination of contraceptive technology it is useful to have some method of comparing the success of the chosen method in preventing unwanted pregnancies; in other words, to be able to calculate its use-effectiveness. A method which has been available for the past 40 years is that devised by Raymond Pearl, and usually referred to as the Pearl index. The index calculates the unintended pregnancy rate from the formula

$$\frac{\text{The number of unintended pregnancies}}{\text{Total months of exposure to pregnancy}} \times 1,200.$$

The result is expressed as the *failure rate per 100 woman-years*. The number of pregnancies in the numerator must include all known pregnancies, whatever the outcome. The factor 1,200 is the number of months in 100 years. The total months of exposure to pregnancy in the denominator is obtained by deducting all those months when coitus did not take place for reasons of separation, sickness or whatever. By convention, ten months is deducted for a pregnancy which reached 30 weeks, and four months for a pregnancy which ended before that time.

A valid criticism of the Pearl index has been made by Dr. Lasagna who had 'a harsh look at current practices', and concluded that the index has the disadvantage that it disregards motivation, the fact that couples vary in respect of their monthly risk of conception, the socio-economic status of the subjects, their ages and the finding that the index can be calculated in several ways. He claims that the index 'blithely assumes that the rates for groups of women under observation for different periods are comparable and can be lumped together'. He writes: 'One is reminded of the play which included a minister, a prostitute, and a man paralysed from the waist down so as

228

to represent a cross-section of humanity.' Unfortunately, the alternative, more accurate, method suggested by Lasagna is neither easy to calculate nor is it easy to understand, whilst Pearl's index does enable the reader to appraise the relative efficiency of the different methods of contraception available.

In the following discussion, methods which can be used by men will be discussed first, and those used by women will be considered later.

2

CONTRACEPTIVE METHODS FOR MEN

Coitus interruptus

Apart from abortion and infanticide, coitus interruptus is probably the oldest method of birth control. It is used in all cultures and is known by a variety of names, 'withdrawal' and 'being careful' being the most usual ones. The Bible in a memorable phrase refers to it as 'winnowing inside and threshing without'. As I noted in the last Chapter, coitus interruptus played an important part in the transition from a high to a low birth rate, which occurred in many European nations between 1820 and 1890, but its use has now diminished, even in Britain where it was previously popular, particularly amongst working-class men. A social survey into sex and marriage, carried out in England and Wales in 1957, showed that coitus interruptus was the method of choice of birth control of 20 per cent of a random sample, but by 1969 the proportion using the method had fallen to 5 per cent.

The reliability of coitus interruptus, as a method of birth control, depends on the ability of the man to recognize the pre-ejaculatory phase of coitus and his agility in removing his penis from the vagina before ejaculation occurs. It also demands that he directs the ejaculate away from the vulva, as pregnancy can follow sperm deposition in the entrance to the vagina. Provided that the man can exercise this degree of control, coitus interruptus is relatively efficient. The method requires no prior preparation and is without cost, which is an advantage.

Claims that coitus interruptus is physically or psychologically injurious to either partner cannot be substantiated, although a woman with a high libido may fail to reach orgasm and may become sexually frustrated unless her partner brings her to orgasm by digital or oral manipulation of her clitoral area, after he has ejaculated.

The Condom

The history of the condom, its method of manufacture and the standards required have been considered in the last Chapter. Modern condoms made of fine latex or plastic, prelubricated by adding silicone, and individually packed in hermetically sealed aluminium foil sachets, are efficient and hardly noticeable contraceptives. They have a store life of at least five years, and can consequently be made available through a variety of outlets. In Britain, for example, over 65 per cent of sales are made through pharmacies and men's hairdressers, a fact which led Dr. Malcolm Potts, then Medical Director of the International Planned Parenthood Federation, to state: 'This is a matter of considerable importance, and a possible reason for the continuing popularity of the condom, as it can be purchased without a prescription and from a variety of outlets, including the impersonal vending machine.' In 1972, the American A.I.D. programme, in an effort to popularize the method in a variety of nations, introduced coloured condoms. It is now possible to choose a red, a blue, a black, a yellow, a green or a white condom, whichever the user feels the most appropriate. Already the jokes are starting. For example, the man who used a black condom, when seeking sexual relief after his wife had died, was greeted with the remark from his partner that he showed 'great delicacy'.

The reliability of the condom is difficult to evaluate, for it depends on the technique used, although its simplicity should reduce this factor. In general, the condom is drawn on to the erect penis, which means that its use must be related to immediate coitus. The rolled condom is unrolled on to the penis, care being taken to remove air from the closed end, which may be teat or plain-ended. There is no difference in effectiveness. If air is left in the closed end, its pressure, together with the ejaculated semen, may lead to the condom bursting. Although the risk is slight, couples using the method for whom an inadvertent pregnancy would be disastrous, should also make sure that the woman has used a vaginal spermicidal pessary, or cream, before sexual intercourse takes place.

As well as its ready availability, the condom has medico-social advantages. If the couple have only infrequent and un-predictable coitus, it is more logical for the man to use a condom than for the woman to use a method such as oral con-traceptives or the IUD. One such situation may be when the man is away from home for the greater part of the year, or if he returns unexpectedly. A condom should be used for preven-tive reasons if the man seeks coitus with a prostitute, although its protective value is by no means absolute. It should also be used if the woman, but not the man, has psychological or religious reasons for not using a contraceptive method. The condom can be used by any man, provided he can get an erection; and if he can't he has sexual problems which need help. Modern condoms are virtually undetectable to either partner during coitus, and there are no side-effects from their use.

Because of its ready availability, its cheapness, and its ease of use, the condom remains a very popular method of birth control in the developed and in the developing nations. In the former, its use varies with the culture, the age and marital status of the user and his socio-economic group. More older men use condoms than younger men, and more men of the lower socio-economic groups than those of more affluent groups. In the most recent survey in Britain, Geoffrey Gorer found 29 per cent of the married population habitually used the condom for birth control. It was particularly favoured by older men, who belonged (on his assessment) to the skilled working class or lower middle-class, and who lived in the South of England. In the U.S. the use of the condom has declined considerably since the Pill became available, but sales continue to remain high. In Japan, nationwide surveys conducted in 1950 and 1959 showed that the use of the condom increased from 38 per cent to 58 per cent in the population studied. This increase coincided with a fall in the number of abortions performed. A calculation made in 1970 indicated that more than 100 million condoms are manufactured annually in the world.

The reliability of the condom as an effective birth control method has been difficult to estimate because most surveys have been made on selected groups. The American gynaecologist,

Christopher Tietze, has reviewed the available literature and has concluded that when used by couples who already had children and who were motivated to prevent a further pregnancy, the pregnancy rate calculated by Pearl's formula, was 3 per 100 woman-years. In most investigations, however, the pregnancy rate lies between 10 and 20 per 100 woman-years.

Vasectomy

Interest in vasectomy is increasing at the moment, and it is accepted that it is a highly effective, easily performed, permanent method of birth control. It is, in fact, easier to do the operation on a man than to operate to cut and tie a woman's tubes, although not all men would accept this viewpoint.

Most of the opposition to vasectomy is the fear that the operation is painful, and to the hidden fear that it reduces a man's sexual drive. Investigators have been astonished at the degree of ignorance about the male genital tract even amongst supposedly intelligent people. To a significant number of people vasectomy is confused with castration, which is the erroneous basis of the hidden fear of reduced sexual potency after the operation. A man thinking about having a vasectomy can be reassured that there will be no reduction in his sexuality after the operation, as the operation does not interfere with his testicles but merely divides the vas deferens, the tube which carries the spermatozoa from the testicles to the penis. Some men are also concerned about what happens to the sperms which are manufactured by the testes after vasectomy. They know that every time they ejaculate a considerable amount of semen spurts from the penis, and fear that after the operation this will distend the testes and lead to trouble. What they do not realize is that the spermatozoa only contribute a small amount to the ejaculate. Most of it is from the secretions of a small gland which lies near the base of the bladder. These, of course, continue to be made after vasectomy so that ejaculation continues but the ejaculate contains no spermatozoa. Because the quantity of spermatozoa is so small, there need be no fear that the testicles will blow up like balloons. The testicle is made up of fine tubes, and as the spermatozoa fill these tubes, further production ceases. However, the male sex hormone, androgen, continues to be produced and there is some evidence that increased quantities are made after a vasectomy, so that a man need not fear that his virility will be lost. Perhaps the most successful proof of the lack of side-effects of vasectomy is for a man, who proposes to have the operation, to meet a man who has already had a vasectomy performed.

Since fear of the unknown is a dominant human trait, a description of the operation should reduce this fear. If a man gently palpates his scrotum, at the level where it joins his body, by putting this thumb in front and his index finger behind, he

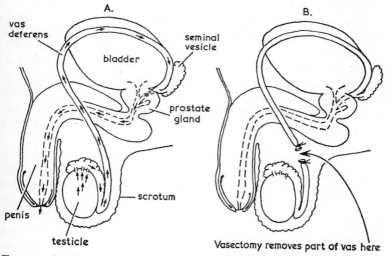

FIG. 10/1. Vasectomy. A. The route followed by sperm in the male before operation. B. As a result of vasectomy this route is interrupted.

will feel a cord-like tube in the midst of the tissues. It is easiest to feel this if he roles the folds of skin between his finger and his thumb. The cord-like tube is the vas deferens. If he repeats the experiment on the other side of his scrotum, he will discover that he has two vas deferens, one on each side.

The operation merely cuts out a short segment of each vas, and ties the cut ends (Fig. 10/1). It can be done under a general anaesthetic or under local anaesthesia. In most developed nations the man is admitted to hospital for the day and given a general anaesthetic. In India, where more than 4 million vasectomies have been done, local anaesthetic is usually used.

Once the man, or his scrotum, has been anaesthetized, two small incisions are made, one over each vas, and a loop of it is brought into view. The vas is separated from the blood vessels which make up the spermatic cord, and two small clamps isolate a segment, which is then cut out, and the ends are tied. The whole operation takes about 15 minutes, and ends when the skin is stitched with fine stitches which are removed about 4 days later. During this time the man wears a testicular support, or jock strap, but need not stay in bed.

Sexual intercouse can be resumed whenever the man or his partner wish, but one of the couple must continue to use other contraceptive measures as the man is not sterile until all the spermatozoa accumulated in the seminal vesicles have been ejaculated. This may require twelve ejaculations, and until a sperm test has been made the man is potentially fertile. Where it is not possible to do a semen analysis, the couple should continue to use other contraceptive measures until the man has had 15 ejaculations. Once this period is past, vasectomy is 100 per cent effective, and the Pearl index is zero.

The psychological effect of vasectomy has been studied in several nations. The consensus is that if the operation is socially and culturally acceptable in the society, and if the patient himself has been properly prepared for the operation, the effects are minimal. Those who are most disturbed are men who were psychologically unstable before the operation. Over 70 per cent of men interviewed claimed to have a more satisfactory sex life after vasectomy, and only 2 per cent were unhappy. There is no evidence to support the myth that vasectomized men become increasingly unfaithful to their wives.

In general, the operation should be considered irreversible, although it is possible to do a reconstructive operation if too wide a wedge has not been excised. A novel idea, as yet little developed, except in the U.S.A., is for a man to deposit a quantity of his spermatozoa in a 'sperm bank' where it is stored under liquid nitrogen for use later should he wish for some reason to have a further child.

In Britain vasectomy is now available at no cost under the National Health Scheme; in India men who have had vasectomy performed are given a money grant so that they may take time off work; but in most nations the operation must be paid for

Vasectomy is becoming increasingly acceptable in the developed nations of the world. The increase in the number of operations has coincided with concern about the effects of population growth and about the side-effects of other contraceptive measures.

3

CONTRACEPTIVE MEASURES FOR WOMEN

The old adage 'never trust a male' applies particularly to birth control. After all, it isn't the man who becomes pregnant. Unfortunately (for women), in many societies, the decision about contraception is taken by the husband, although it is hoped that he and his wife discuss the problem. The male dominance in sexual matters, which is the norm in most developing nations, is also met in the developed nations. One of Gorer's respondents in his survey of sex and marriage in England and Wales was a 22-year-old grocery assistant who had first met his wife on a blind date. He considered that 'a wife should always agree with her husband, always do as her husband wishes, and always agree with him'. In Australia a 28-year-old woman, with five children, who recently came to me seeking an abortion, when asked why she hadn't used contraception said, 'my hubby doesn't approve. He's not Catholic or anything like that, but he doesn't think it right that a woman should be examined by a doctor, and anyhow he had always taken care of that sort of thing.' Her five children belied the quality of the care!

But a change is occurring. Increasing numbers of women are making the decision that they will use birth control methods, and will protect themselves against an unwanted pregnancy. The choice of method used depends on a variety of circumstances, and the method must be tailored, when possible, to the needs of the particular woman. In certain situations even relatively ineffective measures which are easy to use may be preferable to no contraception at all.

Locally used chemical contraceptives (vagitories)

In the previous chapter it was pointed out that chemically impregnated intra-vaginal plugs have been used for contraceptive purposes by many primitive tribes. The plug delayed the spermatozoa's transit to the cervix, and the chemicals were spermicidal. The method had a period of popularity in Britain between 1885 and 1935 due to the persuasive (but discreet) advertising of Rendell's cocoa-butter and quinine vaginal pessaries, and other chemicals have been suggested from time to time. Currently, there are over 50 suppositories, pessaries, gels, or foams available. The solid vagitories (to use the word recommended by the IPPF for pessaries and suppositories) use a spermicide in a base of soap, gelatin or cocoa-butter which is designed to melt at body temperature. The vagitory is inserted just prior to coitus. The gels which are made up in a water-soluble gelatinous base disperse easily in the vagina, and are usually used as an additional protection if the male uses a condom, or in conjunction with a vaginal diaphragm. The gel or cream is usually introduced high into the vagina through a plastic plunger applicator which is provided in the package. The foams are either in foaming tablet form or in containers from which the appropriate amount can be introduced into the vagina. They are theoretically more efficient than other types of vagitory.

Used alone, locally applied chemical contraceptives are inefficient; but used in conjunction with condoms or vaginal diaphragms they add to the protection given by the contraceptive appliance. Their main advantage is that they are easy to buy and easy to use, but against this must be set a failure rate of 40 per 100 woman-years usage (range 18–48), which is too high for most women to accept.

Even less effective is a post-coital vaginal douche, which usually contains vinegar or some proprietary spermicide. Logic should tell a woman that using a douche as a contraceptive measure in this way is unaesthetic, ineffective and stupid. Since the ejaculated spermatozoa begin their transit through the cervix within one minute of ejaculation, it is like washing the stable door with the sperm well inside.

The 'Safe Period'

In a woman with a normal cycle, ovulation will occur approximately 14 days before the anticipated menstrual period. The ovum can only survive for 2 days unless it is fertilized, and the ejaculated spermatozoa survive, and are able to fertilize the ovum, for 4 days at the most. It is obvious from these facts that if coitus is avoided for 4 days before ovulation to 6 days after it has occurred, pregnancy should not occur. Coitus should therefore be restricted to the 4 to 6 post-menstrual days and the 10 pre-menstrual days. The physiological concepts of ovulation were independently observed in 1929 by Dr. Knaus in Austria, and Dr. Ogino in Japan. The so-called Ogino-Knaus method was enthusiastically adopted by Roman Catholics who could argue that they were not preventing conception, but were regulating births in a 'natural way'. The original observations have been developed in recent years but the principle is the same: that is, for the couple to restrict coitus to times of physiological infertility. Unfortunately, the method, despite the improvements, requires considerable motivation and is not particularly safe, as the average woman does not have an exactly regular cycle, and ovulation may occur at other times of the cycle, especially if the emotions are stirred.

Since the method is the only one permissible to Roman Catholics, it requires further, and rather detailed, consideration in its four modern forms—the 'rhythm method', the 'temperature method', the 'mucus method' and the 'predictable ovulation' method.

The calendar rhythm method. If a woman is prepared to use a calendar, and over a period of 6 menstrual cycles to record the duration of each cycle, she can determine her own safe period by calculating the date of ovulation in each cycle, and then subtracting 3 days from that day in the shortest cycle and adding 3 days in the longest cycle (Fig. 10/2). Coitus should be avoided during the danger period. If a woman has a cycle of less than 20 days, or if the duration of her cycle varies by more than 10 days, she will only be able to have 'safe' sexual intercourse at infrequent intervals and sexual frustration is likely to occur. A careful study in Washington D.C. of 30,000 cycles in 2,316 women showed that only 30 per cent of them would qualify for the calendar rhythm method on the basis of a cycle range of 8 days or less. The cycle range varied with age, the smallest variation being in the age group 30 to 34, when 40 per cent had a cycle with a range of 8 days or less. However, if the couple are prepared to accept that coitus takes place in accordance with the calendar, not with desire, then the method is reasonably successful.

The temperature method. This is a more accurate method of pinpointing ovulation. It is based on the physiological observation that when ovulation has occurred the body temperature rises slightly. To detect this temperature rise a woman has to be

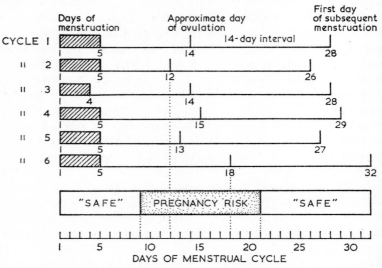

Fig. 10/2. The 'calendar method' of birth control: calculation of the 'safe period'. In this example the shortest cycle was 26 days, the longest was 32 days. Ovulation in the shortest cycle was calculated to take place on day 12, in the longest on day 18. Three days on each side of ovulation are potentially fertile (as the spermatozoa and ovum live for three days). For this particular woman, the days on which coitus should be avoided are from day 9 (i.e. the day of ovulation in the shortest cycle, less three days) to day 21 (i.e. the day of ovulation in the longest cycle, plus three days).

sufficiently motivated to take her rectal, or vaginal, temperature each morning on waking and before she gets out of bed (which may be difficult for a woman with a young family), or has any food or drink. From the daily reading she makes a chart, and can have coitus safely 3 days after the temperature rise has occurred. The problems are that not all cycles show 'ideal' temperature rises and if the woman has a cold, flu or some other infection, the method cannot be used. It also requires considerable motivation to remember to take the temperature each day (Fig. 10/3).

The mucus method. In this method, which was developed by an Australian physician, the woman learns to examine her vaginal orifice for the presence of mucus. Immediately after a menstrual period the vaginal orifice feels dry, but as ovulation time approaches mucus can be detected. Initially, it is cloudy and sticky, but as the level of oestrogen rises, the cells of the neck of the womb, the cervix, are stimulated to secrete more mucus and its character changes. It becomes clearer, strands stretch without breaking and it 'feels slippery'. The peak of the clear mucus is reached on the day of ovulation, after which the mucus becomes cloudy again. The physiological concept of this

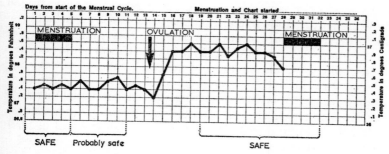

FIG. 10/3. The 'temperature method' of birth control.

sequence is correct, but the detection of mucus at the vulva requires considerable motivation, and perhaps the eye of faith. As well as this, vaginal secretions, either physiological or pathological, can confuse the issue. The motivated woman is given a chart and enters her findings each day using differently coloured stickers for different types of mucus. Coitus is 'safe' when there is no mucus, and more than 3 days after the last day of the clear mucus. Between these times coitus should be avoided. Patients trained by Dr. Billings claim considerable success with his method, but in the one investigation reported the failure rate was 25 per 100 woman-years, and I have seen several patients for whom the method failed. The problem is one of motivation. If the couple avoid coitus whenever there is any mucus, the woman will avoid pregnancy; she may also have to avoid coitus for most days of the month, which can be remarkably frustrating to both husband and wife.

The predictable ovulation method. It will be appreciated that the safety of the safe period depends on ovulation occurring on a predictable day during the menstrual cycle. Increased safety would be ensured if ovulation time could be regulated to within 3 days, and unexpected ovulation eliminated. There has recently been a break-through which may enable women to achieve this. If a woman takes a very small daily dose of a particular oestrogen hormone from days 9 to 15 of the cycle (counting day 1 as the *first* day of menstruation) she will ovulate between days 13 and 17 in over 95 per cent of cycles. Sexual intercourse need only be avoided from days 10 to 20 of the cycle, and the woman does not need to take her temperature daily, or to inspect her vagina for mucus. Conjugated equine oestrogen (sold under the trade name, Premarin) is rapidly absorbed from the gut, and rapidly stimulates the pituitary gland to secrete the hormone, gonadotrophin. This in turn causes ovulation on a predictable day. The method, if adopted, should improve the efficiency of the 'safe period' method of birth control for those women who are unable to use more efficient methods; but there are disadvantages, and the method is currently experimental.

It will be appreciated that the 'safe period' method of birth control requires considerable motivation, whichever method is used to determine the safe days. The method is now only used by those Roman Catholics who wish to avoid pregnancy and whose conscience does not permit them to use other contraceptive methods. Despite the fact that 'safe period' users are a select group, the pregnancy rate varies between 14 and 40 per 100 woman-years, depending on their motivation. In well-motivated patients, a Roman Catholic gynaecologist has reported a pregnancy rate of 5 to 19 per cent.

In Latin America, where it was hoped the method would help limit the rate of population growth, it appears to have been a failure. Information from Bogota and Cali in Colombia indicates that despite a large number of consultations, home visits and short courses conducted by Roman Catholic Family Planning Organizations, only 8 per cent and 3 per cent of the 1,800 and 2,400 women initially recruited in those two cities continued to use the method.

Contraception

Diaphragms and cervical caps

The early birth control clinics, and the few physicians at that time who offered birth control services both in Europe and North America, adopted the vaginal diaphragm as the main method of contraception. The reasoning was good. If the spermatozoa could be prevented from being sprayed onto the cervix during ejaculation, and if they could be immobilized in the vagina, pregnancy would be prevented. The vaginal diaphragm or the cervical cap, combined with a spermicidal cream, did both things: insemination of the cervix was prevented by the diaphragm, and the sperms were eliminated by the spermicide.

The enthusiasm of the workers in family planning clinics, who were mainly middle-class, was matched by the enthusiasm of their mainly middle-class clients. For many years, many middle-class women in the U.S.A. and in Britain used the diaphragm, although since the introduction of the Pill its popularity has waned. Amongst the lower socio-economic groups it was never as popular, partly because of prudery, most women feeling it improper to introduce an object into their vagina, and partly because many of the women lacked a bathroom to enable them to insert the diaphragm with comfort and privacy.

In the developing nations, the lack of privacy was even more marked, and the diaphragm as a method of birth control made little impact in birth control programmes.

Nevertheless, it is a good and fairly efficient method. Its advantage is that it is completely without side-effects (although some spermicidal creams cause vaginal irritation, which disappears when the cream is changed). Its disadvantage is that for maximal efficiency the diaphragm should be inserted each evening whether coitus is anticipated or not. The psychological problem to a sexually aroused couple of the woman needing to go away to 'put in my diaphragm' is obvious. Not only is the night air often cold, and the bathroom freezing, but on her return to bed she may find a snoring partner, not a sexually stimulated, exciting and excited bed-mate. The doctor's instruction to his patient should be: 'Put in your diaphragm when you clean your teeth each evening.' In Australia and Britain, where dental health is deplorable, the slogan is even more brief: 'Put in your diaphragm when you take out your teeth.'

Once inserted, the diaphragm must remain in for at least six hours after coitus.

There are basically three devices, although because of a falling demand the last two are becoming increasingly difficult to obtain. They are: (1) the vaginal diaphragm (Dutch cap) (Fig. 10/4), (2) the vault cap, and (3) the cervical cap. The vaginal diaphragm is the easiest to fit and to use, and is the most efficient as a protective against unwanted conceptions. It

FIG. 10/4. The vaginal diaphragm in position.

consists of a thin latex rubber dome attached to a circular flat or coiled wire spring. Because the capacity of the vagina is different in different women, the diaphragm is made in a series of sizes from 45 to 100 mm, usually in steps of 2·5 mm.

The doctor examines the woman vaginally, and may take the opportunity to make a cancer test on the cervix. This is called a 'Pap' smear. He then selects the appropriate size from a fitting set, and puts it in the vagina. The patient should not be aware that it is there.

The patient is next shown how to introduce the diaphragm and how to remove it by hooking it out with her finger. Since

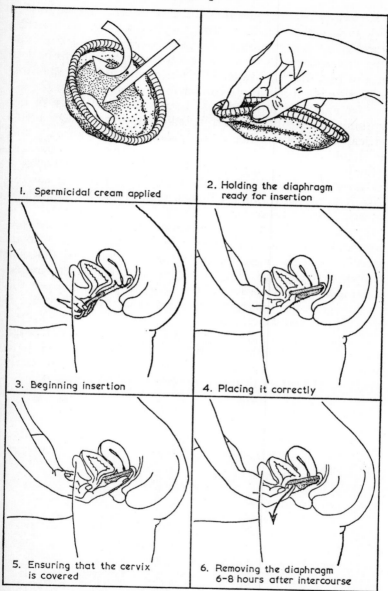

1. Spermicidal cream applied

2. Holding the diaphragm ready for insertion

3. Beginning insertion

4. Placing it correctly

5. Ensuring that the cervix is covered

6. Removing the diaphragm 6-8 hours after intercourse

FIG. 10/5. The technique for using the vaginal diaphragm in birth control.

243

it is essential that a spermicidal cream is used in conjunction with the diaphragm, she learns to place a large blob in the centre of its upper surface and additional cream around the rim. This also makes its introduction easier. She learns how to be sure that the diaphragm is in place, and to know she must feel her cervix through the rubber to be sure that it is.

A woman generally needs to have some knowledge of her anatomy, many quite incorrectly believing that the vagina runs vertically upwards rather than upwards and backwards, and she should practise introducing and removing the diaphragm at home (Fig. 10/5). If she can, she should revisit her doctor a few days later, wearing the diaphragm, so that she can be reassured that her technique is good, and so that her additional questions can be answered.

It will be realized that the complexity of fitting the dia-phragm, the necessity for the patient to use intelligence in its insertion, and the need for her to be so motivated that she makes sure it is in place every time she expects coitus, has limited its popularity. Used properly, the pregnancy rate is 3 per 100 woman-years, but unfortunately the average pregnancy rate is 15 to 25 per 100 woman-years.

The place of the diaphragm in a birth control campaign should not be minimized, as it has no side-effects, is perhaps protective against cervical cancer, and if maintained properly can be used for one to two years before being changed.

CHAPTER ELEVEN

Avoiding Unwanted Pregnancy

The fact itself of causing the existence of a human being, is one of the most responsible actions in the range of human life. To understand this responsibility—to bestow life which may either be a curse or a blessing—unless the being on whom it is to be bestowed will have at least the ordinary chances of desirable existence, is a crime against that being.

'On Liberty',
JOHN STUART MILL.

I

In the past 15 years, contraceptive technology has made considerable advances, which have led to the development of the two most reliable contraceptive methods available—the hormonal contraceptives (the Pill and the Injectables) and the intra-uterine contraceptive device (the IUD). These two methods have a high index of reliability, and have been widely accepted by women. They give to a woman the right to choose not to become pregnant. Whilst the better educated women in all the countries of the world can make this choice for themselves, the less educated, particularly in the developing nations, usually defer to their husbands, accepting their advice, and often their prejudices. Education is ultimately the key which will give women the right to choose; but until patriarchal attitudes change, many myths and misconceptions about the Pill and the IUD will continue.

Today, in the nations of the world, over 50 million women are using hormonal contraceptives and over 15 million women have an IUD neatly hidden in their wombs.

The use of a birth control measure by a woman gives her a feeling of relief that she can avoid an unwanted pregnancy with efficiency, and without any loss of her dignity. It may also give rise to feelings of guilt, that she is denying her cultural or biological destiny to propagate the race. The feelings of guilt can be insidious: she may feel that by preventing a natural body function, she is doing 'wrong'. She may also be strongly influenced by the gossip of neighbours, or by sensational newspaper reports about the real or imagined hazards of the method of contraception which she has chosen. In Singapore a most efficient campaign to introduce the IUD immediately after confinement failed because sensational newspaper reports claimed, quite erroneously, that the devices were moving through the wall of the womb and being carried to the liver. Over a period of ten weeks, the demand for IUDs fell so much that the Government, who were very conscious of the need to control population growth, had to offer the more expensive Pill in place of the suspect IUD.

Birth control arouses irrational emotions. Those opposing the use of contraceptives on religious or demographic grounds, seek to inflame opinion against them; those who believe that modern contraceptives give women a new freedom, seek to minimize the complaints. On both sides emotion replaces objectivity, and imagination replaces investigation.

In this chapter the evidence obtained from a very large literature about the efficiency, the side-effects and the value of modern contraceptive methods is discussed.

HORMONAL CONTRACEPTIVES

To most people, hormonal contraceptives mean the Pill. Although the Pill is the most commonly used hormonal method, the hormones may be given singly or in combination, and taken by mouth or given by injection. In fact, two hormones are used in the Pill. These hormones are laboratory-produced substitutes for the two female sex hormones which are produced throughout the fertile years by a woman's ovaries. The two hormones, oestrogen and progesterone, make a woman what she is. Not only do they give her feminine contours, but each month they prepare her uterus to receive a fertilized egg and to encourage it to develop into a child. In the correct sequence, and in the correct balance, the hormones lead to ovulation. This occurs about half-way between two menstrual periods.

Ovulation is controlled by a special area of the brain—the hypothalamus. From cells in this area, hormones travel to the pituitary gland, at the base of the brain, and stimulate it to release a hormone, called follicle-stimulating hormone, into the blood. This, in turn, stimulates between 12 and 20 egg cells (or follicles) in the ovary to grow. As they grow they produce oestrogen. The oestrogen levels rise and 'feed-back' to the hypothalamus. This has the effect of reducing the amount of follicle-stimulating hormone released, and of causing the release of a second hormone, the luteinizing hormone. The sudden surge of this hormone in the blood causes an egg, and usually only one egg, to escape from one of the growing follicles. The egg is expelled and the follicle, which looks like a tiny thick-walled balloon, collapses. It quickly undergoes conversion into a yellow-coloured structure which produces not only oestrogen, but also progesterone. If pregnancy occurs the yellow-coloured structure continues to live, but if pregnancy does not occur it ceases to produce hormones after a life of about 12 days. When this happens, menstruation starts (Fig. 11/1). The hormonal control of menstruation is discussed at greater length in my book, *Everywoman*.

The hormonal contraceptives upset this sequence. There are two main types. In the first, both oestrogen-substitute and pro-gesterone-substitute are given from soon after menstruation. At the dose chosen, the hormones 'feed-back' to the hypothalamus and prevent the release of the follicle-stimulating and of the luteinizing hormones, so that ovulation is prevented. In addition, they alter the lining of the uterus so that it is not receptive to a fertilized egg; and they alter the secretions of the cervix so that they become thick and sticky. This prevents most spermatozoa from travelling upwards from the vagina and entering the cavity of the uterus. The 'combined' hormonal contraceptives protect a woman against an unwanted pregnancy in these three ways. But if a woman takes the Pill by mouth, she must remember to take a pill every day, as the hormones are rapidly inactivated in her body, and the level may fall too low for the protection to occur, should she miss more than two days.

The second type of hormonal contraceptive avoids the use of

oestrogen, and contains only the progesterone-substitute, which is called gestagen. The gestagen hormonal contraceptives do not prevent ovulation consistently, but do alter the secretions of the cervix so that sperms cannot penetrate it, and also alter the lining of the uterus so that the egg, if fertilized, is unable to

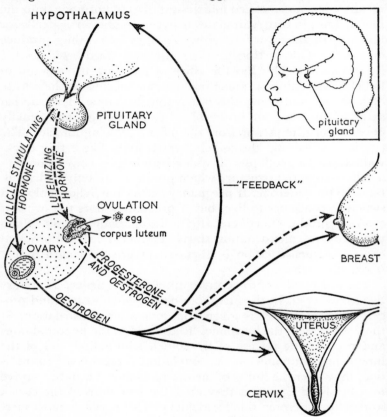

FIG 11/1. The regulation of menstruation.

implant itself. The gestagen hormones can be taken by mouth each day, or can be given by injection at one-monthly, three-monthly or six-monthly intervals. Given by injection, they are claimed to be more convenient, as the woman has no longer to remember to take her daily pill, but unfortunately in about 30 per cent of women the injection prevents menstruation, and in a further 25 per cent it leads to quite irregular and unpredictable bleeding. In certain circumstances, particularly with good motivation, the injectable contraceptives are fairly satisfactory, but most women prefer to take an oral contraceptive each day.

As I mentioned, the gestagen can also be taken by mouth, each day. The advantage of this type of hormonal contraceptive, which has been called the 'mini-pill', is that it can be taken by those women who, for medical reasons, should avoid oestrogen. The gestagen pill can also be taken when a woman is breast feeding. Combined oral contraceptives reduce the milk supply in a few women, but the gestagen 'mini-pill' is thought to increase the flow of milk. Unfortunately, the gestagen mini-pill disturbs the menstrual cycle in a large number of women, so that it is not so convenient or acceptable as the combined pill.

In exceptional circumstances oestrogen alone can be used as a contraceptive. Scientists have established that if a woman has sexual intercourse during the time of expected ovulation (that is about half-way between menstrual periods in a normal woman), she has a considerable chance of becoming pregnant unless she is protected. If she takes large doses of an oestrogen-substitute, such as stilboestrol, starting within 72 hours of the unprotected intercourse, she will avoid pregnancy. Dr. Kuchera, working amongst College students in California, gave big doses of stilboestrol for 5 days to 1,000 girls who had had unprotected coitus at ovulation time. No pregnancies occurred, although she estimated that 40 might have been expected. It is not a pleasant method of contraception. The larger doses of stilboestrol make the women very sick; all have severe nausea, and most vomit off and on over the 5 days of treatment. The method has attracted considerable publicity, and has been called the 'morning after' pill. The side-effects of a prolonged severe hangover make the name all the more appropriate.

2

For the majority of women, the combined oral contraceptive, or its stable-mate, the so-called sequential contraceptive, prove satisfactory and efficient. Of the two, the combined oral contraceptive is superior, and the so-called sequential contraceptive should only be chosen if the woman has severe acne or scanty menstruation.

In the combined oral contraceptive, both the oestrogen-substitute and the gestagen are taken daily from day 5 (day 1 is the day menstruation starts) to day 25 of the menstrual cycle. Some manufacturers add a further 7 tablets to the pack, so that a woman takes a pill 'every day'. These seven tablets either contain sugar, or in some cases, iron. This is of value, of course, in countries where anaemia is common. In the sequential contraceptive the patient takes the same dose of oestrogen each day, but only a small dose of gestagen for the first 10 days, and thereafter a rather large dose.

Since the investigations in Britain by Professor Scowen, most oral contraceptives contain the same dose of oestrogen-substitute. The dose of gestagen appears to vary, at least if you examine the doses marked on the packs. The differences in gestagen content of different oral contraceptives are more apparent than real. This is because the biological effects of different gestagens vary, and the dose in milligrams is without meaning. The biologically stronger gestagens have a smaller milligram dose than the weaker ones—but the total effect on the secretions of the cervix, and on altering the lining of the uterus, is identical. There are at least 25 competing formulations available, each of which is claimed by its manufacturer to have the fewest side-effects. These claims have rarely been assessed in a scientific way. The only properly controlled scientific studies have shown that there is little, or no, difference between the brands in efficiency in preventing pregnancy, or in the incidence of side-effects. For example, at a meeting of the International Planned Parenthood Federation held in Copenhagen in 1969, Dr. Richter reported that when he changed the appearance of the Pill he was prescribing every 6 months, without changing the content of the hormones in it, his patients complained of very considerable increases in headaches and nausea, a reduction in sexual desire and changes in other symptoms. Since the drugs were unchanged, the only reason for the complaints was a psychic one due to visual stimuli. The new Pill looked different!

The incidence and severity of side-effects is influenced by gossip and by sensational articles in women's magazines which are high on anecdotal speculation and low on scientific observations.

The side-effects which are commonly attributed to oral contraceptives are listed in Table 11/1. The table does not

TABLE 11/1

The side-effects attributed to oral contraceptives (The Pill)—
an A.B.C.

Acne	Some increase in some women who take the combined Pill; reduction if a sequential Pill is taken.
Blood pressure	Generally no change, except for a few susceptible women, generally over the age of 30, who do get some rise in blood pressure.
Depression, mood changes	No increase, except amongst women who were depressed before taking the Pill, or who feel guilty about taking the Pill.
Headaches and migraine	In carefully controlled investigations, no increase has been found. However, if a woman taking the Pill develops severe migraine which is localized, she should consult a doctor.
Menstruation	Tends to be reduced in amount, and often the colour changes from red to dirty brown. This is unimportant and does not mean that toxic substances are collecting in the body. Menstruation occurs on a predictable date, but a few women have spotting of blood, or a small bleed, on an unexpected day. If this is repeated in another cycle, a doctor should be consulted.
Nausea and vomiting	Fairly common in the first and second cycles on the Pill, thereafter unusual.
Pain with periods	Women taking the Pill usually have painless periods; this is a beneficial side-effect of the Pill.
Sexuality	Despite a good deal of anecdotal information, sexuality and sexual desire are unchanged.

Table 11/1—*Cont.*

Vaginal discharge	The vagina is normally kept moist by secretions from the cervix. Women taking the Pill may expect increased vaginal moisture, and some discharge. If this is not irritant, it is of no consequence. If it is, a doctor should be consulted at once.
Weight gain	Most women, whether taking the Pill or not, gain weight from retaining fluid in the few days before menstruation. This disappears when menstruation starts. Some women taking the Pill gain weight after a few months of use. This may be due to the hormone, gestagen, or to an increased appetite when the fear of pregnancy is lifted. Weight gain is controlled by eating a proper diet.

prove that the Pill causes a particular side-effect, as many women have similar complaints when using other contraceptives.

This particular problem was recently investigated by Dr. Goldzieher working in the Southwest Foundation for Research and Education in Texas. He conducted a trial in which he compared the side-effects attributed to three types of combined oral contraceptives, one type of sequential and one gestagen-only contraceptive. The patients were all volunteers who had never used oral contraceptives before, and all agreed to cooperate. All the tablets were made up to look identical, so that neither doctor nor patient knew who was taking which formulation. In addition, after four months of treatment, the drug was changed to one of the other formulations without either patient or doctor knowing. To make the trial even less biased, the patients unknowingly took a sugar pill for the first month and one group used sugar pills for four months. The technical name for the procedure was a double-blind cross-over trial.

When the trial was completed and the code was broken, Dr. Goldzieher found that the true incidence of side-effects usually attributed to oral contraceptives was 'far lower than indicated by the usual uncontrolled investigations'. He added, 'An incredible amount of effort, investigational time, money and printed paper have been wasted on oral contraceptive trials which uniformly failed to include the necessary controls.' Dr. Goldzieher investigated the frequency of nausea, vomiting, abdominal bloating, breast tenderness, headache, nervousness, depression, reduced libido, weight gain and changes in blood pressure in his 400 patients. Apart from some extra nausea and vomiting in the first cycle of a combined oral contraceptive, none of the other symptoms occurred with greater frequency in patients taking combined pills, gestagen-only pills or sugar pills. In his conclusion Dr. Goldzieher felt that the true incidence of side-effects attributable to oral contraceptives was far lower than generally supposed, and many were due to coincidence, to feelings of guilt or to misinformation given by the woman's doctor.

3

One side-effect of oral contraceptives has received an immense amount of publicity over the past four years, and has caused great anxiety to many women. This is the side-effect of venous thrombo-embolism or clotting in veins. Biochemists working with oral contraceptives discovered that oestrogen causes the liver cells to synthesize, and secrete, certain chemical substances involved in blood clotting. Since these substances make the blood more likely to clot, it was argued that the Pill caused the formation of blood clots. Clotting of the blood is a most complicated and little understood process, but it is known that the liver and other organs also produce chemical substances which prevent blood clotting. A rise in clotting substances is balanced by a rise in anti-clotting substances.

Even so, the chance that oral contraceptives lead to an increased frequency of blood clotting was sufficiently worrying for Drug Evaluation Committees in several nations to seek information. In Britain Drs. Vessey and Doll looked through hospital records of patients admitted with venous thrombosis, and compared them with women of the same age and characteristics who had been admitted for other reasons. They reported that women taking oral contraceptives had about seven times the chance in any year of being admitted to hospital with venous thrombosis, and seven times the risk of dying from a clot carried to the lung, a pulmonary embolus.

They did point out that the risk was very low, and was related to the age of the woman. It was more likely to occur if the woman was overweight and a heavy smoker (Fig. 11/2). Of 100,000 women taking the Pill, 3 might die each year from thrombo-embolism. Moreover, pregnancy carried a far greater risk. Of 100,000 pregnant women, 27 would die in a year. In

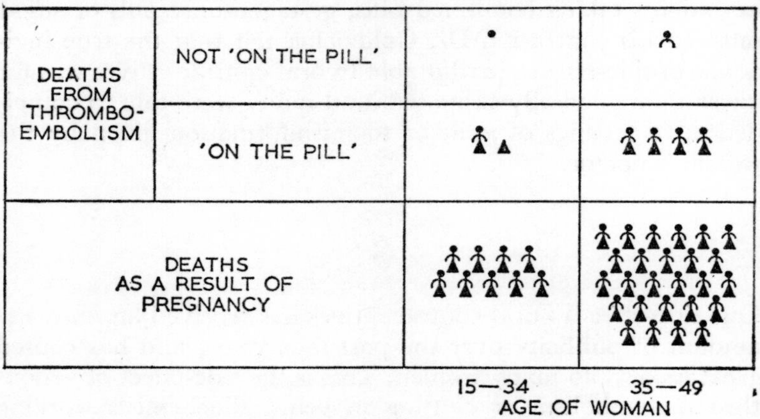

DEATHS FROM THROMBO-EMBOLISM	NOT 'ON THE PILL'	•	♠
	'ON THE PILL'	♠ ♠	♠ ♠ ♠ ♠
DEATHS AS A RESULT OF PREGNANCY		♠ ♠ ♠ ♠ ♠ ♠	♠ ♠
		15—34	35—49
			AGE OF WOMAN

FIG. 11/2. Thrombo-embolism and the Pill, estimated deaths per 100,000 women in Britain. Source: (Maternal Deaths 1964–66) Rep. *Public Health and Medical Subjects* **119**, H.M.S.O., London, 1969; Vessey, M. P. and Doll, R., *Brit. Med. J.* **2**, 651, 1969.

other words, it was 9 times safer to take the Pill for a year than to be pregnant.

In another, but similar, investigation in the U.S.A., Dr. Sartwell and his colleagues calculated that a woman taking oral contraceptives had four times the chance of developing thrombo-embolism as had a non-user.

These reports were not universally accepted, and two investigators from the U.S., Dr. Drill and Dr. Calhoun, criticized both their statistics and their conclusions.

At this point the Committee on Safety of Drugs in Britain reviewed the relevant data, and concluded that the risk of thrombo-embolism was related to the dose of oestrogen-substitute in the oral contraceptive. Unfortunately, the findings were leaked to the media before publication, with resulting scare headlines, and a very considerable discharge of emotion. It had the beneficial effect of causing manufacturers to reduce the oestrogen content of the Pill. It had the unfortunate effect of scaring many women. As the President of the Royal College of Obstetricians and Gynaecologists wrote in the British Medical Journal in April, 1971:

'Leaving aside thrombo-embolism, none of the other reported side-effects of oestrogen-progestogen contraceptive pills has yet been shown to have any serious significance, provided women known to be at special risk are screened out, and provided those who take the pills are kept under supervision to exclude the occasional development of glycosuria (i.e. sugar in the urine) or hypertension (i.e. raised blood pressure). . . .

'. . . Unfortunately, the dangers of oral contraceptives have sometimes been grossly exaggerated and distorted in the medical and lay press and by radio and television. At times, there has appeared to be almost a campaign to discredit the Pill, and the views of prejudiced if well-meaning individuals have been given disproportionate emphasis and allowed to outweigh scientific evidence. The result is that many women, and also their husbands, have become unreasonably alarmed about continuing a method of contraception which has hitherto suited them well. . . .

'. . . . The oestrogen-progestogen oral contraceptives so far available are admittedly not perfect. Something better may be produced any day. So far, however, they provide the most efficient method of contraception known, and they constitute a group of drugs whose effects have been subjected to closer study than most, if not all, others available to the medical profession. Such study has shown that their efficacy : safety ratio is probably as high as, or higher than, that of any other drug, other than placebos, ever devised.'

This very reasoned comment by an eminent gynaecologist should have calmed anxious women, but articles continued to pour out in women's magazines. No doubt these articles sold copies, but most were 'grossly exaggerated and distorted', so that women continued to be concerned about taking oral contraceptives. The conclusion by most experts was that the risk of thrombo-embolism due to the Pill was small; but it was present.

255

Then in 1972 the whole argument was reopened. Dr. Drill, who had attacked the original findings, published a new report in the prestigious *Journal of the American Medical Association*. In this article he pointed out that a retrospective study, made by looking at old hospital records, cannot establish a cause and effect relationship: it can only suggest further investigations to be made prospectively. That means that the investigators follow the course of patients from the time they take the drug over months or years. This is what Dr. Drill claimed he had done. He concluded from his prospective investigation that there was no evidence that users of oral contraceptives had an increased risk of developing venous thrombosis. He claimed that if a cause and effect relationship existed, a higher proportion of cases would occur in the first months of use of the Pill, larger doses should be more likely to cause the disease, and a higher incidence should be found in pregnancy when oestrogen levels are very high. Dr. Drill could find no evidence of any of these occurrences (Table 11/2).

TABLE 11/2

The estimated chance of a U.S. woman aged 15 to 44 developing thrombo-embolism.
Source: Drill, V. A., *J. Amer. Med. Ass.* **219**, 583, 1972.

	Rate per 10,000 women per year
Not pregnant, not taking the Pill	3·1
Pregnant	3·6
Post-partum	4·5
Taking the Pill	2·1

Whether the Committee on Safety of Drugs or Dr. Drill is correct, it seems reasonable to state two things. Firstly, in general, oral contraceptives containing the lowest dose of oestrogen which suppresses ovulation should be used, as the side-effects, possibly including thrombo-embolism, are less frequent. Secondly, if an association exists between thrombo-embolism and the use of oral hormonal contraceptives, the risk of death from the disease in women of reproductive age is low, and is much less than that due to pregnancy. In Britain, as I have mentioned, pregnancy is nine times as likely to cause death as are oral contraceptives, whilst in the developing nations, where maternal mortality is considerably higher, the risk of death due to pregnancy is between 70 and 100 times more than that due to oral hormonal contraceptives.

4

Many women worry that taking oral contraceptives for a long period will cause harmful effects. There is no evidence that this is so. The three most frequently reported fears are that fertility will be reduced, that cancer may develop and that the liver will be damaged. Women can be reassured. There is no evidence that the long-term use of the oral contraceptives reduces fertility. Indeed fertility may be temporarily increased for a few months after ceasing to use the drugs, as coitus occurs more frequently in couples who have used oral contraceptives. There is no evidence that the risk of cancer of the uterus or of the breast is increased. There is no evidence that the incidence of diabetes or of liver damage is increased.

Two further questions arise. At what age can a girl, who is having sexual intercourse, take the Pill with safety and at what age can a woman safely stop taking the Pill and avoid becoming pregnant? Over the past one hundred years the age of puberty has declined from 17 years to about 12 years. Girls are becoming physically mature earlier, and begin to ovulate at a younger age. When ovulation occurs a girl is at risk of becoming pregnant and, as is discussed in Chapter 14, unexpected, unwanted pregnancy in the young teenager is of considerable consequence. For this reason, a girl of 15 or 16 who is at risk of becoming pregnant should take contraceptive measures. The Pill is the only reliable method.

A question often asked is how long need a woman approaching the menopause take the Pill? The age of the menopause is about 50, and ovulation ceases a variable number of years before this age. The time of the menopause is individual for each woman and is unaffected by the previous use of oral contraceptives. Oral contraceptives have two advantages in women approaching the menopause. Firstly, they protect her against a late unwelcome pregnancy; and secondly, they assist in carrying her through the hormonal changes which precede the climacteric. A safe guide is that a woman should continue to take oral contraceptives until her 50th birthday.

5

Oral contraceptives are the most effective and the most widely used method of family planning. Despite this, a large number of women abandon the method because of imagined fears, misunderstandings or sensational newspaper articles. A woman should not suppress these fears, but should discuss possible side-effects with the doctor or other health worker whom she consults, and he must try to reassure her. An educated woman may fear that the hormones in the Pill will upset her natural hormonal balance. Less educated women, and particularly their husbands, have a variety of anxieties, based on misunderstood physiology, folk lore, and the fear that the drug will reduce sexual desire, activity or response. The particular fear varies from place to place and from time to time.

A woman seeking contraceptive advice should be prepared to answer certain questions before she obtains the Pill. She will be asked if she has diabetes, a high blood pressure (or if her parents have either), or if she has had a clot in a deep vein in the past. It is usual, particularly in women over the age of 30, for the medical attendant to take the woman's blood pressure and to examine her vaginally. This examination is to make sure that she has no tumours in her uterus or ovaries, and often the doctor takes the opportunity to do a cancer test, so that cancer of the cervix is excluded. An older woman should expect to have her breasts palpated so that early breast cancer, which is the commonest cancer in women, may be detected.

In the state of our present knowledge, certain women should be advised to use methods of contraception other than oral contraceptives. These include women who (1) have previously developed thrombo-embolism, (2) have liver disease, (3) have blood disorders, (4) have severe migraine particularly if the pain is localized, (5) have a very high blood pressure.

Present-day oral contraceptives are supplied in packs which make it easy for the woman to take the pills appropriately, and which hinder children from inadvertently taking the drug. Directions for taking each formulation are given by the manufacturers, and should be studied.

Although in the developed nations only qualified doctors usually prescribe oral contraceptives, there is no good reason why their distribution and prescription should not be in the hands of trained health workers.

The final question to be answered is how efficient are oral contraceptives? The answer is easily given. They are the most efficient protection against unwanted pregnancy available, provided that they are taken as prescribed. A woman may forget to take a pill for one day without much risk of pregnancy, but if she forgets for more than one day, ovulation may occur. If taken daily, as prescribed, all combined oral contraceptives currently available are over 99·9 per cent effective in preventing pregnancy.

Despite this evidence myths about the Pill persist.

The first myth is that the Pill leads to promiscuity. This is untrue. Permissive attitudes to sex, and the Pill, appeared in industrialized societies at about the same time. The myth started because it was believed (mainly by men) that girls only remained virgins because of fear of pregnancy, fear of venereal disease and fear of public opinion. The Pill has removed the fear of pregnancy, but the other two remain. Venereal disease is more frequent amongst promiscuous people. The Pill does not make women promiscuous. That is a myth propagated by opponents of contraception. The facts are the opposite. A study in London of unmarried women taking the Pill showed that only 5 per cent had had more than two partners in a period of two years after being prescribed the Pill.

The second myth is that a single girl can't get the Pill. This is true up to a point. A few doctors won't give an unmarried woman contraceptive advice. But many will, and those who do know that the Pill provides the single girl with a very much higher degree of security against an unwanted pregnancy than any other form of contraception. And if a woman can't find a doctor, the Family Planning Association will give advice to anyone who goes to their clinics.

259

The third myth is that the Pill doesn't protect. The low dose combined oral contraceptives do protect, provided a pill is taken every day as directed. In Sweden, a national survey found that only 17 out of 300,000 women taking the Pill for a year became pregnant. Some women who take the Pill have no periods. Provided that they continue taking the Pill as directed, they won't get pregnant.

The fourth myth is that a woman must stop the Pill after taking it for a year. This is nonsense. If a women takes the Pill, and it suits her, she can stay on the Pill, *without a break*, for as long as she wants to prevent pregnancy.

The fifth, insidious myth is that if a woman takes the Pill before she is married, she will never have a baby. This is untrue. A few women, on ceasing to take the Pill, fail to have periods for a few months. Then the periods return, and ovulation occurs. Most women get pregnant easily and readily when they decide that they want to, after stopping the Pill. In the first month, ovulation is often delayed from 7 to 21 days. This means that a slightly different calculation has to be made to find the expected date of birth of the baby if the woman becomes pregnant. By the second month after stopping the Pill, ovulation and menstruation become normal in most cases.

The Pill was first developed by a research scientist, Dr. Pincus, and a Roman Catholic gynaecologist, Dr. John Rock. The first trials were made in Puerto Rica. Since those days, nearly 20 years ago, the quantities of oestrogen and of gestagen contained in the Pill have been reduced, and the efficiency of the Pill has increased. Women, all over the world, should be grateful to these scientists for producing an efficient and safe way of avoiding compulsory pregnancy.

THE INTRA-UTERINE CONTRACEPTIVE DEVICE

Although not as popular as the Pill, the intra-uterine contraceptive device, the IUD, is being used increasingly by women who want to avoid compulsory pregnancy. The IUD has a distinct advantage. Once it has been placed inside the uterus, and it has been accepted, the woman hasn't got to do anything else. She doesn't have to remember to take the Pill each day. She can have sexual intercouse with reasonable safety and without worry.

The idea that an object, inserted into the cavity of the uterus, would prevent pregnancy, is not new. The Arabs, at least 500 years ago, put a small round stone, the size of a large pea, into the uterus of their female camels. The camel then repulsed the advances of male camels, as if she were pregnant. This was a considerable advantage as saddle camels were used for long journeys, and pregnant camels were difficult to manage. They either travelled too fast, or, more often, refused to move.

Nobody thought of putting an object into the uterus of the female human until the 1920s, when a German gynaecologist, Dr. Grafenberg, made devices of gold, silver and silkworm gut. His results were claimed to be spectacular, but his imitators were not so fortunate. Numbers of unfavourable reports appeared. Patients using Grafenberg's ring were reported to develop pelvic infection, to have severe cramping pains and to become pregnant. In Australia the method was popular in Melbourne and condemned in Sydney, which led to the comment that 'women had their Grafenberg ring put in in Melbourne at considerable cost, and the abortion performed in Sydney at even greater cost'. It is impossible, thirty years later, to find out the truth of the statement. Because of the problems associated with Grafenberg's rings, the method of contraception was condemned by most American and British gynaecologists and fell into disfavour.

Then, in 1959, interest was revived. Dr. Oppenheimer, who practised in Israel, reported that he had recommended Grafenberg rings to over 300 patients, who had used them with extraordinary success for up to 18 years. By coincidence, in the same year, Dr. Ishihama reported his experience from Japan. He had used a metal ring which resembled a wedding ring, with equal success.

These reports stimulated the Population Council in the U.S.A. to restudy the intra-uterine devices. They were looking for a method which would give good protection against pregnancy and could be used on a large scale. The IUD seemed to have considerable potential, particularly as polythene was now available. All the devices made of metal had caused a reaction in the tissues of the uterus. Scientists thought that this reaction was the cause of some of the unfavourable side-effects. Polythene causes very little tissue reaction. If an IUD could be made of polythene, and was an efficient contraceptive, the scientists at the Population Council reasoned it would make a cheap, easily distributed method of birth control. The IUD was on the way to acquiring a new respectability.

Since that date, a large number of intra-uterine devices have been made in a bewildering variety of shapes. It is difficult to analyse which is the best, as many reports are inadequate, but three seem to be superior. These are Lippes Loop, the Dalkon Shield, and the Copper-7 (Fig. 11/3).

The Loop, the Shield and the Copper-7 are made of flexible plastic, which regains its original shape once the stress has been

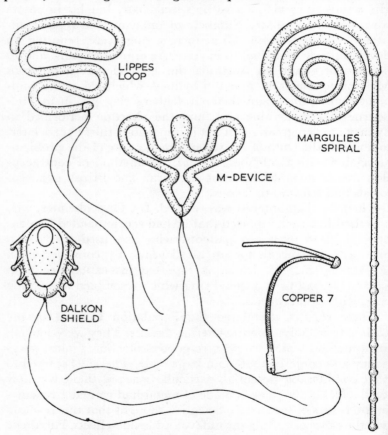

LIPPES LOOP

MARGULIES SPIRAL

M-DEVICE

DALKON SHIELD

COPPER 7

Fig. 11/3. IUDs in common use, actual size.

removed. This is a great advantage, as it permits the device to be straightened out and loaded into a narrow tube, or introducer. If the introducer is then gently pushed through the cervix into the uterus, and the device expelled, it will regain its shape inside the uterus. The devices are provided with nylon threads which project through the cervix and permit the woman to reassure herself that the IUD is in place.

No one yet knows how the IUDs work. The most recent evidence suggests that they cause a change in the environment inside the womb which makes its lining 'hostile' to the egg. It is known that the larger the device, the lower the pregnancy rate. Unfortunately, the larger the device, the more likely is the woman to have cramping pains and to have heavy periods, which are a considerable disadvantage. This was the reason for adding copper wire to the device. Inside the uterus the copper slowly ionizes, and this affects the lining of the uterus so that it rejects the egg. Copper has permitted scientists to make the device smaller, and consequently to reduce the side-effects whilst giving the same protection against pregnancy as with the larger devices. The smaller device is also easier to introduce into the uterus of a woman who has never had children. There is one problem with the Copper-7. It is that as the copper slowly ionizes, the device becomes less efficient. At the moment, scientists think it should be changed every 24 months, whilst the Loop and the Shield can stay in the uterus and give protection against pregnancy for as long as a woman wishes.

6

It is quite surprising how many women are misinformed about their anatomy. If a woman chooses to use an IUD she should know that it lies snugly within her uterus, and will neither 'get lost inside' nor 'move through the womb and affect the heart', to quote two fears told me by patients. Before the IUD is inserted it is important that the woman should talk with the health worker—doctor or nurse—so that she may have the opportunity to ask questions. The health worker will also examine her vaginally so that the size and position of the uterus can be determined. Once this has been done the IUD is put into the womb easily and painlessly. Modern devices are pre-packed in sterile packs and it is simplicity itself to introduce it into the patient's uterus (Fig. 11/4). Usually she lies on her

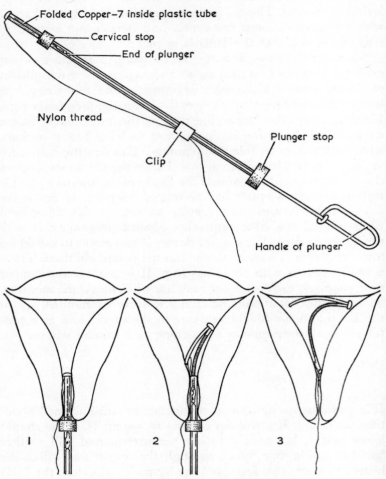

FIG. 11/4. The introduction of the IUD.

back with her legs apart. The health worker puts a small instrument into her vagina so that the cervix can be seen. It is cleaned with a gentle antiseptic, and then the introducer, preloaded with the IUD, is slowly pushed along the canal of the cervix so that its tip lies in the cavity of the uterus. The plunger is pushed, and the device is expelled to lie in the womb. There is no need for an anaesthetic, and the patient can go home immediately after. In one hospital in Bangkok, more than 60 patients have IUDs inserted each morning.

The best time to put an IUD into the uterus is in the last days of menstruation; at a postnatal visit, which usually takes place six to eight weeks after childbirth; or just after an abortion. At these times the canal of the cervix is wider and it is easier to introduce the IUD.

A few women feel a little faint during the procedure, and some have cramping pains for a few hours, as the uterus adjusts to its new occupant, but most have no trouble at all.

7

If this was all the IUD would be the perfect contraceptive. But, unfortunately, it isn't. There are side-effects, and pregnancies do occur.

In the first few months after insertion most patients report an increase in the amount and duration of menstruation. Whilst this is fairly unimportant amongst affluent women, it can lead to anaemia amongst undernourished women. There is no treatment, despite extravagant claims by various enthusiasts for Vitamin C or other pharmaceuticals, and the periods settle quite quickly.

Menstruation tends to start one or two days earlier than usual. The blood loss is light initially, and then becomes heavy, when clots may be expelled. The heavy loss may continue for four or more days, after which the period ceases, or drags on with irregular bleeding and spotting for a few days. Usually menstruation becomes normal in three or four months. Heavy periods occur less frequently if the Copper-7 device is used.

Apart from some cramp-like pains after the initial insertion, and some pain during menstruation when clots are expelled, pain is not common at other times. Its presence and severity depend to some extent on uterine sensitivity and on the patient's personality. About one woman in every ten asks for the IUD to be taken out in the first year of use because of bleeding or pain.

In some women the activity of the uterus leads to the device being expelled. This usually takes place during menstruation, but can occur at other times. About 5 per cent of the Loops, about 3 per cent of the Shields, and about 2 per cent of the Copper-7's are expelled. If the expelled IUD is replaced it is less likely to be expelled again.

Of course, if the device has been expelled, the patient is no longer protected against pregnancy. This is the reason for the threads. They are made of soft nylon so there is no danger of spiking the penis of an active male partner; in fact he won't notice them. But a woman who uses the IUD can reassure herself that it is in her uterus by feeling in her vagina for the threads from time to time, and especially at the end of the menstrual period.

The major side-effect, if it can be called a side-effect, is that pregnancies do occur. Some even occur with the IUD still in the uterus, but there is no truth in the story of a baby being born chuckling and holding the IUD in his hand. If a pregnancy does occur, the IUD is pushed aside between the lining of the uterus and the bag of membranes. It cannot damage the baby.

Using Pearl's index, the pregnancy rate with the recommended IUDs is between 0·5 and 1·5 per 100 woman-years, which is higher than that of combined oral contraceptives, but comparable with that of sequential oral contraceptives. And the IUD is a much cheaper method of contraception.

TUBAL LIGATION

Increasingly, couples who have completed their families are seeking permanent methods of birth control. In many cases the husband chooses to have a vasectomy, as the operation is simple to do, relatively painless and highly efficient. In other cases the wife chooses to take the permanent measure. In her case the operation consists of cutting out a portion of the oviducts. These are the tubes which stretch from the upper corners of the uterus towards the ovaries. The egg, whether fertilized or not, passes along the oviduct. The sperms swim through the cavity of the uterus and along the oviduct where, when conditions are favourable, one of them fertilizes the egg (Fig. 11/5). If a segment of the tube is excised, and the cut ends tied, the sperms cannot reach the ovum and pregnancy will be prevented.

This is the principle of the operation of tubal ligation. It is also called sterilization, as the woman is permanently prevented from having children. Unfortunately, to many women, sterilization is thought to mean castration, and confusion occurs. The ovaries are never removed in tubal ligation operations and after the operation continue to function normally,

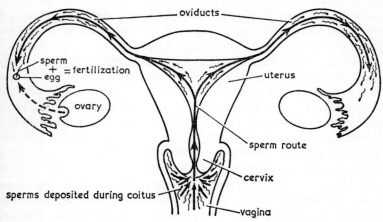

FIG. 11/5. Fertilization of the ovum.

producing the hormones which make a woman a woman. Neither her femininity nor her sexuality is diminished. Some women who contemplate having tubal ligation are anxious lest the eggs, released from the ovary each month, collect in the abdomen 'like frog spawn', as one of my patients said graphically. This fear is unfounded. At the most, only one egg is released each month, and it at once migrates into the oviduct where it is destroyed by other body cells.

Before deciding on the operation a woman should talk it over with her doctor, who will be able to answer all her questions. He will also need to examine her vaginally as certain conditions make tubal ligation inadvisable. These conditions include uterine 'fibroids', a marked prolapse, or a history of irregular menstruation which has not responded to hormones. If a woman has any of these conditions, and also wants permanent birth control, a hysterectomy is the preferable operation.

Nowadays, tubectomy (as the Indians prefer to call the operation) is a relatively simple procedure requiring only a short stay in hospital. The operation can often be done very conveniently in the first days after childbirth, or it can be done apart from childbirth. Many doctors refuse to do the operation if the woman has less than four children. This is, of course, arrogant of the doctors. If a couple decide they want no more children, and are aware that the operation produces permanent sterility—so that if they change their minds later it cannot be readily reversed—then they should have the right to choose.

The operation can be made with an instrument like a periscope, called a laparoscope, or by making a small cut in the lower part of the abdomen. The laparoscope is introduced through a 2 cm cut at the lower side of the umbilicus, after filling the abdominal cavity with gas. Looking through the lenses, the surgeon gets a very clear view of the uterus and the oviducts, and by inserting a narrow instrument, rather like a meat skewer, through a tiny hole made in the lower part of the abdomen, he can grasp the oviducts with it. He connects the instrument to an electrical supply, and burns a segment of each oviduct, so that a blockage is created. The cut below the umbilicus is closed with a couple of tiny stitches, and the patient can go home after 36 hours.

The other method is to make a cut just at the hair line above the pubic bone. Again this need only be 2 to 4 cm long. The abdominal cavity is opened and the oviducts are seen. Each one is grasped and a wedge is cut out, after which the cut ends are tied (Fig. 11/6). As with laparoscopic tubal ligation, the patient need only stay in hospital for 36 hours, but often chooses to stay a few days longer.

Tubal ligation is a most successful operation. It is most efficient as a method of birth control. It has no side-effects, and once it has been performed the couple need take no other contraceptive measures. A few myths persist, and there is no truth in any of them. They are that after tubal ligation a woman's menstrual periods cease, she becomes fat, and she loses all sexual urge. It is also believed by some women that after a few years the oviducts open up in some miraculous way and pregnancy is possible. All these myths are untrue. The one which worries women most is the effect of the operation on their sexual desires. This has been investigated extensively. Despite the difficulty in interpreting some of the results, the sexual urge

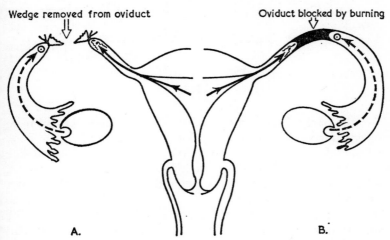

Wedge removed from oviduct   Oviduct blocked by burning

A.   B.

Fig. 11/6. Tubal ligation. This is a permanent method of birth control.

is unchanged in over 70 per cent of women, it is increased in 10 per cent and reduced in 20 per cent of women.

Investigations in the past 10 years show that over 99 per cent of women are satisfied that they had tubectomy performed. The degree of satisfaction is greater if the woman chose to have the operation than if it was suggested by her medical attendant, and is less amongst women who had psychosexual problems before the operation. Provided that the woman understands the nature of the operation, adverse responses postoperatively are few.

CHAPTER TWELVE

Where England Went Wrong—
A Study of Abortion

I

After the party, Pete said he would drive me home. It had been a great party—lots of fun and lots of grog, and I liked Pete, so I said I would go with him. Well, we went off, about one in the morning I suppose it was. He said what about a swim, and I said I hadn't got a costume, and he said it didn't matter, I could keep my bra and panties on, so I said yes. We went to the beach, and Pete parked the car, and we walked out on the sand. It was quite dark but for the stars, they were so bright, you never see them like that in the city. Well, we walked for about a mile, and the surf was beating in white foam on the sand. Then Pete stopped and started kissing me, and I wanted him to. So we lay on the sand and he started playing with my breasts, and I said he shouldn't. But I liked it and then he stopped and said let's swim. The water was great, warm, and I had my bra and panties on so I was decent. Pete took all his clothes off and his thing was quite little except when we kissed in the water. And he said he wanted me and I wanted him. It was romantic like in the books. He chased me up the beach, and undid my bra and I kicked off my wet panties, and he kissed me all over, and then he did it. I wanted it, but I was scared he would make me pregnant. He said he'd be careful, and he came all over my belly, and it was warm and lovely and I loved Pete. When we got home, Mum was mad I'd stayed out so late, and Dad was asleep. But he wouldn't say anything, he never did. You could tell from Mum they'd been rowing.

I saw Pete a lot after that but we only had sex twice more

that month, and he said he'd get a french letter and that would make it safe. I loved Pete.

Then my period didn't come, and I didn't know what to do. Pete said it would be all right because he'd been careful, and I couldn't be pregnant. But days went by and it didn't come. I couldn't tell Mum, she would have belted me, and I know it's wrong to have sex when you're not married, the priest kept telling us that. And Dad wouldn't have helped, he didn't take any notice of me, all he's interested in is his car and the pub and the footy. Mum would have been fit to burst.

Anyhow, two weeks went by, and still no period, and I felt sick, so I went to the doctor. That was embarrassing. I felt ashamed. He examined me and took some of my water, and he told me I was pregnant, and I said I couldn't be, and he said I was and I was a stupid, foolish girl and it served me right. I asked him if anything could be done and he said I should have the baby, it was God's punishment for being immoral.

I went and saw Pete, and I told him, and said I loved him and he went all cold. He said he didn't love me, and he wasn't going to be caught up with an eighteen-year-old tart, and if I was pregnant it couldn't be him because he'd been careful. And I started crying and that made him mad, and he left me, and he won't see me now.

I didn't know what to do. I couldn't tell Mum. It would have killed her. She's always been so strict, going to Mass and Confession and all. I was that worried. One of my girl-friends said that if you took castor oil and hot baths it brought it on, so I did and all I got was a guts-ache, and Mum wanted me to go to the doctor but I wouldn't. Another girl friend said gin did it, so I bought a half bottle and drank it, and all it did was make me sick. I don't like gin. I thought of doing something to myself but I was scared. I don't know much about my insides.

It was nearly four weeks since I missed my period and I was frantic. Then one of the older girls at the factory was boasting how she'd had two abortions, so I asked her about it, and she said you had to have $150. I'd been saving to go to Surfer's for a holiday and I had that much anyway. And she gave me an address that I went to.

It was this old man. He was a dirty devil. He said he was a doctor but I don't know. He said I'd left it a bit late but he'd do it. I had to bring the money in cash, and if anyone asked I had to say that I had gone to see him because I was bleeding heavily. He said he'd do it for half price if he could have sex with me, but I wouldn't have that. Then he got all cold and business-like. He said I was to go to a certain address the next day and see the woman there and he'd fix it, and I had to take two days off work. And I asked him could I go home after, and he said yes I could. Then I wondered what I'd say to Mum. I couldn't tell her and she might be suspicious, so I decided I'd stay with one of the girls, and when I went home all that would happen was Mum would wallop me for staying out.

I tried to ring Pete, but they said he was out.

I went next day with the money, and I was scared. I kept bursting into tears on the bus, and my legs were quaking when I went into the house. It was clean and there were two other girls there waiting like me. After an age the woman made me take off my panties and gave me an injection into my arm. Then I was taken into a small room and put on a table with my legs held up in a frame. The doctor was there, wearing a gown and washing his hands. He put a thing into my passage, and then said he was going to give me an internal injection, and it wouldn't hurt much. But it did, and I was scared, and it was bleeding. Then he said it was done, and I was faint and the woman said I was to lie down but I had to get out of the house within two hours, and she gave me an injection.

I went to my girl-friend's and the bleeding got less, so next day I went home. Mum was mad, but I didn't care what she did. I wasn't going to have the bloody baby, that's all I wanted. But I felt awful and said I'd go to bed, and Mum said it was because I was leading a loose life. If she'd only known!

Next morning I still felt awful and hot and shivery so instead of going to work I went to the hospital. They said I had an infection and took me in. I asked them not to tell Mum, but they said they had to tell her, but they'd only say I was in hospital. Mum came that night, and was nice to me. I almost told her about the abortion. I wanted to tell someone, but I was scared so I didn't. The next day they took me to the operation theatre, and cleaned my womb, they said. I got better after that but I'm scared I'll never be able to have a baby because I read about infection, or VD or something, in a magazine.

And perhaps God will punish me for having sex and for having an abortion. I'm really worried about it.

2

Induced abortion, usually in defiance of the law, is the oldest method of birth control and the most common method by which women prevent the birth of unwanted children. Surveys have been carried out in many nations in the course of which women have been asked if they have ever had an induced abortion. In countries economically and culturally diverse as the U.S.A. and Chile, as England and Iran, as Greece and Korea, between 15 and 45 per cent of the women surveyed admitted that they had had at least one abortion induced. This would suggest that each year women of all races, of all religions and in all regions of the world seek to terminate unwanted pregnancies. Although any estimate is really a 'guesstimate', such evidence as is available suggests that between 20 and 25 million women abort themselves, or obtain an abortion, each year. And this is likely to be an underestimate.

In primitive cultures abortion and infanticide were necessary to keep the tribe at an optimal size. When food was plentiful, pregnancy was welcomed; when food became short, either because of drought or because of population pressures, a pregnancy could lead to a disaster for the tribe. That induced abortion is world-wide amongst primitive peoples has been documented by anthropologists who found that only one tribe or cultural group of the three hundred studied, denied using induced abortion as a method of birth control. Anthropologists have also found that abortion was performed for two main reasons. In the first, abortion was induced for strictly social reasons. For example, Hottentot women in Southern Africa practised abortion as too frequent pregnancies would limit their ability to work and would make their nomadic life more complex. A more poignant reason is that if they didn't abort themselves, the new baby would have to replace its older brother or sister at the mother's breast. The Hottentots know all too well that the displaced child (and they breast feed their

273

babies to the age of three or more) would have a good chance of dying from starvation.

The second reason for seeking an abortion is a personal one. For example, it is reported that Masai women in Kenya obtain an abortion if they have been made pregnant by an old, or an unfit, man as they believe that the child will be a weakling. In South America, Chagga women seek an abortion when they consider themselves too old for having children.

Primitive peoples tend to be an interesting half hour's entertainment on a television programme, and nothing more, to most people living in the affluent, developed world or, indeed, to the peoples of the hungry, developing world. Yet in both groups of nations, and particularly those whose Governments have not introduced 'liberal abortion' laws, illegally induced abortion is widespread, despite a general condemnation on social and moral grounds. There is not so much difference between primitive and so-called civilized women.

The reason for the condemnation of abortion is cultural and religious. Until recently, as has been pointed out in Chapter 3, children were needed. Children proved a man was virile: the more children he had the greater was his virility. Children were an economic asset, at least in rural communities. When they were young they could take on tasks, such as seeing that the ducks didn't stray too far, or herding the sheep. As they grew older they could help cultivate the land, plant the crops and scare away predators. Children were a social asset. When a man grew old he knew that his land would be cared for, and he would be fed and housed until his death. Children were a religious asset, for a man's son could complete the ritual needed so that he had an easy passage after death. Children were needed because so many died.

These beliefs led to the development of a pronatalist culture, and this was encouraged by the religions to which people belonged.

Of the older religions, Christianity has the most adherents, with 800 million nominal or actual Christians in the world. Roman Catholics hold that you may not kill an innocent human being (except it must be assumed in self-defence—which includes all wars, for no nation ever attacks another except in self-defence!). To be human implies to a Christian that you possess a soul. This is where the discussion begins. When does the soul enter the body? For before it enters, the fetus is non-human and therefore its abortion would not be a moral crime. Until 1869, just over one hundred years ago, Roman Catholics were not sure. Thomas Aquinas, the great theologian of the middle ages, had argued that the soul couldn't enter the body until the body had a human shape, and possessed basic human organs, since without human shape it couldn't be a human being. This idea came from the concept of hylomorphism. According to this theory the soul is the substance of man, whilst the body is the result of the union of the soul with amorphic or shapeless prime matter. The logical development of this argument is that an actual human soul can only exist in an actual human body, just as a statue can only exist when it has been created out of an indifferent block of marble. This argument was codified by the Catholic Church in A.D. 1312, at the Council of Vienne, which forbad the baptism of any birth which did not have a human shape. In general, this was held to occur only by the twelfth week of pregnancy. Despite this theological argument most Roman Catholics accepted the teaching of the early churchmen who had written in the Didache, in the first century after Jesus, that 'you shall not kill the child by abortion. You shall not kill what is conceived.'

However, moral dilemmas did occur. The Church recognized no difference between abortion (which was held to mean termination of pregnancy up to the seventh month after conception) and infanticide, in which a formed child, capable of living, was killed. But it was realized, very early, as far back as the third century A.D. that the child might kill the mother. In such cases, Tertullian had argued 'sometimes by cruel necessity, whilst yet in the womb, an infant is put to death when lying awry in the orifice of the womb he hinders parturition; and kills his mother'. It was considered lawful by most theologians that in such a case the mother should be saved.

In 1895 these opinions were finally reversed. Ensoulment was held to take place at conception, although embryologists had by now determined that the fetus was unrecognizable as a human in the first 35 days after its conception. This dogma was

275

re-emphasized by Pope Paul in 1968 in his encyclical 'Humanae Vitae' in which he wrote 'we must once again declare that the direct interruption of the generative process already begun, and above all, directly willed and procured abortion, even for therapeutic reasons, are absolutely excluded as licit means of regulating birth'.

Despite this prohibition in the predominantly Roman Catholic nations of South America, where contraception has been generally prohibited, investigators have found that induced abortion is common, particularly in the congested urban slums. The women feel no regret, and have no moral anxiety. They do not associate the act of abortion with killing a human being. When a woman has an abortion she feels, if she feels at all, like a soldier killing an unknown, unseen enemy.

The danger is that, as in war, both sides suffer. The fetus is inevitably killed, but the mother, too, has a high risk of damage or death. In Brazil one woman dies of every two hundred who abort themselves, or are aborted illegally. And 20 per cent of women's beds in hospitals are occupied by aborting women. Of course, some of these are spontaneously occurring abortions— and about 10 to 15 per cent of all pregnancies are known to end in this way—but most are due to illegally induced abortion.

The Protestant churches take a less rigid view on abortion and generally encourage contraception. The Anglicans hold that the soul enters the fetus at the time the fertilized egg plants itself in the uterus, but accept that abortion is licit when it threatens the life of the mother, for she then acts in her self-defence. The non-conformist Protestant Churches tend to be more liberal in their attitudes to abortion. Both Churches leave the decision to the individual who is expected to think for himself and form his own opinion. Lay Protestant opinion in recent years has supported a more liberal attitude to abortion, and in many predominantly Protestant nations the abortion laws have been liberalized recently. Much of this change has been occasioned by the knowledge that a wealthy educated woman has always been able to obtain an abortion, performed safely and skilfully. A poor woman has not had this facility and has had only three choices. She could induce the abortion herself, or submit to a cheap, crudely performed, dangerous abortion, or bear an unwanted child.

The stereotype of the woman seeking an induced abortion is not, as might be expected, an unmarried woman. It is a woman aged 25 to 29, who is underprivileged, under-educated and fatalistic, who has three children already and has lived in an urban slum for five years. At least this is the experience in the U.S.A., where it has been calculated that between 1960 and 1965, 4 million illegal abortions were obtained, and 5 million unwanted, unwelcome children were born.

The desperate American woman either tries to abort herself by introducing soap solution, a caustic substance, or a wooden stick into her uterus; or else she goes to an unqualified person, who inserts some object into the uterine cavity. In either case she has a considerable chance of developing infection, often has to submit to undignified acts—including in some cases coitus with the abortionist—and is generally disadvantaged. The inhumanity of the process has led to the changes in the law to permit abortions to be performed with dignity and safety.

The second largest religious group is Islam with about 500 million adherents. Islam holds that it is permissible to take medicine to procure an abortion as long as the fetus is unformed. The duration of pregnancy when abortion is permissible differs in each Islamic nation. Those countries which formed the old Turkish Empire generally believe that life starts 40 days after conception. In addition, many Islamic jurists add that for abortion to be licit a reason must exist, but most are generous in their interpretation of the reason. For example, in 1964, the Grand Mufti of Jordan quoted an ancient Islamic authority, that an abortion might be procured in the case of 'the mother who has a baby still unweaned and who becomes pregnant and thus her milk ceases and the father is unable to hire a wet nurse to save the life of the baby'.

In two surveys in Islamic nations a considerable percentage of urban women interviewed admitted to one or more induced abortions. In a survey in Turkey the percentage was 40, and the corresponding figure amongst Iranian women was 25 per cent. In Egypt, in 1969, it was calculated that 180,000 abortions were induced, and the medical care of induced abortions consumed over 50 per cent of the budgets of maternity hospitals. It is unfortunate that the vast majority of abortions in Islamic nations are performed on middle-class women, who have the

277

knowledge to use contraceptives. The poor, as elsewhere, resort to self-induced abortions or bear unwanted children.

Hinduism is adhered to by 400 million people. There is no distinct religious prohibition against abortion, nor is it encouraged. However, urban women in India seek abortions and this has recently been recognized by the Government who have introduced legal abortion. The attitude of the Buddhists is similar. In theory Buddhists hold that all life, human and animal, is sacred and consequently abortion is prohibited. But Buddhism recognizes that man is imperfect, and finds it hard to strive for the Way, so abortion is tacitly accepted, especially if a medical reason exists.

The Jewish belief is that the human soul is only discernible from the moment of birth to the moment of death. Prior to birth the fetus is simply a part of its mother and has neither individual life nor personality of its own. The modern Jewish view is that there is no objection to any sort of abortion in the first 40 days of life and it may be performed later if the fetus threatens the life of the mother.

I have left to last the faith under the guidance of which live the largest number of people on this earth. This is communism. In all communist nations abortion is permitted, on liberal grounds, as part of a programme to emancipate women from constant childbearing. Although illegally induced abortions occur, their numbers are few. Perhaps Czechoslovakia has the most enlightened approach to abortion of all nations in the world, and the Czech experience will be reported later.

3

The observation, repeated again and again, that in the affluent developed nations the educated, the wealthy and the knowledgeable woman can obtain an abortion safely and with no loss of her dignity, whilst the poor woman is disadvantaged, was a major reason for campaigns to make the laws against induced abortion less restrictive. The poor woman is disadvantaged because she is not only uninformed about human reproductive physiology, but is also ignorant of contraceptive methods, fatalistic in her attitude to unplanned pregnancy and unable to move easily through the institutional maze which would enable her to obtain an abortion. If she chooses to procure an abortion by an unqualified abortionist she runs the risk of developing the complications of an unskilfully performed operation. The

TABLE 12/1

Sociological constraints in preventing conception and obtaining an abortion in countries with laws against abortion

Factor	Poor (lower socio-economic groups)	Affluent (upper socio-economic groups)
Sex education or knowledge of reproductive physiology	Limited	Some
Knowledge of contraception	Limited	Some
Access to contraceptives	Limited	Good
Referral service for abortion	Poor	Good
Medical system	Complicated, time-consuming maze in public hospital	Simple, early access to private gynaecologists
Attitudes of staff	Hostile and punitive, especially nurses	Friendly
Abortionists sought	'Para-medical' or non-medical	Medical
Abortions	Dangerous	Safe
Incidence of sequelae	High	Low
Money to obtain safe abortion	Insufficient	Sufficient
Counselling after abortion	None	Available

main problems are the chronic ill-health, and the pelvic pain, due to infection, following an induced abortion (Table 12/1).

The current laws discriminate against the under-privileged woman. Moreover, if she fails to obtain an abortion and

is forced to continue with the pregnancy and to deliver an unwanted child, the child is likely to be disadvantaged. A very
carefully documented investigation was carried out in Sweden
by two doctors, Dr. Forssman and Dr. Thuwe, in 1966. They
followed up the children of 120 mothers who had been refused
an abortion in 1939 to 1941 and compared their performance
with 120 children selected from hospital records. The next
same-sexed child born in the same hospital was chosen as the
'control' for each unwanted child. Over the 21-year study it
was apparent that the unwanted child had to face far greater
problems. The unwanted children had more health problems,
more psychiatric problems and their education attainments
were invariably poorer. They were more likely to show anti-
social and criminal tendencies, and were less likely to be loved
as much as the wanted child. 'All the investigations', declared
Dr. Forssman, 'indicated the handicapped position of the unwanted child.' And this study was made in Sweden which has
the most enlightened social welfare services amongst Western
democratic nations. It is, of course, true to say that the problems of the unwanted child are far less amongst societies which
pay less attention to Judeo-Christian morality. In the Caribbean, in South America, in Asia and in Africa, an unwanted
child is accepted into the extended family group, and despite a
far greater chance of dying in infancy and childhood is no more
or less disadvantaged than his brothers or sisters.

In Western nations, particularly since 1965, changes have
been made in laws prohibiting induced abortion, so that the
unfortunate, the unlucky and the ignorant woman might
avoid bearing an unwanted, unwelcome child (Fig. 12/1).
Previously, at least since 1935, legal abortion had been available in the Protestant nations of north-west Europe and North
America, if, in the opinion of a qualified physician, the con-
tinuance of the pregnancy would cause danger to the mental
health of the mother. But it was apparent that this loophole was
available to the rich, but not so readily to the poor. In studies in
Australia, in Canada, in Britain and in the U.S.A. before
1965, the overall ratio of legal abortions to deliveries amongst
private patients varied between 3 and 10 per 1,000; but amongst
public patients it was between 0·5 and 1·5 per 1,000. Either
the affluent were more affected mentally by a pregnancy, or

someone was bending the law. It was not difficult to discover who that was. It was said that if a rich woman wanted a pregnancy terminated, she sought a co-operative psychiatrist, but a poor woman sought a backyard abortionist.

Sweden had recognized this injustice since 1939, when more liberal abortion laws were introduced, and these were relaxed

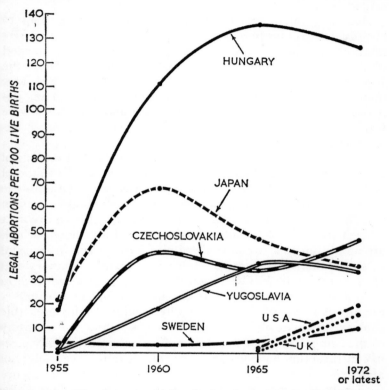

FIG. 12/1. The increase in legal abortions per 100 live births in selected nations, 1955–72.

still further in all Nordic council nations between 1952 and 1960. Meanwhile, public opinion was changing in most Protestant nations, and from 1960 on increasing pressure was being brought to bear on governments to liberalize their laws against abortion. In 1967 the dam broke. Britain introduced a more permissive law towards abortion, which became effective on

27th April, 1968. New York State and Colorado enacted abortion law reform at about the same time, and by 1972 twelve other states of the U.S.A. had modified their restrictive abortion laws. In 1973 the U.S. Supreme Court ruled that constitutionally no state could hinder a woman from obtaining an abortion. Abortion on request, with some controls, is now permitted in the U.S.A.

However, Japan was the first of the developed nations to introduce legal abortion as a social policy. In 1948 in the aftermath of total defeat, and very conscious of their overcrowded island, and the absence of any hope of relief by emigration, the Japanese introduced liberal abortion laws. Four years later these were relaxed even further to provide abortion on demand. Between 1953 and 1962 over one million abortions were legally performed each year, but since then the number has dropped.

Legal abortion is also available in the communist nations of East Europe, in the U.S.S.R. and in the People's Republic of China. Although the conditions vary between the nations, the objective of the amended laws has been to emancipate women from the burden of constant childbearing, and to 'protect women from perilous and unhealthy illegal abortions—which are an affront to a woman's dignity'. Abortion was made legal in the U.S.S.R. in 1955, in Bulgaria, Poland, Romania and Hungary in 1966, in Czechoslovakia in 1957, in Yugoslavia in 1960 and in China in 1962. It can be seen that at the time of the introduction of the laws no really reliable, readily available contraceptives existed, and abortion was made the mainstay of the campaign. Since the early 1960s, technological advances in contraception have led to modifications in the availability of abortion, and with the exception of Hungary the numbers are falling. In Hungary, in 1970, 127 abortions were performed for every 100 live births, but in all other communist nations the ratio is far lower, lying between 20 and 40 abortions per 100 live births. This is almost exactly the legally induced abortion ratio in New York. Perhaps what is even more important to the health of the women of the communist nations is that the technique used is very safe—safer than that used in Western Europe and North America—and illegal abortions virtually have been abolished.

4

In Western nations many women have been misled by friends, and friendly pharmacists, when they have tried to obtain drugs to induce the abortion of an unwanted pregnancy. An investigation by Dr. Martin Cole in Britain in 1964 showed that 'female remedies' could be purchased in 12 out of 15 pharmacies chosen at random, and in 17 out of 22 shops selling condoms or diaphragms. Most of the drugs were claimed to bring on menstruation suppressed 'due to colds, shock, fright, strain, etc'; but they were sold as abortifacients, and were not cheap. The drugs studied contained iron, quinine, purgatives or herbals which tradition held brought on menstruation. Examples of the last group are aloes and pennyroyal. They are, of course, all quite useless if a woman is pregnant. None will procure an abortion.

The lack of efficacy of these drugs led women, who could not afford proper care, to try to induce an abortion using the easily available enema (or vaginal douche) apparatus. With considerable contortions, women have introduced the nozzle of the douche into their cervix and have tried to fill their womb with mixtures of soapy water or caustics. In all too many cases this led to a medical disaster, and often to the death of the mother. In other instances desperate women have ingeniously introduced domestic instruments—crochet hooks, knitting needles, or pieces of wood—into their womb in the hope that an abortion would follow. Often it did—but often the woman also became infected.

When a woman went to a back-yard abortionist, her chance of obtaining an abortion, whilst avoiding death from haemorrhage, or sterility from infection, varied with the training and skill of the abortionist. The best trained were fairly efficient and used gynaecological instruments skilfully. The others used the enema syringe, or introduced an object into the womb to start bleeding so that the woman could then go to the hospital claiming that she was aborting spontaneously.

Accurate statistics of the deaths, and damage which occur after self-induced or back-yard abortions are almost impossible to obtain. Such information as is available suggests that in South America a woman has a 1 in 100 to 1 in 200 chance of dying after an illegal abortion. This means that 1,000 to 2,000 women die for every 100,000 illegal abortions performed. In 1968 it was calculated that over 2 million illegal abortions were performed in Latin America. In the U.S.A., before the more permissive abortion laws were introduced, the rate was much lower, only 50 to 100 women dying for every 100,000 abortion performed. However, the death rate was more than twice that due to childbirth.

The death rate following an illegal abortion performed without haste by a skilled practitioner is much less, and the mortality after legal abortion is even lower. To a large extent it depends on the period to which the pregnancy has advanced, the method used, the skill of the doctor and the health of the woman.

The safest abortion is that which is performed on a healthy woman, whose pregnancy is less than 10 weeks advanced, by a skilled physician, in a well-equipped hospital or clinic. If the physician uses the method of suction, rather than the traditional dilatation and curettage, both the death rate and the complication rate are even lower. The suction curette was first used in China over 20 years ago. A narrow metal, glass, or plastic tube is introduced through the cervix into the womb under local analgesia, it is connected to a vacuum bottle, and a vacuum is created, either mechanically (as in the developed nations who have a readily available electricity supply) or by burning alcohol (as in China) or, in pregnancies which have not reached 8 weeks after the last menstrual period, by attaching it to a specially designed syringe (Fig. 12/2). The vacuum created in the womb causes the conception sac to be sucked along the connecting tubing into a collecting bottle. Research scientists have found that suction curettage is much less damaging to the uterus, is followed by less bleeding and is less painful than ordinary curettage. In East Europe only 1 woman died for every 100,000 abortions done in this way. This is lower than the deaths due to childbirth. It is one-hundredth the death rate of illegal abortions reported from developed nations, and two hundred times as safe as an illegal abortion done in one of the developing nations.

After the tenth week of pregnancy the risk of death increases considerably, as does the difficulty of performing the abortion. As will be seen later, this is one of the ways in which England went wrong. The Registrar-General of England and Wales reported on the 165,000 abortions performed in 1970–71 and found that the mortality rate was three times higher after the twelfth gestational week than before it, and was five times higher if an abdominal operation was performed to end the pregnancy. As well as this, the morbidity—that is ill-health caused by the

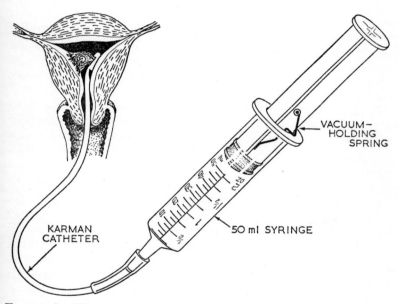

VACUUM–HOLDING SPRING

50 ml SYRINGE

KARMAN CATHETER

FIG. 12/2. The suction curette and the Karman catheter with its attached syringe.

operation—rises fivefold if the abortion is performed after the tenth week of pregnancy.

The problems of getting the larger, more formed fetus out of the uterus are considerable. Although some surgical sportsmen will 'have a go' and use the curette, even if the pregnancy is fourteen weeks advanced, their results are not good, and they are dicing with their patient's health and their own reputations.

Because of this, other methods have been advised to end a pregnancy which has advanced to the tenth week of pregnancy.

In one, a miniature Caesarean section is performed. This is a clean operation, but it leaves a scar in the mother's uterus, on her abdomen and perhaps on her mind. The operation is called a hysterotomy—which merely means 'an opening of the uterus'. Because of the problems associated with it, the operation is now being performed less often.

Two newer methods are now recommended. In the first, a thin needle is introduced into the conception sac, through the abdomen. Some of the liquid surrounding the fetus is withdrawn and is replaced by a special salt solution. The salt solution can also be introduced into the uterus through the cervix when it separates the conception sac from most of the wall of the uterus. It is believed that the salt solution reacts with the lining of the uterus, causing it to release prostaglandins, which induce the abortion. The injection must be made by a skilled doctor, as there is a considerable danger to the woman if the salt inadvertently enters her bloodstream. Between 7 and 50 hours after the injection, the fetus is aborted, but in about one-fifth of women a curettage is needed to remove the after-birth.

The other method is to introduce a solution containing prostaglandins into the conception sac, or through the cervix of the uterus, rather in the way in which the special salt solution is used. Prostaglandins are strange substances, which chemically are long chain fatty acids. They were first found in male semen in 1935 by the eminent German physiologist, von Euler. But, in fact, they occur in many tissues of the body. His discovery was ignored for nearly thirty years until, in 1964, workers began to investigate the intriguing and ubiquitous fatty acids. They found that they had many properties. One of them was that they make smooth muscle contract. This means that they should make the bowel and the uterus contract, and therefore they should be useful in causing the womb to expel a fetus. Dr. Karim, working with prostaglandins in Uganda, found that their theoretical properties were also practical ones. In a series of patients he found that he could induce labour by giving solutions of prostaglandin intravenously, and also that the prostaglandins would induce abortion if given intravenously, or injected into the uterus. Unfortunately, one half of patients given prostaglandins complain of nausea or vomit, and about one in every ten develops diarrhoea, so that the drugs have to be used with care. If the patient doesn't mind these side-effects, prostaglandins are very effective in inducing abortion. At the moment there seems little to choose between using the special salt solution or prostaglandins, but with either method the dangers are greater than if the abortion is performed in the first ten weeks of pregnancy.

Many newspapers and journals have hailed prostaglandins as the ultimate do-it-yourself birth control method. Research and development may prove this to be so. One intriguing idea is that vaginal pessaries of prostaglandins will induce an early abortion if inserted at hourly intervals should the menstrual period not occur. The delay in menstruation may be due to pregnancy or to other reasons. The woman doesn't wait to find out. When her period is five days late, she inserts the prostaglandin tablets into her vagina and waits for bleeding to occur. The suggested name of the method is 'menstrual regulation', which is a euphemism. Unfortunately, the use of prostaglandins in this way is not so simple, and the associated nausea and diarrhoea are annoying complaints, so that contraception to prevent pregnancy is a far more sensible, and less traumatic, approach. To induce abortion between the fifth and tenth week of pregnancy, their use is less efficient, has more side-effects, and is potentially more dangerous than the use of the suction curette. But after the tenth week of pregnancy, they give promise of being the safest, and best, method of producing an abortion, especially if injected into the uterus itself. Even so, the mortality is three times higher, and the morbidity five times higher, than that which follows a legally induced abortion performed in the first ten weeks of pregnancy. And both are higher than the mortality and morbidity of the use of efficient contraceptives. That is where England also went wrong.

5

On 27th April, 1968, the Abortion Act, 1967, became law in England, Scotland and Wales. The Act, as is now well known, permitted doctors to perform abortions in certain well-defined circumstances without being charged with a criminal offence under the Offences Against the Person Act of 1861. The law made abortion legal on certain grounds, but contrary to the popular belief, it did not provide for abortion on demand. The doctor had to make two decisions when consulted by a pregnant woman who desired an abortion. He had to decide firstly, was the abortion permissible under the Act, and secondly, was it in the best interests of the woman and her family that the pregnancy should be terminated. Despite the concern of many doctors, these decisions have had to be made with increasing frequency between 1968 and 1971. The numbers of legally induced abortions have risen from 25,000 in 1968 to 59,000 in 1969, to 89,000 in 1970 and to 120,000 in 1971. To many people these figures indicate that Britain is becoming morally decadent, sexually irresponsible, and the abortion centre of the world. None of these beliefs is true. In fact, the number of abortions, as a percentage of the number of live births, in Britain remains low.

Yet the English experience needs study. The liberalized abortion laws were introduced prematurely, without sufficient thought and without being a part of a programme to prevent unwanted and unwelcome children being born.

For a long time it had been recognized that in Britain a knowledgeable woman who had the proper contacts, and the appropriate fee, could obtain an abortion easily. It would be performed by a qualified doctor, in pleasant surroundings and with safety. But if a woman was neither knowledgeable, wealthy nor wise, and had conceived an unwanted child, her only recourses were to have the baby, to seek to abort herself or to obtain the services of an unskilled, inefficient abortionist. Since the ignorant and unfortunate women made up the majority of those unhappily pregnant, the dangers of illegal, ill-managed abortions became obvious, as infection, subsequent sterility and occasionally death occurred. No one knows how many illegal abortions were carried out in Britain before 1967. Estimates range from 50,000 to 200,000 a year, and at least three-quarters of patients admitted to hospital with infection after an abortion had had the abortion induced.

It was clear that in Britain there was one law for the rich and one for the poor, and that much unnecessary illness was caused to the poor. The unsatisfactory nature of the law about abortion led to the formation of the Abortion Law Reform Association in 1936 and to its strenuous efforts against obscurantism, obstruction and obloquy to obtain a more humane and equitable approach. Between 1948 and 1965 five bills were introduced into Parliament but none reached the statute-book.

But the climate of opinion was changing; more people were in favour of abortion law reform and the arguments of the reformers were becoming increasingly sophisticated. On 13th July, 1966, David Steele, the member for a Scottish constituency, introduced a private bill 'to amend and clarify the law' about abortion.

The debate both inside and outside Parliament was intense. Predictably, the Abortion Law Reform Society mounted a campaign in favour of the Bill, and equally predictably the opponents of the Bill, and particularly the Roman Catholic community, attacked the proposed Bill holding that the fetus as a potential human was entitled to its rights, and that to abort it was to commit murder. One Roman Catholic lawyer was so incensed that he published a pamphlet in which he wrote that if the Bill was passed 'Herod will laugh in hell'— which showed a somewhat injudicial attitude to Herod and to modern Catholic theology. The effect of the debate was to make the public aware of the Bill, and opinion surveys revealed widespread support for it. By early October, 1967, the end of the parliamentary debate was in sight. Each clause of the Bill had been thoroughly discussed, concessions had been made, the House of Lords had returned the Bill to the House of Commons. On 27th October, 1967, it received the Royal Assent, to become law on 27th April, 1968.

If anything, the debate since the Act became law has increased, as the numbers of women seeking abortion have increased. The Roman Catholic Church, of necessity, has continued to campaign for 'the rights of the innocent unborn'. The Anglican Church has taken an equivocal stand. The men and women who have had to do the terminations—the gynaecologists, and to a lesser extent, the general practitioners—have been split in their views.

The only in depth survey of doctors' attitudes to abortion was made in late 1969 by the Royal College of Obstetricians

289

and Gynaecologists. It showed that 94 per cent of gynaecologists had no conscientious objection to terminating pregnancy, although over 50 per cent wanted the law amended to 'restrict

PEOPLE POPULATING
J. D. Llewellyn-Jones

PUBLISHER'S NOTE

On page 290 there is a reference to Sir Norman Jeffcoate which is inaccurate and misleading. During his term of office as President of the Royal College of Obstetricians and Gynaecologists from October 1969 to September 1972 he gave no interview to the B.B.C. on the subject of abortion, nor did he at any time express views other than the official ones of the Council of the College.

The author and publishers apologise to Sir Norman for the inaccuracy and are glad to publish this correction.

In all future editions of this book lines 19-28 on page 290 will read as follows:

"informed concern was exaggerated by the more vocal opponents of the Abortion Act who claimed, publicly, that it had been sponsored by a small but strongly organised band of agitators who had sought to sway public and parliamentary opinion by propaganda and misrepresentation of the position existing at the time. However, this extreme opposition was not supported by facts; dangerous illegal abortions continued to occur. It was these that the sponsor of the Bill, David Steel, wished to eliminate. In the words of one proponent of reform, Mrs Madeleine Simms, the President of the Abortion Reform League, 'the law ..."

pregnancies they were expected to terminate, had cause to complain. And the fault was due to the way in which the Act had been introduced. It had not been preceded by a campaign to make knowledge of contraceptives available to all women at risk—and that meant any women aged between 14 and 49 who were having sexual intercourse. It had not been preceded by schemes which made the contraceptives themselves freely available. Deprived of facilities to prevent conception, the restrictions of the Act forced many women to beg to have the pregnancy terminated. An American, Dr. Garrett Hardin, has asked, 'Do we promote human dignity by requiring women to beg?'

In fact, in Britain, it was possible to offer contraceptive advice. In 1968, the Family Planning Act gave local authorities the power to establish birth control clinics, although it was not mandatory for them to do so. In fact few did. The reasons were many but most might be summed up as moral reasons, one Councillor stating that 'It is not the duty, nor the obligation of the council to protect loose women from the consequences of their promiscuity'. By the time the Abortion Act became law, only one third of local authorities had taken any action, and even then the action was minimal, the councils pleading 'shortage of funds'.

Rather dismayingly, the services offered have not always been 'consumer oriented'. Yet sociological surveys have indicated that a 'consumer demand for contraceptives exists in Britain'. Surveys seeking information about birth control get a higher response than those seeking information about income and expenditure. Newspapers and magazines find a ready readership for articles emphasizing sexual exploits, although they seemed less willing to emphasize the value of contraception in preventing pregnancy. Despite Lord Longford's views there is no evidence that the dissemination of contraceptive knowledge encourages promiscuity. The main constraint which prevents many women, particularly in the lower socio-economic groups, and the unmarried, from accepting birth control, seems to be the fear of being snubbed by predominantly middle-class doctors, or health workers. Not only are the women anxious about their reception, but they tend to be deterred by the documentation required, and are particularly deterred by the fact that they have, in the case of Family Planning Association clinics, to walk into a building which exists solely to give contraceptive advice. This attitude is due to the prudery of many British women, particularly regarding sexual matters. This in turn is due to a cultural conditioning that human sexuality is something to be ignored largely, and to the relative lack of sex education in schools. In consequence the number of unwelcome, often unwanted, children is considerable. In 1970, the Select Committee on Science and Technology estimated that between 200,000 and 300,000 unwanted children were born each year in England and Wales alone; and a study of the 120,000 pregnancies terminated in 1970 showed that in 70 per cent the failure to use contraceptives was the reason the woman became pregnant.

It was clear, even to the most reactionary and obtuse person, by 1972, that there was something bad in the state of Britain. Even the British Medical Association, which could hardly be said to be a radical organization, in its submission to a committee set up to inquire into the working of the Abortion Act noted that it seemed 'illogical to make provision for an abortion service (under the free National Health Scheme) without providing similarly for a contraceptive service including male and female sterilization. Moreover it is less hazardous for a woman to practise contraception than to undergo an abortion or proceed with a pregnancy which could involve risk'. This is an excellent summary of the moral and medical aspects of the problem and was in direct conflict with Government policy in Britain at that time. This was exemplified by the British Minister of Health's Statement in 1971 that free contraceptives would be a 'gratuitous waste of taxpayers' money'.

But the British Medical Association had more to say, and all of it pertinent, if critical, of the Government. 'Every woman', the report stated, 'who has proper grounds for an abortion under the terms of the Act, should be able to obtain it in a National Health Service hospital within reasonable reach of her house.' What is implicit in the report, although not stated, is that the organizational facilities should be such that every woman who was to have an abortion could be sure that it would be done before the tenth week of pregnancy had been reached. It has been quite evident that in Britain and the

U.S.A., in contrast to Eastern Europe, far too many women only reach the gynaecologist after the twelfth week of gestation when termination of pregnancy is increasingly hazardous.

One such woman was Mrs. Pobble. Mrs. Pobble, whose husband was permanently incapacitated because of severe asthma, had four children. She didn't believe in contraceptives, 'They're not safe, are they?' she said. 'It may be all right for people who are single, but it's not proper for married women.' Her husband used a condom with fair success, although as she admitted, they sometimes took chances when 'he was usually careful'. On this occasion he wasn't. When six weeks had elapsed since her previous period she began to get worried and went to her general practitioner. 'I told him that I thought I might be pregnant, and he said he wouldn't be able to tell, and didn't I think I might be worrying too much. I told him my nerves were bad, so he gave me some tablets for them and said I was to go back to see him the next week. I couldn't go then because my Lana got 'flu and I had to stay home, but I did go the week after. He took some of my urine and sent it off to be tested.' Mrs. Pobble was now eight weeks pregnant, and when she reported back to her doctor the next week he confirmed that the test was positive and that she was indeed pregnant. 'I told him that I knew that I was pregnant and that I couldn't go on with it. He said he couldn't see any reason why not. I was quite healthy, but if I really wanted it he'd try and get me to see a psychiatrist. I didn't like the idea of that, but if it was the only way to help I'd do it. Mind you, I'd thought that the law was meant to help people, I told him.' It took two weeks to arrange the psychiatric appointment, and a few days for his letter to go back to Mrs. Pobble's general practitioner. By now she was nearly eleven weeks pregnant. The psychiatrist had recommended termination as he believed that to continue the pregnancy would affect Mrs. Pobble's health. On this evidence, the general practitioner referred her to the nearest hospital to see the gynaecologist there. She saw him a week later, and it was agreed that her pregnancy would be terminated. There was a problem, no bed was available for ten days. Ten days later, when nearly fourteen weeks pregnant, Mrs. Pobble had her pregnancy terminated. She bled heavily, developed an infection, and was ill for some time.

As the British Medical Association point out, when writing about problems similar to those of Mrs. Pobble, in some areas it is difficult to find hospital accommodation within reasonable access of the patient, but that 'those able to afford private consultation are always able to obtain an abortion, especially if they are prepared to travel away from their home area'.

As well as proposing that some important medical and demographic implications of legally induced abortions should be studied, the B.M.A.'s report also observed that 'after-care facilities and follow-up with contraceptive advice must be established', matters considered of great importance in Eastern European nations, as I have shown.

If this excellent advice had been available in 1968 when the Act was made operative, many of the problems which have occurred in Britain could have been avoided. Other nations considering more liberal abortion laws may profit from Britain's experience.

6

It is not sufficient to consider abortion as a surgical procedure without giving some attention to the psychological aspects of being refused an abortion, and of having an abortion. Evidence has been accumulated on both of these matters.

Women refused a legal abortion commonly seek to terminate their pregnancy elsewhere. For example, in Forssman and Thume's study, 36 per cent of the women refused the abortion failed to deliver at term. In Britain, a study of 105 women refused an abortion between 1968 and 1970 showed that 10 per cent had a supposedly spontaneous abortion, 50 per cent accepted the decision and continued with the pregnancy, and the remaining 40 per cent obtained an abortion elsewhere. Four of the 41 women doing this became seriously ill, one girl nearly dying from infection. Two of the 52 women who continued their pregnancy developed significant mental illness.

The high complication rate following the abortion performed 'elsewhere', and the sinister effect of the continued pregnancy on the woman's mental health emphasize the seriousness of refusing a request for abortion. In the case of the pregnancies which were terminated subsequently, a delay must inevitably have occurred during which time the woman desperately looked for a more sympathetic gynaecologist. This delay would advance the gestation period into the hazardous time zone.

A woman seeking an abortion should be given a definite answer, whether of agreement or refusal, as soon after she seeks medical aid as possible. If she is refused the abortion, the medical attendants should give her advice regarding the social services available to her, and should try to ensure that she is put in touch with the appropriate social workers. It is not sufficient for the gynaecologist to be moralistically intolerant and to feel that what the woman does is none of his business. It is. The desperation of a woman refused an abortion can be seen from these statistics, and the serious impact on her mental and physical health is apparent. The effect of being an unwanted child, on its physical and emotional development, has been mentioned earlier in this chapter, and is further considered in Chapter 14.

The effect of having an induced abortion on the woman's emotional state has also received a good deal of unscientific, often biased, study. Those opposed to abortion, those supporting the rights of the innocent fetus, usually found that induced legal abortion occasioned considerable mental trauma. Those who supported abortion on demand invariably found that abortion was without any emotional effect on the woman. Experience should indicate that neither extreme view is correct. Investigation of the literature shows that about one-quarter of women have transient grief, but that this is more likely to occur if the pregnancy has advanced beyond ten weeks, and the woman has begun to become aware that the fetus has an identity. However, very few women develop psychiatric illness after an abortion. Dr. Kummer, who has made one of the most thorough surveys, holds that induced abortion 'far from being precipitor of psychiatric illness, quite to the contrary is actually a defence against such an occurrence in women who are susceptible to mental illness'.

But do women feel guilt that they have had an abortion? Some obviously do, and unfortunately the degree of the guilt and its duration can be influenced considerably by the attitude of the doctors and nurses caring for the patient. If she is treated with odium and contempt by the nurses, if she gets the impression that they consider her to be immoral, and only just to be tolerated, her guilt will be magnified. If the administrative procedures are complicated and bureaucratic, the woman may feel that she is being 'got at' and this may increase her feeling of guilt.

It should follow that once legal abortion is accepted by the community, the administrative procedures to achieve it should be as simple as possible, the medical attendants should be as sympathetic as possible, and should certainly avoid imposing their own moral standards on the patient. A woman should be allowed to retain her dignity.

Supporters of women's liberation may think, from these remarks, that the writer supports abortion 'on demand'. He does not—and for what he thinks good reason. An example may make this clear.

Sadie Thompson was a 20-year-old who didn't approve of society, who did her own thing and who couldn't be bothered to use contraceptives. After all she could always get an abortion on demand. If she demanded it she expected society to give her an abortion. It was only right. Even if it meant that she had three abortions a year, and occupied the time and energy of a gynaecologist and nurses three times each year. If a woman takes no contraceptive measures, and has frequent sexual intercourse, she is likely to become pregnant within three months. She waits four weeks until she is sure she is pregnant, and if abortion on demand is available, then obtains a termination, only to become pregnant again within four months. Repeated induced abortions are not without danger, and even if the woman is as vacuous as Sadie, physicians try to avoid increasing the danger to their patients. This is the situation which could develop, on a large scale, if 'abortion on demand' were accepted.

Equally it is ridiculous to advocate contraception if the 'back up' of legal abortion is not also available for the woman whose contraceptive fails, or who becomes pregnant through ill fortune or ignorance.

Perhaps the most enlightened approach to the place of abortion in a birth control programme is that adopted by the Czechs.

In Czechoslovakia, 'education for planned and conscientious parenthood', which includes knowledge of contraceptive techniques, begins at school. Girls and women at risk of becoming pregnant are told where they can obtain contraceptive advice and appliances. These are available either free of charge or at cost. Abortion on medical grounds is permissible if there is a substantial risk that to continue the pregnancy would gravely impair the health or life of the mother. Abortion is permitted on social grounds, but only if it is sought before the end of the tenth week of pregnancy. After an abortion a woman is given contraceptive advice and materials, and is told that a further abortion on social grounds will not be permitted within the next twelve months. This has the effect of encouraging contraceptive usage and deterring the woman who can't be bothered to protect herself from becoming pregnant inadvertently.

This seems more sensible, more humane and more realistic than advocating 'abortion on demand' which could encourage vacuous femininity; or refusing abortion as a back-stop to contraception, which is inequitable and will do nothing to reduce the incidence of dangerous, undignified illegal abortions. Moreover, it places abortion in its proper place in any movement which seeks to make sure that all children are wanted children, and which encourages a reduction of the present reproductive growth rate.

CHAPTER THIRTEEN

Death in the Afternoon

However strong a mother may be, she becomes afraid when she is preg-
nant for the third time.

Chinese Proverb

I

They brought Sundraletchumy into the hospital at about five
in the afternoon. She was a short woman, in late pregnancy
unconscious, her face and body bloated with fluid, her flowered
sari dirty from vomit. Her husband had come with her. It was
he told us, her sixth pregnancy, and she had had no trouble
with the deliveries of her first five children, although two had
died in the first two years of life. She hadn't expected this
pregnancy to be any different. He was a landless harijan, but in
good times was able to get enough work to keep his family
reasonably fed. Their needs were few: rice, dung for cooking
cloth for saris and for his garments. The people in their village
let them alone, and there was no real trouble. Yes, there was a
Government Maternity Clinic, but Sundraletchumy didn't
go there. It was in the next village and she didn't like the
midwife. Anyhow she had too many things to do. Like helping
him, and getting water from the special well the harijans had
to use, and looking after the children—the second was afflicted—
she could not do much for herself. And anyhow, why would she
go to the Clinic, she had had no trouble with the other pregnancies.

We asked him what had happened. She was near her time

298

he said, and a week back she began to get swollen. First her legs swelled up, but she went to a medicine man and he gave her something to soak and to drink. It hadn't done much good, her hands had got swollen and then her face, but she said she felt all right. Then today when he was in the fields one of the children had come running to say that her mother had suddenly fallen to the floor and had begun twitching. He had come home and found Sundraletchumy breathing deeply, so he'd decided to get the help of the Government, that was what they were there for. Some women, including the traditional midwife, had seen Sundraletchumy and told him that was what he should do. He'd run, through the midday heat, along the bunds dividing the rice paddies to the Clinic, and the Government midwife had come.

The midwife confirmed what Sundraletchumy's husband had said. She had been sitting, completing the family planning records, when Munisamy had come in. Although Sundraletchumy wasn't one of her patients, she had gone at once with him to see her. And when she had got to the whitewashed, mud-walled hovel in which Munisamy lived, she had known at once that Sundraletchumy needed to be got to hospital. She called the lady medical officer, but she was away at the other side of the development block and wouldn't be back till night-fall. So she had got the jeep and had brought Sundraletchumy in. The midwife's face showed her anxiety, her large breasts heaved under her white sari as she told the story. Would she be criticized for what she had done? We assured her that she had done well. The fault was that Sundraletchumy had become pregnant in the first place, and hadn't taken family planning advice. And once she had known she was pregnant, the fault was that she hadn't gone to the prenatal clinic. No, the midwife was not to blame. In a way, Sundraletchumy was.

But she couldn't hear. Whilst we had been getting this information the doctor had been examining Sundraletchumy in the labour room. It was a bare room. And hot. A stained concrete floor, whitewashed plastered walls, a wooden roof—that was the labour room. In it were three metal beds, a washbasin, and some obstetrical instruments in a cupboard. Utilitarian rather than elegant. Functional rather than well-equipped. Stained walls rather than gleaming stainless steel instruments.

The doctor, too, was rather stained. He and his wife looked after the hospital and each year supervised the obstetric care of 3,000 women with complicated obstetrical problems. His annual salary was rather less than the amount an American obstetrician gets for looking after 15 women with no obstetric problems.

Sundraletchumy was unconscious. Her breathing was slow, deep and snorting. Her eyes were fixed, the pupils tiny, even in the darkened labour room. The swelling of her legs was gross. If you pressed your thumb into the flesh below her knee and then took your thumb away, a curved pit was left in the water-logged flesh. Her baby was dead. The doctor couldn't hear its heart. And she was in labour. The midwife had said she had had six fits in the jeep during the 20 km journey from the village to the hospital. She had stopped Sundraletchumy from biting her tongue, but with each fit her colour had become worse—a sort of dusky, greyish blue in her dark skin. The doctor also noted that she was very anaemic, her eye sacs were very pale, almost white. And he noticed her pupils were like pin points. He took her blood pressure, and the column of mercury rose up and up whilst he checked the reading. It was far, far too high. He gave her an injection and got one of the nurses to pass a catheter into Sundraletchumy's bladder. There was very little urine, and what there was, was dark, blood stained, and loaded with protein when the nurse tested it.

The diagnosis was clear. Sundraletchumy had had eclamptic fits, and from her condition it looked as if she had had a brain haemorrhage. They would try to do something. But they could only hope.

At 5.15 p.m., on that afternoon, Sundraletchumy had another fit, became blue, her mouth filled with froth and she died.

2

The death of a mother in pregnancy, in labour or after child birth, is one of the greatest tragedies which can befall a family for its entire structure is temporarily or permanently disorganized. In the days when both maternal and infant death were common, the custom of polygamy had much merit, for its enabled the family group to continue even if one mother died in childbirth, or failed to rear her child.

The likelihood of death due to complications of pregnancy or childbirth has only been computed in relatively recent times, and then only in certain nations. Nobody knows how many women died in England, for example, in the sixteenth century, although students of parish records can obtain some information. The rate was fairly high, perhaps one mother dying for every two hundred births. But no real statistics were available until 1837 when a Government Act required the registration of maternal deaths. In such registration, Britain was well in advance of most other nations. The lessons were there to be learnt, but it took over a century for them to be learnt, and for the maternal death rate to drop significantly.

It was realized at the very beginning that a very considerable danger to newly delivered women was childbed fever. The fever was attributed to bad air, or to evil humours in the mother, or to a visitation from God. But the real cause was unknown.

In 1847, a significant advance occurred. This was in Vienna, when a 30-year-old doctor, Ignaz Philipp Semmelweis, was appointed Assistant to the First Obstetric Clinic in Vienna's famous hospital—the Allgemeine Krankenhaus. The hospital was indeed famous. It was also feared, particularly by pregnant women from the slums. The hospital was a charitable institution and cared for the confinement of women too poor to employ and pay a midwife. In return for being attended in the lying-in wards, the women agreed to be used for the instruction of medical students and midwives. But as it was considered improper and indecent for male students and female midwives to be together at such an intimate sexual matter as childbirth, two separate obstetric 'clinics' (which were really lying-in wards) were established. The First Obstetric Clinic was used for the instruction of medical students, and the Second Obstetric Clinic for the instruction of midwives. There was no need for published statistics to show why the Allgemeine Krankenhaus was feared. If a woman was confined in the First Obstetric Clinic, she had a one-in-ten chance of dying. Regularly, childbed fever swept through the wards, from one bed to another, decimating the mothers. Oddly, in the Second Obstetric Clinic, which was conducted by the midwives, the death rate was one-fifth that of the First Clinic. Women would beg to be sent there rather than to the doctors' clinic. In 1846, the year before Semmelweis was appointed, 459 of the 4,010 women confined in the First Obstetric Clinic had died, that is a mortality of 11·4 per cent. In the Second Obstetric Clinic only 105 of 3,754 women had died—a rate of 2·7 per cent. Those who delivered at home were even luckier—fewer than one in every two hundred women confined died in childbirth. Semmelweis decided he would try to discover why the death rate in the First Clinic was so much higher. He examined and rejected the traditional causes of childbed fever: poisonous air, constipation, delayed lactation, seasonal influences, noxious humours and the will of God. None explained why the women died, and why more died in the First Clinic than in the Second Clinic. The conditions were the same, the patients were similar. Why? Semmelweis started doing autopsies on the women, spending more and more time in the mortuary. Each time, always, he found the same changes in the bodies he examined. At the necropsies, medical students assisted and did obstetric manipulations on the bodies as part of their training in midwifery. After the session, which took place early each morning, the students went to the lying-in wards to examine the patients. And the deaths continued no matter what measures were taken. Semmelweis tried changing the position of the beds, he tried closing and opening the windows, he tried prohibiting foreign students. The deaths refused to fall. Then in 1847, a strange event occurred. His friend and colleague, the Professor of Legal Medicine, Joseph Kolletschka, became ill. He had cut himself doing a necropsy. With astonishing rapidity he had developed a high fever, and had shown all the signs of childbed fever before dying. A necropsy was performed on Kolletschka's body which Semmelweis, deeply unhappy, attended. The necropsy showed that the changes in Kolletschka's body were identical with those that Semmelweis had found in his autopsies of the mothers who had died after childbirth. The truth dawned on him. Kolletschka had died of poisons entering his body from the body of the person on whom he had done the necropsy. The medical students carried the same poisons from the dead bodies on whom they did obstetric manipulations, to the women whose genitalia they examined directly afterwards. The cause of childbed fever was 'cadaveric poisoning'. It was due to poisons which developed in the dead tissues of corpses. The medical students carried the poison on their unwashed hands and gave it to the mothers they examined as they lay in rows in the lying-in ward. The midwives did not attend autopsies, and they examined their patients less frequently. This must be the reason for the greater number of women who died in the Doctor's Clinic.

Semmelweis checked and checked again. He could see no flaw in his reasoning. If this was so, the answer should be to insist that every medical student and every physician must wash his hands in chlorinated lime solution and thoroughly scrub them with clean sand to remove the dissecting room poisons. Only then might he examine the mothers. As with many medical innovations, Semmelweis' views, his integrity and his honesty were attacked by his colleagues. They said that he was irreligious, he was a trouble-maker, he was a crank. No sensible, intelligent, educated doctor could believe in cadaveric poisons. 'Cadaveric poisons, indeed!' they said, it was absolute rubbish. In a similar manner philosophers had refused to believe, centuries earlier, the earth was not flat. But Semmelweis persisted in his views and insisted on hand washing—and the death rate went steadily down. It fell from 57 deaths in April, 1847, to 6 deaths in June and to only 3 deaths in July. Put another way, in April, 18 per cent of the mothers died, in July, 1 per cent. Semmelweis believed he was vindicated, and, more important, mothers were living. Then in August, in one week, the death rate shot up: 11 women died. Semmelweis was dumbfounded, his medical colleagues were dismayed about the deaths, but jubilant that the upstart doctor had been proved wrong. He checked all the possible reasons—and found no answer. The medical students had obeyed his rules and had carefully washed their hands after doing the necropsies. The poison couldn't have been carried from the corpses in the mortuary. Then he spotted what had happened. The answer was under Semmelweis' nose, lying, slowly dying, in a corner bed of the ward. It was a woman who had an advanced, foully discharging, cancer of the uterus. Her bed was nearest the door. On entering the ward the students washed their hands. Then they examined the cancer patient first before going on to examine the maternity patients. Semmelweis reasoned that the poison could come from gangrenous tissue in live patients as well as from corpses. He ordered that the students were to wash their hands in chlorine solution after each examination. With increasing annoyance the staff and students obeyed, and the death rate obligingly went down.

Semmelweis was urged to report his findings but he refused. He was a poor writer, he said, and an indifferent speaker. Amongst the hostile medical colleagues were two friends. They agreed to report Semmelweis' discovery to the local medical society. They did and were abused, scorned and belittled. His arguments were ridiculous—said his colleagues. There was no need for washing. Semmelweis, dispirited, left Vienna. And the maternal death rate in the First Clinic in the Allgemeine Krankenhaus rose to the previous levels.

It was not until 1857, eight years after leaving Vienna, that he was induced to write a book—*The Causes, Concept and Prophylaxis of Childbed Fever*. His views were still attacked, he was becoming more eccentric and obsessed about the prevention of childbed fever. In 1865, at the age of 47, he was admitted to a mental hospital, and there in August he died—of blood poisoning, the very infection he had studied, and fought to prevent lying-in mothers from developing. And by a quaint irony, on the day before Semmelweis died, Joseph Lister was operating in Glasgow. Acting on the conclusions reached in a paper which Pasteur had written, Lister used carbolic acid to treat the infected wound of a broken leg. The era of antisepsis had begun; the era of bacteriology was about to start.

Although Semmelweis' theory had met with a hostile reception in Vienna, in Paris the great obstetrician, Tarnier believed in it, but was unable to convince his colleagues. In his hospital, the number of women dying in the years 1857 to 1869 was 93 per 1,000 live births. Nothing was done to prevent the spread of childbed fever during those years. Semmelweis' views were ignored. Then, in 1869, Pasteur reported finding microbes in 'little chains' in the blood and vaginal discharges of women dying of childbed fever. Semmelweis' 'cadaveric poison' had been identified. It was a microbe! Tarnier now had a much stronger case. The cadaveric poison was a microbe and moreover, it had been discovered by a Frenchman. H colleagues began to accept his views, and agreed that he should attack the problem. Tarnier at once separated the feverish patients from the others, and insisted that separate staff attend them and hand-washing was instituted. The mortality between 1870 and 1880 dropped to 23 per 1,000. In 1881, he added Lister's carbolic antiseptics to his regimen, and the maternal death rate dropped to 10·5 per 1,000. Tarnier's authority, his persistence and his knowledge had vindicated the eccentric Semmelweis. Because of this, fewer women would die from childbed fever in maternity hospitals. Childbirth was becoming safer.

Luckily, at that time, most women were delivered in their homes by midwives who did no other jobs, so that overall mortality from sepsis was far lower. But in Britain between 1838 and 1938, sepsis accounted for half the maternal deaths, and throughout the century the death rate hovered around 4·5 per 1,000 births. Then in 1935 Leonard Colebrook, working in London, noted that bacteria could be transferred from patient to patient, or from medical attendant to patient by infected droplets coming from the nose, or introduced into the dust and the air from infected bedding. By taking action to isolate infected women, and by preventing the spread of infected dust, the deaths from sepsis halved.

Later, with the development of the antibiotics the deaths from sepsis fell still further. But they still occur, particularly amongst women who undergo illegal abortions by unqualified abortionists, or who try to abort themselves. Indeed in South America, 20 per cent of all maternity beds are occupied by women infected during an abortion.

3

Since 1935 in Britain, and paralleled in other affluent developed nations, there has been a steady reduction in the number of deaths of women during and after childbirth (Fig. 13/1). Deaths from haemorrhage occurring in pregnancy and after confinement, which 30 years ago caused great concern, have been reduced because of better obstetric care and, as important, because of the availability of blood, provided through blood transfusion services. In the hungry, developing nations, deaths from haemorrhage continue to cause maternal deaths all too frequently. In these nations, too, a large number of women are anaemic. Anaemia in pregnancy adds to the danger of any haemorrhage which may occur. An anaemic woman is unable to cope with the sudden loss of blood, and what would be annoying, but not dangerous, in a well-fed non-anaemic woman, is life-threatening to an anaemic mother. The tragedy is that anaemia is completely preventible. If all pregnant women living in the developing nations took iron tablets every day during pregnancy, and in addition were given special vitamin tablets called folic acid tablets, in the second half of pregnancy, anaemia would disappear. Unfortunately, a campaign to achieve this is not dramatic; it does not count as real research. In fact it requires good organizers with persuasive tongues, rather than academic medical researchers. However, many doctors—particularly those in positions of power—although concerned with the problems of anaemia in pregnancy, are anxious to keep up with the medical Joneses, and engage in abstruse research on obscure obstetrical problems. Such research, although intellectually satisfying, requires great expenditure in equipment and in the employment of laboratory technicians, and diverts funds from projects more applicable to the nation. Furthermore, many large, lavishly equipped, well-funded research institutions, geared for doing this type of investigation, already exist in the developed nations. An argument can be made for having one or two such institutes in each developing nation, to act as a spur to health workers, and to investigate problems peculiar to the nation, but the desire for each medical school to get into 'big scientific' research is counterproductive.

Sundraletchumy's death from eclamptic fits is another pregnancy condition which is largely preventible. Eclampsia is the final, and often lethal, stage of a disease process peculiar to pregnancy. It is called 'toxaemia', although no toxin has ever been found. The disease complicates about 10 per cent of all pregnancies, but is more common in first pregnancies and amongst women pregnant for the fifth or subsequent time. Research workers have spent uncountable hours, and expended considerable sums of money, over the past half century, attempting to find the cause of 'toxaemia'. They have failed. In the entrance foyer of the Chicago Lying-in Hospital, plaques around the walls commemorate those doctors, such as Semmelweis, who have made far-reaching discoveries to make pregnancy and childbirth safer for women. One plaque remains blank. It has been left blank so that the name of the man, or woman, who discovers the cause of toxaemia of pregnancy may be carved into the marble.

Although the cause of 'toxaemia of pregnancy' is unknown, it is known that if the first signs are spotted early, the progress to the more severe form of the disease can be prevented. These early signs—a rise in blood pressure, marked swelling of the legs or hands, and the presence of protein in the urine—are looked for by midwives and doctors in prenatal examinations. But if the woman, like Sundraletchumy, fails to attend prenatal clinics, eclampsia can result.

The key to much of the reduction in the maternal death rate over the years, in most developed nations, has been the increased acceptance by women of the need for antenatal care. A woman who obtains regular, high quality, antenatal care has one-tenth the likelihood of dying in pregnancy, in childbirth or in the lying-in period, than a woman who fails to seek antenatal care. This was studied in Malaya in the 1950s where we found that in the maternity hospital in Kuala Lumpur, the death rate of women who had had antenatal care was 1·3 for every 1,000 births; but if they failed to seek antenatal care it rose to 15 per 1,000 births. This finding not only applies to the developing nations. In New York, investigators have identified women who are at 'high risk' of dying in pregnancy. These patients are girls who become pregnant under the age of 17 (when they are often unmarried), and women over the age of 40 who often have had more than 5 previous pregnancies. Single women, of all ages, are at higher risk than average, as are those who are grossly overweight (more than 90 kg) or grossly underweight (under 45 kg). One such woman died recently in Australia. She was aged 34 and it was her fifth pregnancy. Her husband was a heavy drinker so that the housekeeping money was limited. She was overweight for her height and had 'lost' two of her five children. Both had died in the first year of life—from bronchitis—she said. Her mother, who was still alive but lived in a country town, was a diabetic. The patient didn't seek antenatal care because she was too busy, she said. She had tried to induce an abortion on herself using a knitting needle but had failed. The pregnancy had continued, the money was short, she was depressed and fatalistic. In late pregnancy her legs and hands began to swell, but she took no notice of this. Labour began prematurely and she went into a small nearby hospital. There it was found that she was severely anaemic, and had a raised blood pressure. A blood transfusion was given to correct the anaemia, but unfortunately the patient became breathless, fluid filled her lungs and she died. Her death was preventible. If she had sought antenatal care, the anaemia would have been treated by tablets or by iron injections. In addition, the 'toxaemia of pregnancy' which she also developed would have been treated. As well, she was a 'high risk' patient who should have been referred to a larger, better staffed hospital. There the staff would have avoided a blood transfusion to treat her anaemia, as this undoubtedly overloaded her circulation and caused the heart failure.

An interesting, and depressing, finding in the New York study was that of 40 women dying amongst 40,000 pregnancies investigated between 1959 and 1965, 28 were 'high risk mothers' and 20 stated that they had not wanted to become pregnant. In their case the pregnancy was not only unwanted and unwelcome—it was lethal.

In addition to antenatal care, a significant factor in the reduction of maternal deaths has been the establishment of Committees on Maternal Mortality. Initially established in the State of New York, most American States now have such Committees, as have Sweden, Australia, England and Wales. These Committees investigate all maternal deaths. They seek confidential information from all those who attended the patient in labour—from the midwife, the doctor and the hospital. The information is collected and analysed by the Committee and every few years a report is published. In Britain reports are now available for the years 1952 to 1969, whilst in Australia two reports covering the years 1964 to 1969 have been published. The purpose of the reports is not to pass judgement on doctors and nurses for their neglect of care, but to educate all those who look after pregnant women. The reports are read and discussed by those who care for pregnant women. Their value is confirmed by the finding that in each of the successive 3-year periods the number of deaths in which the general practitioner or the hospital staff were considered to have made a faulty decision has fallen. Over the years the maternal death rate has also fallen.

Mothers still die in pregnancy and childbirth, although fewer do so each year in the developed nations. Since the death rate is so much higher in the developing nations and amongst

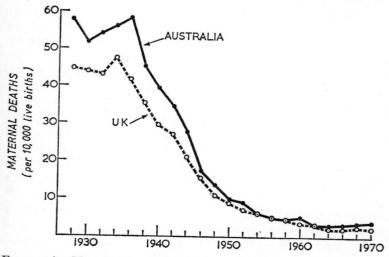

FIG. 13/1. How maternal deaths have fallen in Australia and in England and Wales since 1930.

the submerged 20 per cent of the people in the affluent nations, there is much to be done. For the action to be effective, knowledge of the problem and concerted action by all concerned citizens to change it, is required. Two groups are involved—firstly, the public and the politicians, and secondly, the medical profession.

The public should insist that the politicians take action. They should make sure conveniently sited antenatal clinics are built and that a continuing educational campaign is started to induce all pregnant women to use the facilities provided. The clinics must be convenient for the patient, and open at a time which suits her. She must not have to wait too long to be seen, because this will deter her, particularly if she is anxious about what is happening to her other children. With good organization, and by using health centres, as is being done in Britain, these conditions can be met quite easily. Whilst the State and family doctor can provide antenatal clinics, it is up to the community leaders, the press and all educated people to show the poorer and less educated sections of the population that care during the 40 weeks of pregnancy is as important as care during the 10 hours of labour.

Unfortunately, evidence from several nations, and most recently that of Dr. Klein and Dr. Karten in New York, shows that inability to induce high risk mothers to seek prenatal care is a most significant factor in maternal death. They report that 'Forty per cent of the current deaths, or 3.8 deaths per 10,000 live births, occurred in women who either failed to obtain medical care prior to their hospitalization, or death, or received inadequate care. This group included self-inflicted complications and criminal abortions. This is unbelievable in view of the availability of prenatal and family planning clinics in municipal and voluntary hospitals, as well as neighbourhood satellite clinics that are open evenings in order to accommodate those women who cannot attend the usual clinics. Evidently, availability of medical care is not the only factor contributing to patient welfare. Socio-economic status appears to be a more potent force affecting patient attitude as well as outcome. Seventy-two per cent of the patients who died in the various institutions were in the "low socio-economic" category. Thus, poverty with all its complications contributed disproportionately to our current mortality rate. The decline in maternal death rate has been significantly greater among the higher income groups than among the poorer class.' In another survey of deaths occurring over a 14-year period in Chicago, Dr. Webster concluded that poverty, rather than race, is the major factor in the maternal mortality rate. Poverty is associated with poor education; with fear of institutions, particularly if the staff are distant, dictatorial and condescending; and with a lack of motivation to seek medical care. Help is only sought when the disability or discomfort becomes sufficiently severe to constitute a crisis, which is invariably late in the disease process. The remedy lies in a multidisciplinary health education programme which starts at primary school and continues after school in community educational enterprises, involving local key persons, and the full utilization of radio and television. Even this will fail unless the health staff of clinics are trained to deal with problems without condescension. As a first step the pejorative terms 'public' (i.e. charity) patient and 'indigent' patient must be replaced. The ability to pay for medical care should not produce a higher standard for the affluent, and a lower standard, charity medicine, for the poor.

The politicians should also ensure that properly designed, adequately equipped district obstetric hospitals are provided, which will receive from the peripheral hospitals, health centres, maternity homes, family doctors and specialists, all patients who would more suitably be delivered in units where specialist care is available. Where this is economically possible these would include all women pregnant for the fourth or subsequent time; all primigravidae over the age of 30; all women with a multiple pregnancy; all women who have had an abnormality in a previous pregnancy or labour, or who develop an abnormality in the present pregnancy; and all women whose labour has lasted more than 18 hours, for whatever cause. Within the hospital the system of medical service, whether it is prepaid, or fee for service, will depend on the circumstances in the country. But all patients should receive equal service based on need, not on ability to pay.

The politicians must also make sure that in each region there is a central obstetric hospital with medical staff in sufficient numbers to permit teaching and research to be conducted as well as routine clinical care of patients. The specialist obstetricians and gynaecologists in the hospital should have undergone a course of training of not less than three years in their speciality.

The director of the hospital, who might well also be the Professor of Obstetrics, would organize the obstetric services of the area, in conjunction with the health authorities. He would ensure that good person-to-person communication existed between specialists, family doctors and his staff. He would make visits to the peripheral units, and to midwives working in the field, to assess the quality of obstetric care (including family planning) and to encourage the obstetric health workers at all levels in their endeavours. He would make sure that ready, easy, transfer of problem patients could be effected from the periphery to the centre should this be required, and that skilled expert attention from the centre could be brought to the seriously ill patient at the periphery without delay.

It is realized that such a scheme would interfere with current patterns of 'free enterprise' obstetric care which is in evidence in Australia, Canada, the U.S.A. and some European nations. But there is no doubt that the 'team-concept' of obstetric care will do much to reduce maternal mortality, to reduce unnecessary operating and to improve the obstetric services. This is the last quarter of the twentieth century. It is ridiculous to suppose that the nineteenth century corner shop-keepers' attitudes, usually considered normal by most doctors, can retard the provision of maternity care. The public and the politicians have a duty to see that it does not.

In the developing nations, and in nations where patients are delivered in their homes, good obstetric care presupposes the development of a mobile obstetric flying squad. The idea behind the flying squad is that in cases of emergency, skilled medical attention is better given in the patient's home, before transferring her to hospital. The team would consist of a trained obstetrician and a nurse who has been trained to give anaesthetics (or in developed nations, an anaesthetist). The team travels by ambulance Land-Rover as far as is possible, and then by foot and takes with them previously packed equipment. Experience has shown that resuscitation by blood transfusion and the removal of a retained placenta are the most common procedures required. The obstetric squad can be life-saving.

In one report a patient delivered a normal baby after a short labour. She was delivered in her home by a trained midwife. Soon after the birth of the child the afterbirth was expelled, but following this severe bleeding occurred from the uterus. The midwife examined the afterbirth and found that a piece was missing. Presumably it was still in the uterus. She gave the patient an injection to make the uterus contract. But the bleeding continued and the patient became pale, weak and shocked. The midwife telephoned the hospital and within minutes the obstetric flying squad was on its way. It took 20 minutes of fast driving to reach the patient's house. The doctor at once assessed the problem. He set up a blood transfusion and gave a further injection. When the patient's condition had improved, he got the nurse to give an anaesthetic and explored the inside of the uterus with his hand, removing the missing piece of placenta. The bleeding then ceased. The patient was taken to hospital for observation. Her condition improved rapidly and she was discharged after three days. Since then she has had two more children. In certain nations, notably Malaysia, this service has been supplemented by the use of a helicopter air ambulance to bring in help and to evacuate the ill patient.

The central hospital is 'linked' to the district hospitals, and both are linked to a web network of prenatal clinics held in health centres or in doctors' offices or surgeries. In the developing nations the smaller clinics would be conducted by midwives, under supervision; the clinics in health centres by midwives or doctors, those in the hospitals by doctors and midwives. In this way the patient is 'screened' and can be transferred rapidly and safely to the next link in the chain should an abnormality arise in pregnancy or labour. At all levels of the chain, health education, nutritional information, child health care and motivation to family planning is undertaken by the appropriate person.

To be effective, the organization of the obstetric services demands that at all levels there is an awareness of the social problems of obstetrics, and the staff function as a co-ordinated team—specialist obstetricians, family doctors, and midwives working in a close relationship with frequent contacts, so that each knows his strengths and his limitations.

The medical profession in its turn would ensure that there were sufficient permanent senior trained nursing staff in the larger obstetric hospitals and, in the developing countries, that there was intensive training of sufficient midwives to work in the hospitals, the towns, the villages and the rural areas, so that one midwife was available to every 1,000 of the population.

They would try to make sure that facilities existed for all family doctors, who intend to care for pregnant women, to spend 6 months to 1 year after graduation in a selected, properly equipped and adequately staffed obstetric hospital, where continued education is possible. It is also recommended that all family doctors practising obstetrics return every 3 to 5 years for a 2 to 4 week organized course of instruction in the subject.

Both public, politicians and the medical profession would see that facilities for family planning and population control were provided in convenient locations so that the hazard of frequent, repeated childbearing was minimized. Such family planning information, advice and supplies are best introduced in the lying-in period, when patients are more motivated to accept birth control, or in conjunction with maternal and child health services. The death of a mother in pregnancy or childbirth is the greatest tragedy which can befall a family, and the reduction of the maternal mortality is one of the most important indications of the efficiency of the medical care provided in any country. It is a challenge which can be met, and is being met increasingly in all nations.

Singapore provides a good example of what can be done. Over 2 million people live on the island, which is only 585 km² in size. Most of the people are Chinese and live in the city, but 10 per cent are Malays living in rural conditions. In 1955, 8 mothers died in every 10,000 births; by 1967, this had fallen to 3 per 10,000 births, making the mortality rate as low as that of the U.S.A. Even more significant, the deaths of Malay mothers which in 1957 had been 41 per 10,000 births, had fallen to 6 per 10,000 births by 1965 (Fig. 13/2). This had been

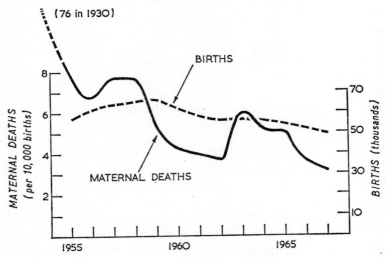

Fig. 13/2. The fall in maternal mortality in Singapore since 1930

brought about because the Government had taken maternity care to the people. Thirty-six antenatal clinics had been built, mostly in the rural areas with 'the objective of carrying health services to the people'. As well as this, all women had been encouraged to use the free maternity services. In 1967, the main maternity hospital delivered over 30,000 women. This is a world record for any hospital. In addition, the hospital and the clinics were supervised by highly qualified, well motivated staff, and a campaign to eliminate unwanted pregnancies by free birth control measures had been most successful.

Singapore is a model of what can be done to reduce maternal mortality. And because the women of Singapore know that they will be cared for in pregnancy, and that their child is likely to survive to reach adult life, they have readily accepted family planning as a health measure. The success of Singapore's attack on the deaths of women in childbirth has improved the Government's desire to control the rate of population growth. Other nations can learn from Singapore.

CHAPTER FOURTEEN

Unwanted, Often Unwelcome

I

By the time Gaye was ten days over, and feeling a bit sick, she knew that she was pregnant. She also knew that she couldn't be. Jim had said that he'd be careful, and he had said he knew what to do and she wasn't to worry. But now that her period hadn't come on time, she was worried. She was always so regular. Of course, it might be because she had just started at College. One of her friends had said that leaving home often upset your periods. It was the first time she'd been away from home properly, so that might be it.

It had been an effort to get to College. She was the first one in her family to have managed it. But then her teachers had always said she was an intelligent girl. Her parents had been so proud when she had got the Scholarship. They had gone round the village, almost crowing with delight. And for a village postmaster, who had married rather late in life, and who rarely showed emotion, the obvious joy at Gaye's success had been astonishing. Mum was a good woman, everyone said so, she worked hard, helping Dad in the shop, and she helped in the Church, but she never seemed to have had much time to talk, really talk, to Gaye. Gaye didn't really get on with her. Particularly not in the last year at school when Mum had insisted she was in by nine in the evening. When the other girls were out at the pictures, or with boys, Gaye had to be back at home. She was an attractive girl, too, tall and dark and slim. The other kids said she was stuck up. But what with Mum, and the work and everything, she had had a 'nervous breakdown' in the term before the exam, but she got over it and did so well in the exam that she was given a Scholarship to the College.

She'd liked College. The work was interesting, and the petty restrictions she had had at home were absent. She was treated as an adult. Then she met Jim.

More accurately, she saw him. She went to watch the local football team, and Jim was playing. He was the star of the team, and kicked both the goals. After that she went to most of the games, just to watch Jim.

By chance, quite by chance, she met him in the College. The desk in her room had come away from the wall, and the housekeeper had sent up a carpenter to fix it. He came when she was studying one afternoon. It was Jim. That's how it began. They got talking and he invited her out, and she went. They went out a good deal over the next few weeks, and she thought she loved him. And now she was ten days over, and she could be pregnant and she didn't know what Mum would say. But she hoped she wasn't. It could be going to College. She'd wait a bit longer just to see.

Nothing happened. Two weeks later she went to a doctor. He told her that she was pregnant. She knew she couldn't marry Jim, much as she liked him. She wanted to be a teacher and nothing was going to stop her. Marrying Jim would mean that she could never be a teacher. Anyhow, he didn't seem keen on marrying. He said he was prepared to stand by her, and support her emotionally, and see her as often as he could, but he wasn't going to marry her, at least not yet. He had been careful, he couldn't understand how she had got pregnant. Perhaps . . . but he left the rest unsaid. Gaye knew what he meant.

She went home and with great difficulty told her parents. As she expected, there was a scene. Mum flared up, Dad was silent but very upset. Both parents told her she couldn't come back to the village. The shame of having a pregnant daughter, and she not married, would be too much. They were quite adamant that no one in the village should know of it, not even the vicar. Gaye would have to go elsewhere.

She returned to the College sicker than ever. The doctor in charge of student health was sensible and able to communicate.

She suggested that Gaye went to the city, and made arrangements for her to see the social workers at the maternity hospital there. She also arranged that Gaye would be permitted to take a semester off from College, and then could return if she decided to have the baby adopted.

The comments of the social worker who helped Gaye summarize what happened:

'Gaye came down in April and was accompanied by her parents who were fairly silent, country people, I think embarrassed and upset by the whole situation. They agreed with any suggestions that were made, and Gaye was placed in a live-in position with a local vicar who lived with his wife and two small children fairly near the hospital.

'She started in the live-in job in May, knowing that she would probably be there about three months as the baby would be due in August. Then followed a very difficult time for Gaye. She became distressed, tearful, nervous, and couldn't sleep. The job was not a particularly arduous one, and she admitted that her employers were extremely nice to her, but she didn't like being in the job, as it was a confirmation of the situation in which she found herself. She was often aggressive to the antenatal clinic staff when she came up to the hospital, and thus brought the wrath of various members of the staff down about her own head. On one occasion she was brought up weeping because she'd refused to leave a specimen, and this sort of thing, which was very distressing for her. She was seen by a social worker regularly, and in July referred to the hospital psychiatrist as she really did seem to be extremely depressed, was not sleeping, and things were becoming very, very difficult for her. She found the psychiatric consultation helpful and supportive.

'She was delivered of a girl baby in late August, whom she surrendered for adoption. She was the usual short time in hospital, and then she returned home to the parents in the country. She found the adjustment to the loss of the baby rather difficult, particularly because as soon as she left hospital the father of the baby ditched her. He said that he had only really stood by her while she was pregnant in order to be of some support, but he didn't see any future in their relationship. At the same time as she was getting over this and also girding herself up to face her return to College, she had a visit from

Child Welfare Department officer who said the baby had not been progressing too well and might have to be made a State ward. This, coinciding with all the other difficulties, caused her to be very distressed and worried. Luckily, the baby did respond well in the Children's Hospital and was able to be placed eventually for adoption.

'By chance, in August of the next year, whilst I was on holiday in the area, I bumped into Gaye. She was looking very well, and although we couldn't have much of a conversation, she was apparently doing well at College, and looking forward to graduating in twelve months' time. I think that this particular patient's pregnancy was a very traumatic episode in her life. It interrupted her studies and did not end in a continuing relationship with the baby's father. She did very sensibly realize that in her circumstances adoption was wisest for the child, and this was able to be accomplished.'

2

For the past 150 years, in all European nations which have statistics, the age of puberty has been falling. In females, puberty is most readily identified as the onset of menstruation—the menarche. In 1840, the average age of the menarche was 16 to 17, by 1880 it had fallen to 15 to 16, and by 1970 it had fallen to between 12 and 13 (Fig. 14/1). The exact reason is unclear, but evidence suggests that it is due to better nutrition in infancy and childhood.

This earlier sexual maturity has coincided in the past decade with what is believed to be a greater sexual permissiveness by girls, and a lesser reluctance to talk about sex. The double standard of sexual behaviour, in which young men, and adult males, were encouraged, either overtly or covertly, to seek sexual intercourse, and to boast about their conquests, whilst girls were meant to be chaste, demure and virginal, has diminished in intensity. But it still persists. Many parents, particularly fathers, confide to their friends about their own, or their sons' sexual exploits, but are incensed if they thought their daughters copulated before marriage. In this the generation gap between today's youth, at least in the industrialized nations of Europe and North America, and their parents, is not a gap but chasm.

This changed attitude to premarital virginity has not bee preceded, or attended, by better sex education (includin education in sexual and family responsibility) or by better an more accurate knowledge about contraceptive practice. Th result has been a startling rise in extramarital pregnancy, par ticularly amongst teenagers.

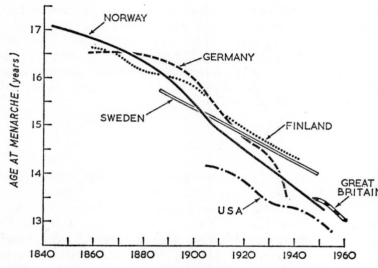

FIG. 14/1. The reduction in the age of the menarche. Source Tanner, J. M., *Growth in Adolescence*, 2nd ed., Blackwell, Londo by kind permission.

In this connection, teenage is taken to cover the period c years between the menarche and the eighteenth birthday. B the age of 18, physical maturity is largely complete, and intel lectual maturity is well advanced, although emotional maturit may not be reached for some years. Moreover, in many Wester nations, 18 is now legally the age when adult responsibilitie are accepted.

Statistics from the European nations and the U.S.A. shov that increasing numbers of teenagers are becoming pregnant For example, in 1960, 189,000 U.S. girls aged 13 to 17 gav birth; by 1965 the number had risen to 196,000; and by 1970 to over 200,000. In the same year, nearly 10 per cent of all births were to girls under the age of 17 and a significant proportion of these births were to unmarried girls.

In the U.S.A., Canada, Australia and Western Europe, be-

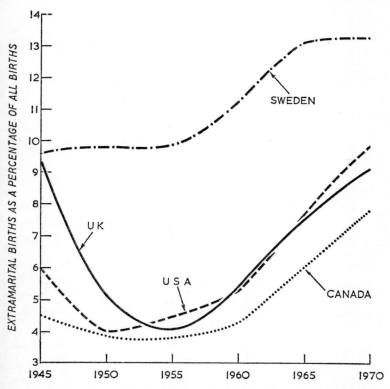

FIG 14/2. The increase in extramarital births in 'western' nations, 1945–70. Source: *Demographic Yearbook*, various years, U.N., New York.

tween 5 to 10 per cent of all births are to unmarried mothers, and in the past decade the proportion has been increasing (Fig. 14/2). For example, in England and Wales, between 1950 and 1965, the proportion of extramarital pregnancies rose from 5·1 to 7·5 per cent of all births and by 1970 it was 9·1 per cent. When the extramarital pregnancies were computed by age of

the mother, a startling rise amongst teenagers was noted (Fig
14/3).

These statistics must be interpreted with caution, and befor
they are accepted as indicating a gross decay in tradition:
Judeo-Christian moral standards in Western affluent nation:

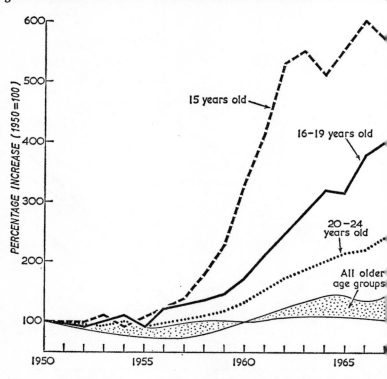

FIG. 14/3. The rise in the proportion of extramarital births t
teenagers in England and Wales since 1950.

greater scrutiny is required. The crude data make no allow
ance for the increasing number of teenagers. For example, i
the U.S.A., the number of young people, aged 15 to 19, in
creased from 13·2 million in 1960 to 19·0 million in 1970. ,
better index of teenage pregnancy is to calculate age-specifi
fertility rates (Fig. 14/4). These, you may remember, are th
ratio of pregnancies per 1,000 females in a particular age grou;
Age-specific fertility rates show that actually there has been

slight decline in the rates for American girls under 17 years of age in the decade 1960–70. This finding is the opposite of that in Britain and Australia, where age-specific fertility rates show an increase in natality of girls under the age of 18. However, in all three nations the number of births to teenagers has risen

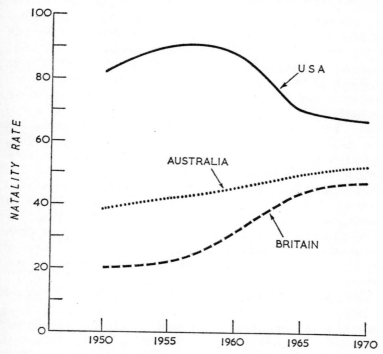

FIG. 14/4. Age-specific fertility rates of women aged 15 to 19 in Australia, Britain and the U.S.A., 1950–70.

proportionately in relation to the total national birth rate, because of the rather rapidly declining age-specific fertility rates for older women, due to the greater use of contraceptive measures in these age groups.

Professor Helen Wallace has summarized some of the social problems of teenage pregnancy and marriage in the U.S.A., and there is no reason to suspect that her findings are much different from those in Europe or Oceania. Basing her findings on the 1960 census, Wallace found that about 25 per cent of

the teenage mothers were unmarried and that between 40 and
60 per cent of marriages of teenagers were because of premarital
conception, which had to be followed, often because of family
pressures, by a hasty marriage.

These observations were confirmed in a study of births
occurring in the U.S.A. between 1964 and 1966. Dr. Kovar,
who did the investigation, found that more than one-third of
the pregnancies were conceived before marriage, but over half
of the mothers married before the baby was born. It was interesting to discover that when the ages of the mothers were
analysed, 42 per cent of babies born to mothers aged 15 to 19
were conceived before marriage, but in the 20 to 24 age group
the percentage had fallen to 14·5 percent, and after the age of
25 to 3 per cent. This gives proof that many of the marriages
were 'forced' by parents to avoid the scandal of illegitimacy,
and without the adolescents having established any real relationship with each other. The effect of this is also shown by
the U.S. and Australian divorce rates amongst couples aged
from 15 to 19. In the United States about 25 divorces or
annulments occur for every 100 marriages each year. The
divorce rate in the 15 to 19 age group is three or four times
higher than that of older age groups. In Australia in 1971, 38
per cent of marriages in which the girl was less than 20 years
old when she married, ended in divorce.

These harsh statistics emphasize the instability of teenage
marriage and stress the necessity for sex education (in the broad
sense of instilling sexual responsibility), and for information
about contraceptives to be given preferably just before, or just
after puberty. They also stress the need for marriage counselling
services to be made easily available to the particularly vulnerable group.

That this is important can be deduced from statistics obtained
from Scandinavia and in Eastern Europe, where the trend to an
increasing proportion of extramarital births has not occurred.
In the Scandinavian nations the proportion ranged between
8 and 11 per cent between 1930 and 1950, but since that time
has declined. In Finland, for example, 9·3 per cent of births
in 1940 were to unmarried mothers but by 1965 they had fallen
to 4·5 per cent.

The reason for the decline in Scandinavian nations and the

increase in other Western nations has been investigated by several authors, notably by Dr. Paavola. He comments that in Scandinavia 'increasing enlightenment, especially sex education, and the ensuing increasingly common use of contraceptives, have generally contributed to the decrease in the number of illegitimate births'.

In Britain, the free distribution of contraceptives to unmarried as well as married women, and men, has been opposed and branded as an incentive to promiscuity. There is no evidence that promiscuity would increase, and the social problems faced by the unmarried mother, and especially her child, would certainly be reduced if the number of extramarital pregnancies fell. There is also a financial benefit which might appeal to those who are too intolerant to see the social problem of the unwanted pregnancy. As I have mentioned, it has been estimated that in Britain 250,000 unwanted children are born each year; half of these children are born outside marriage. Each 'illegitimate' child will cost about £4,000 over the first sixteen years of its life in supplementary benefits, child care, temporary accomodation and health benefits. This compares with the £500 it is estimated to cost in family planning services, over the same period, to prevent a birth. This is a cost ratio of 8:1.

The social problems of the unmarried pregnant woman are largely confined to nations which are predominantly Christian in religion and Judeo-Christian in ethos. Even this generalization requires modification for consensual unions are not uncommon in Central and South America. In consensual unions, the couple do not marry but live together for a shorter or longer time. If the woman becomes pregnant and the association ceases, any children she may have are taken into the family group headed by the woman's mother. The frequency of consensual unions in Latin America was investigated by Dr. Mortara, who found that in the decade 1940–50, only one nation had less than 20 per cent consensual unions per 100 marriages. It is probable that the percentage is declining, but consensual unions still formed a significant proportion of marriages in those nations in 1970. Legally the children of such unions are illegitimate, but because the culture includes any such children in the family group, problems are minimal and neither mother nor child suffers social ostracism.

Unwanted, Often Unwelcome

In the non-Christian nations of Africa and Asia, unmarried mothers form only a minute proportion of all pregnant women, because the cultural traditions of Hinduism and Islam have strict laws against extramarital loss of virginity and most, if not all, girls are married within two years of puberty. Only those families who have received a predominantly Western orientated, Christian education, or who are Christian, do not follow this procedure. Moreover, amongst Hindu, Buddhist and Islamic nations, the culture insists on chastity in girls, and sexual permissiveness amongst females is uncommon, although males may, and do, have recourse to prostitutes.

Whilst proponents of traditional Judeo-Christian values of premarital chastity may agree that the Islamic attitude is highly moral, and consequently good, it has in it the seeds of evil. During the Indo-Pakistani war in Bangladesh, at least 200,000 girls and women were raped by the Pakistani troops. Because of Islamic insistence on premarital chastity, these women have been driven from their villages to swell the populations in the towns. Their only future can be servitude in ill-paid jobs, or prostitution.

China, alone of the Asian nations, seems to have reached a realistic position in the relationship between the sexes. It is one which demands great self-control and a national ethos of service. In China it appears that young people can work together, play together and enjoy each other's company without needing sexual intercourse to weld the partnership. The Chinese government has reversed traditional custom by requesting their citizens to delay marriage, so that now, on average, a man does not marry before the age of 26, or a woman before the age of 23. In addition, contraceptives are made readily available to delay the birth of the first child, and abortion on demand can be obtained. With the social attitudes and public health measures available, extramarital births in China are unusual.

Such evidence as there is indicates that in all the so-called developing nations, the problem of the unmarried pregnant woman is minimal, as few extramarital pregnancies occur, and those women who become pregnant are absorbed into a family group, the pregnant woman being treated as would any other in the group.

The situation in many of the developed nations is rather

different. The influence of the teachings of Aquinas on sexual attitudes in Roman Catholic countries, and that of Calvin on the puritan ethic in Protestant countries, places the unmarried mother at a considerable disadvantage, whilst the putative father suffers far less condemnation. It is surprising that people who continually preach Jesus' ethic of love, find it only too easy to harden their hearts, and to condemn a woman who is pregnant with an unwelcome, unwanted child. It is even more surprising that affluent nations, which can spend millions on weapons of destruction find it possible only to offer inadequate support to unmarried mothers and appear to expect them to lose all human dignity in pleading for that support, rather than being able to obtain it as a right.

3

The socio-medical problems of extramarital pregnancy fall with greatest severity on the teenaged unmarried mother. She is less mature emotionally, more frightened of breaking social conventions, and more dependent on others. The first and major problem is that she is more likely than an older woman, or a divorced woman who becomes pregnant, to conceal the pregnancy for as long as possible, so that prenatal care is often not sought until the second half of pregnancy, if at all. The second problem is that teenage diets tend to lack adequate quantities of protein. An investigation in Chicago of the diets of 1,000 girls who had conceived at the age of 16 or less, showed that nearly 45 per cent were classified as having 'poor' diets and only 30 per cent ate 'good' diets in which the protein, carbohydrate and mineral content was balanced and adequate. One American gynaecologist has complained that too many teenaged Americans eat diets which consist of potato chips, hamburger buns, Coca-Cola, hot dogs and pizza! Such diets are not particularly beneficial to proper fetal growth in utero, and there is suggestive evidence that protein deficiency of the baby in the womb, and in early life, may lead to mental retardation, or at least to reduced intelligence. The third problem is that complications of pregnancy and labour are found disproportionately amongst unmarried teenagers (when compared to all pregnant teenagers) particularly if the girl is in a lower socio-economic group, has a low intelligence, has left school at the earliest permissible age and is occupied in unskilled work.

Since the incidence of pregnancy complications is directly related to the quality of prenatal care received, it is obvious that the social agencies must expand to meet this problem and try to change opinion so that people regard concealment of pregnancy a greater social stigma than the occurrence of conception.

As I have mentioned, the teenaged, unmarried, expectant mother is particularly vulnerable to pregnancy complications if she does not avail herself of prenatal care. In the absence of prenatal care she is more likely to develop 'toxaemia of pregnancy' and anaemia. 'Toxaemia of pregnancy' is a misnomer for there is no toxin, and indeed the cause of the condition remains unknown, despite a great deal of research. The condition is characterized by a rise in the patient's blood pressure swelling of her legs and hands, and the appearance of protein in her urine. Not only is the disease dangerous to her unborn fetus but, in the worst form, it is dangerous to the life of the mother herself. Although the disease cannot be prevented good medical care can prevent the severe form from occurring Anaemia, amongst teenaged pregnant girls, is more common in the U.S.A. than in Europe, and is due to inappropriate dietary habits and a lack of education in nutrition. The unmarried mother is also more likely to give birth either prematurely or to a baby of low birth weight. Once again this is only likely if the girl fails to obtain care in pregnancy. In a study we made in Sydney, we found that problems only arose if the girl failed to obtain the psychological and medical support needed. If she did, then obstetrically her 'performance' was as good as, or superior to, that of her married sister aged 20 to 29.

4

Between 1930 and 1955, most writers about 'illegitimate' pregnancy tended to take the view that unmarried mothers were emotionally immature, were oversexed, had suffered a lack of maternal love and had been brought up in a deprived environment. Even as late as 1952, Bowlby could write, 'In a Western Community it is emotionally disturbed men and women who produce illegitimate children of a socially unacceptable kind. The girl who has a socially unacceptable illegitimate baby often comes from an unsatisfactory home background and has developed a neurotic character, the illegitimate baby being in the nature of a symptom of her neurosis.' Young, working in the U.S.A., concluded that although unmarried mothers came from all socio-economic groups and had a wide range of intelligence, they had similar mental problems. The main problem was that in most cases the girl had had a highly unsuccessful relationship with her mother, a poor relationship with her father, and there was frequently domestic disharmony. However, Young gave no information about the background of a group of controls, so that her conclusions cannot be validated. All these opinions must be criticized today, when sexual permissiveness is more common and extramarital pregnancy increasing. Should all those who have extramarital sexual relations be considered neurotic or 'oversexed'? If so, this will include over 50 per cent of all males and 40 per cent of all females aged 19 or more in Britain, Australia and the U.S.A. Or, should only those who fail to marry after extramarital conception be considered neurotic? Or, perhaps only those who fail to prevent pregnancy by using contraceptives or obtaining an abortion should be considered neurotic. And if the background of the unmarried parturient is so unsatisfactory, is this due to environment or to a poor genetic inheritance? If it is the latter, great concern should be felt as between 30 and 50 per cent of all babies born to unmarried parturients are adopted.

In the study we made in Sydney, Australia, we could find no evidence that unmarried pregnant women were more neurotic, were oversexed, had a greater degree of childhood instability, or had a higher level of sexuality than married expectant mothers. The only factors which seemed of importance was that the unmarried mothers had less sex education from their parents or at school, and their parents' attitudes to sex seemed to have been more rigid and strict. It was also apparent that although the girls had heard of contraception, the information was frequently erroneous, and most had not used reliable contraceptive measures, or had left 'protection' to the male partner.

Similar findings were reported by Dr. Weir of the Scottish Department of Health. Amongst the 228 unmarried mothers she investigated, there was no preponderance in any particular social class, promiscuity was unusual, and venereal disease rare. That the mental stability of the mothers was not disturbed can be deduced from the fact that 65 per cent of the mothers kept their babies, and on follow-up have been proved to make good parents.

The problem which faces the unmarried mother is the scorn which conventional society places on her, her fear of reproach, her fear of shame, and the anxiety that pregnancy may hold dangers because she has contravened convention. In 1950, the eminent American gynaecologists, Drs. Marchetti and Manaker wrote, 'We are convinced from our observations that the most important consideration to be given to the young pregnant girl lies in the management of her antepartum course. There are psychic as well as physical changes that must be borne in mind.'

Informed opinion today concludes that society is failing to meet the fundamental needs of adolescents. As was stated at a conference on *Mental Health of Adolescents and Young People* held in Stockholm in 1969, it was not they who were maladjusted, but rather it was society that had not adapted. It is difficult to ask teenagers to develop responsibility when society seems to be fragmenting, traditional values are being discarded and when national leaders are seen to be intellectually dishonest. It is particularly difficult for young people to maintain sexual responsibility when the mass media constantly emphasize that the relatively affluent adolescent should instantly gratify his or her desires, and much of the advertising uses pseudo-sexual motivations to encourage sales. Dr. Cobliner has observed that current social and cultural changes have had a marked impact on the number of teenage pregnancies. He notes that family and school have relaxed their control over the activities of adolescents and that now they have much more leisure time, but no knowledge of how to fill it. Since sexual permissiveness is a cultural trend, many experiment in sex, and seek to emulate group heroes who boast of their sexual exploits. The group of sexually active school children studied by Dr. Cobliner were of normal intelligence and had good scholastic performances, but lacked 'accurate information on sexual matters', a finding he considered conducive to extramarital pregnancy.

The unmarried mother, often sent away by her family because of their fear that the neighbours will talk, frequently emotionally disturbed because of new, and frightening changes in her physiology and her life-style, needs help. She needs explanation and consideration from her medical attendants, but even more she needs a friend. The role of informed friend and helpful counsellor can often be filled by the social worker. In our type of society the place of the social worker in the care of the unmarried mother may be crucial to her overcoming the ostracism and obstacles of extramarital pregnancy. The experience of my colleagues in the social work department of The Women's Hospital (Crown Street), Sydney, is unique, as the hospital cares for over 1,200 unmarried mothers each year. Their comments in discussions with me form the basis of the remainder of this section.

Pam Roberts, who heads the department, points out that the social worker is able to reduce the impact of the stigma of 'illegitimacy' placed on the adolescent by family and neighbours, or if the girl leaves home for the anonymity of the city, by her landlady. The social worker is a link with normality and friendliness, and can do much to reduce the 'shame' of being pregnant. She can help make the girl feel a worthwhile person. Since between 40 and 50 per cent of unmarried mothers-to-be intend to keep their baby, much counselling is required so that the girl can take a relatively 'dispassionate view of what is likely to be the best course in the child's long term interest'. But, one of Miss Roberts' colleagues points out, the girl must make the decision herself. It must not be made by the girl's parents. Many parents feel that extramarital pregnancy indicates that the girl is immature and incapable of making any decision. This must not be permitted, or a long-lasting period of instability may result.

Second, the social worker can ensure that the unmarried mother obtains financial support and, if living away from home, finds suitable accommodation. In this aspect her counselling can be invaluable. She, more than the girl, knows her way through the mysterious bureaucratic corridors which have to be negotiated before money is available.

Third, the social worker can help educate the girl in human sexual relationships and in contraceptive technology. One social worker reported, 'There is an alarming degree of confusion, superstition and ignorance regarding the nature, function and availability of contraceptives. This is reinforced by newspaper and magazine articles.' This educative function is of great importance in preventing a recurrence of extramarital pregnancy. The social worker can also help to resolve 'the confusion the girl feels by the conflicting values of her peer group, who may, and I think often do, condone premarital sex, and the values of her parents, who usually take a moralistic view of it.'

Both the Australian social workers and the British authors of an authoritative study of the children of unmarried mothers, *Born Illegitimate*, comment that educative measures need to be aimed at adolescents. This means that school curricula should include a course in human relationships, including sexuality and child development. This is especially important as many of the girls come from families which lack love, are broken, or in which the parents are in conflict. To quote one social worker from The Women's Hospital, 'Better sex education, I believe, means not only giving information about physical bodily functions and contraceptives, but also discussing the responsibilities one has in a relationship with someone else.'

An important preventive measure is to make sure that contraceptive advice and facilities are readily available for young people. There is no evidence that this leads to promiscuity. In fact, the opposite is apparent. Two studies in Britain, one amongst University students and the other amongst mainly working girls, showed that over 90 per cent of those who sought contraceptive advice had an enduring relationship with the man, and only 5 per cent had more than two partners in the period of the surveys.

It is also obvious, with a little thought, that the real victim of an extramarital pregnancy may be the unwanted child. Some will grow up unloved entirely; the majority, Dr. Crellin, one of the authors of *Born Illegitimate*, comments, 'will be reared in adverse environmental conditions which may then have long

332

term detrimental consequences in later life. As a result an (at present unknown) number will grow into alienated adults or inadequate parents of tomorrow.'

5

The majority of children born out-of-wedlock are first children born to young mothers, and most are the result of unwanted pregnancies. In recent years increasing numbers of unmarried mothers keep the child and attempt to rear it in a censorious cultural environment, usually with inadequate financial resources. In Australia, for example, about 45 per cent of unmarried mothers keep their child, and similar ratios are reported from Britain and the U.S.

The effect on the child of being 'born illegitimate' has been examined in Britain by Dr. Crellin and her colleagues, as I have mentioned. These investigators have followed the progress of children, born extramaritally, over the first seven years of their lives. Comparisons were made between children retained by their single mother, those adopted and a 'control' group of children of two-parent families. The results were disturbing. To support themselves, most of the single mothers were forced to go out to work, and the quality of the foster day care varied considerably. As well as this, the mothers tended to have a high mobility, changing jobs and housing frequently. Housing conditions were usually inadequate. Overcrowding was common, and decent domestic facilities lacking. The children had a higher mortality rate than the adopted or control children. Although there was no difference in physical growth, they were less advanced at the age of seven in all aspects of ability and attainment. Speech patterns were less developed, the children were more clumsy and had a poorer reading ability. In these early school years the children were backward in ability compared with the average, and were more often rated as unsettled or maladjusted by their teachers. Their mothers showed little or no interest in their educational progress.

In Dr. Crellin's investigation, it was not clear which of the factors she mentioned was the most detrimental to the emotional development of the child. Many psychiatrists believe that the main cause of emotional damage is the child's separation from its mother, although opinion is sharply divided. Mothering is, of course, important, and at the moment society penalizes the unmarried mother who keeps her child, as she is forced to go out to work to provide for it. The best evidence currently available is that the child will suffer no damage provided that the foster care is of a high quality, whether this is provided by a foster mother or at an infant day care centre. As Dr. Crellin mentions, and as was found in earlier studies, the children who suffer are those who have to go through a succession of unsatisfactory child minding arrangements.

Adoption of the child may be in its best interests, but there was no evidence in Dr. Crellin's study to show that the unmarried mother was incapable of successful child-rearing if she was given adequate social and financial support, rather than being treated as a 'fallen woman' deserving to be punished.

Unfortunately, in many Western nations, although not in Scandinavia, Eastern Europe or the U.S.S.R., the unmarried mother continues to be discriminated against financially if she chooses to keep her child.

Enlightened changes in the law regarding 'illegitimacy', and an improved social policy to help the unmarried mother who decides to keep her child, are needed.

In particular, she needs to be given the same financial security which is given to the widow, and to the deserted wife, and the State needs to make available well-staffed, adequately financed and properly supervised child care centres for those mothers who prefer to work.

At a time in history when the exponential growth of population is causing a potential threat to man's survival, it seems an anachronism that extramarital pregnancies still occur, and it is an indictment of our society that the children born to unmarried mothers are deprived of their full potential by a censorious society and by parsimonious Parliaments. In many Western societies, if it were possible to eliminate, or at least drastically reduce, the number of unwanted extramarital pregnancies the objective of zero population growth would be in reach of achievement. In addition, a considerable amount of human unhappiness would be eliminated. And since people are the concern of this book, that would be a most desirable objective.

CHAPTER FIFTEEN

Beyond Birth Control

It is precisely this blocking of alternative thinking and experimentation that makes emphasis on family planning a major obstacle to population control. The need is not to abandon family planning programs but to put equal or greater resources into other approaches.

'Population Policy',
KINGSLEY DAVIS, 1967

I

Even with the most easily available, efficient contraceptive technology, ultimately, the success or failure of a campaign to reduce the birth rate, and to make sure that every child is a wanted child, will depend on the private decision made by millions of couples or individuals. Although, within limits, the decision may be influenced by rewards or punishments, success will only result if the ultimate choice made by a man and a woman is *not* to have an additional child.

Since by far the highest proportion of the people who have to make the decision are poor, middle-class attitudes and values may be inappropriate. To a middle-class couple the reason for delaying conception, or deciding to have no additional children, is based on a reasonably informed opinion, by people who consider planning a necessary factor in many aspects of life, and who have the capacity to wait for the gratification of a need. To many of the poor these attitudes are unaccustomed and luxurious. The women tend to be fatalistic, resigned and more concerned with the present than the future. They want immediate gratification as, all too frequently, calls by authority for them to defer their request have meant that what they sought was never acquired.

In Western societies there is an additional and important factor. This is that an increasing number of pregnancies occur to single girls, and add a large fraction to the total of unwanted, unwelcome pregnancies which occur within marriage. In 1972, in Australia, 26,000 babies were born to unmarried women, in Britain the number was 125,000 and in the U.S.A. it was over 350,000.

Success in any campaign to reduce the rate of population growth depends on two simultaneous approaches. The first is to induce new attitudes about the desirability of having many children, in other words to alter people's attitudes towards their fertility. The second is to make available birth control measures which, if used throughout the population, will ensure that every pregnancy is a wanted pregnancy, and every child is a wanted child. In this chapter those measures which seek to achieve the second aim will be considered, although I believe that the attitudinal changes engendered by adoption of the norms of folk-heroes or trend-setters, and those induced by anti-natalist taxation, need to be more widespread if the goals of a zero population growth, or at least a markedly reduced growth rate, are to be reached. There is a difference between population control and birth control. Population control is the regulation of family size by a society; birth control only regulates the size of individual families who have complete freedom of choice about fertility. Until the attitude of society is changed so that women want fewer children (both in the affluent developed nations and in the hungry developing nations), progress to a markedly reduced rate of population growth will be slow; and those most likely to adopt the new attitudes will be the more affluent women within a nation.

At this time there is an increasing desire by women to limit the size of their family. This is a recent phenomenon. Until about 1880 in the developed nations, and until 1930—50 years later—in the hungry developing nations, high fertility was the desired norm. This was because high infant and childhood mortality reduced the number of children a woman would be able to rear to puberty. When, on average, one in every three children died in infancy and childhood, and when custom demanded two or more sons, a woman needed to have between six and eight children which meant ten or more pregnancies. Today, when infant and childhood mortality has fallen to less than 100 per 1,000 live births in all the developed nations and in many developing nations, a couple can achieve their desired family size by having fewer children, confident that most will survive. Moreover, the introduction of compulsory education, at least to the age of twelve, has reduced the economic value of numerous children. They are no longer potential producers, but are actual consumers.

That the attitudinal change to smaller families is slow, particularly in rural areas, is not unexpected, as the requirement for large families is a product of 10,000 years of tradition. Some 10,000 years ago man learned to cultivate grains and to domesticate animals. With settlement came territoriality; with territoriality came conflict with other tribes. Over the next 5,000 years, as more and better food was produced, more children survived (although the infant mortality must have been extremely high), and children became valued increasingly. The larger the tribe the more hands there were to cultivate the soil and to herd the animals; the more males, the stronger the tribe was to resist attacks; the more females, the larger the annual birth rate. A pronatalist attitude had begun: children became valuable.

Today, conditions have changed dramatically. As a consequence of the impact of environmental sanitary engineering, the improvement of supplies of uninfected water, the better distribution of foodstuffs, the introduction of insecticides which have reduced insect-borne diseases, such as malaria, and the effect of modern medical techniques, which include vaccines and antibiotics, few infants or children die. Never before have so many children reached puberty. This has led to the 'population explosion'. But it has also led, however tentatively, to a change from the cultural pronatal attitude of the past.

The change from pronatalist beliefs has been accepted by the more affluent sections of a society for some time, but it is only now permeating to reach the underprivileged, the poor and the fatalistic. Yet the evidence is that it is reaching them too. In recent years, several organizations, notably the Population

337

Council and the I.P.P.F. have conducted surveys in many
nations to try to find out from women how many children they
actually had, and how many they considered ideal. These surveys are called KAP studies—from the initial letters of the

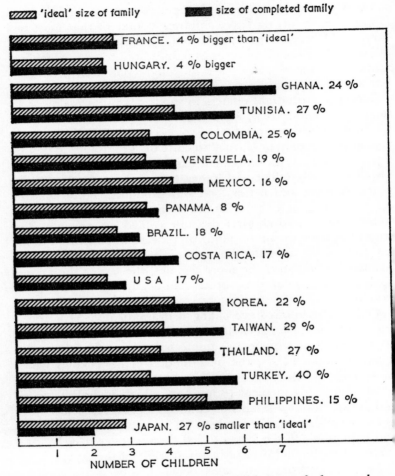

FIG. 15/1. The actual number of children, and the number
woman considered 'ideal' to have, shown in KAP studies. Source
Bernard Berelson, 'KAP Studies on Fertility', in Bernard Berelso
et al., *Family Planning and Population Programs*, University of Chicag
Press, 1965.

words knowledge, attitudes and practice in matters of fertility. Dr. Berelson, who pioneered KAP studies, admits that they are not easy to organize and that the validity of the answers depends, largely, on the ability of the interviewer. KAP studies in a number of nations show that there is a considerable desire to limit family size. Some results are shown in Fig. 15/1 and Fig. 15/2.

MOROCCO 1966
MALAYSIA 1966
BANGLADESH 1968
INDONESIA 1968
PHILIPPINES 1963
COLOMBIA 1963
FRANCE 1966
TAIWAN 1970
USA 1965
THAILAND 1967
VENEZUELA 1963
BELGIUM 1966

10   30   50   70   90
PERCENTAGE OF WOMEN WHO WANT NO MORE CHILDREN

FIG. 15/2. The desire of women to restrict the size of their family, shown in KAP studies. Source: *Studies in Family Planning* **2**, 68, 1972, Table 15B.

Another, perhaps more accurate, method of examining the problem is to try to determine which of a woman's children were unwanted at the time of conception. This is calculated by subtracting the number of unwanted births from the total number of births. From, this, the ideal (or desired) number of children can be deduced. In one study in the U.S.A., this method indicated that women really had wanted fewer children than had been shown in KAP studies. It was significant, too, that the number of unwanted births was much higher amongst the poor than the non-poor, amongst the less educated than amongst the better educated, amongst blacks than amongst whites, and amongst both groups as family size increased. In the U.S.A., 34 per cent of fourth births, 44 per cent of fifth births and 50 per cent of sixth births, or higher, were unwanted in the years 1960 to 1965.

There is some suggestive evidence from KAP studies that the American findings may apply to other nations. The importance of these analyses is that they indicate that in many nations there is a widespread desire amongst women to have fewer children, and if this desire can be stimulated, a considerable reduction of the birth rate should result.

Essentially there are three methods to achieve control of population growth. The first is nihilistic. It is to wait until social and economic change, by increasing the urban population and by more rapid industrialization, leads to a change in attitude to natality, which is what happened during the nineteenth century in the European nations.

This is the approach of those who, like John Maddox, the ex-editor of *Nature*, believe that technology and economics will solve all the problems of the world. He notes that western industrialized nations solved their rate of population growth by increasing urbanization and industrialization between 1790 and 1880, even when birth control methods were primitive and inefficient. From this he argues that nations, which today have a high rate of population growth, can undergo this change, without any direct attack being made on the main problem, that of high fertility. Unfortunately for the nihilists, the demographic situation in the nineteenth century is not really comparable with that of today. First, in the nineteenth century, the scale of population growth was much less, and in no nation did it exceed 1·3 per cent per annum. This meant that the population doubling time in Europe was 54 years in the nineteenth century. Today the population growth rate in most developing nations is over 2·5 per cent which leads to a doubling of the population in less than 28 years. Second, in the nineteenth century the death rate of infants and children were more than twice that of today, and in most nations today it is still falling. Third, excess population in the nineteenth century in Europe led to pressures on land and on food supplies, which were overcome by emigration to the vast, empty lands of North America, Oceania and, to a lesser extent, Latin America. Today the opportunity for emigration to solve a nation's population problems is very limited, as was shown in Chapter 5.

There is grave doubt in the minds of most population experts that there is time for the nihilistic approach to population problems to be effective in the last quarter of the twentieth century. In addition, the nihilistic approach will tend to increase the utilization of scarce mineral and water resources, and to aggravate environmental pollution.

The second approach is to educate people so that their attitudes to fertility alter, and an ideology glorifying small families is developed. This implies that the leaders of society will have to take the lead in encouraging this new attitude. Stycos has written about the problem in Latin America. He has pointed out that amongst the leaders of the 290 million people, three main groups can be identified. The first are the conservatives, who are concerned with preserving existing society, and who hold that people make a nation strong. They reluctantly concede that social change must occur, but resist its onset, and are more concerned with suppressing any revolutionary tendencies. On rational grounds the conservatives might be expected to encourage family planning as this would reduce the social expenditure required for young dependants, without unduly diminishing the labour force of peasants and unskilled workers. The reality is different. The conservatives are split in their attitudes because of their identification with the hierarchy of the Roman Catholic Church. Although many of them use birth control measures themselves, they would oppose the dissemination of contraceptive knowledge and appliances to the mass of the people.

The second group are the revolutionaries who seek violent revolutionary change. If they fail to achieve this, they are anxious that the conservative *status quo* is maintained since it encourages revolution, as the expectations of the people are increasingly ignored. In their opinion social reform, by offering some amelioration of living for the mass of the people, will delay the ultimate revolution. In theory they should reject any population, or birth, control, but since most are Marxist in philosophy they support it to some extent, in so far as birth control leads to the emancipation of women.

The third group comprises the social reformers who wish to see social change brought about by peaceful means, but accept that if this is not possible, revolution is better than the *status quo*. This group is mainly middle-class in attitude, and supports both population and birth control to a large extent, although their attitudes are influenced by the dicta of the Roman Catholic Church.

If the experience of Latin America can be extrapolated to other developing nations, considerable effort will be required to induce attitudinal changes amongst the leaders of many nations, although as will be seen in the next section, attitudinal changes are occurring at an increasing rate amongst them and amongst women of all classes within the countries.

The third approach is not to seek to motivate leaders, or individual women and their husbands, but to make contraceptive technology so easy, and the appliances so readily available, that no motivation is required. Obviously increased research to produce the 'perfect contraceptive' is desirable, even though the goal is unlikely to be achieved. But merely to rely on technology without inducing attitudinal changes is unlikely to be successful.

From this it would appear that the most successful approach is a multiple one. Efforts must be made to change the ideology of the nation's leaders, and of the people, to one of desiring small families. Concurrently, efforts must be made to enable women who have made the ideological change to achieve their new goals with the minimal inconvenience to their social and sexual life.

2

The goals of a birth control campaign can be stated quickly and simply. The first goal is to inform all the people that the current exponential growth rate of population threatens the individual family and all mankind, but that methods are available for couples to make a choice about the size of their family so that the threat recedes. The second goal is to motivate most couples to try, and to continue to use, whichever method they find most appropriate.

Although a few couples, mostly of the more affluent section of society, will choose to use birth control methods after seeking information themselves, the mass of the people will only make the decision if they know that the Government and national and local leaders approve, support and encourage population control.

Leaders of different nations have different political and social philosophies, and each nation may have to use a different strategy to reach its goals. For example, in the communist world, the idea that population growth is outstripping food and resources is not acceptable. Marx, in attacking Malthus whose writing he detested, had written, 'This is a law of population peculiar to the capitalistic method of production; and, in fact, every method of production that arises in the course of history, has its own, historically valid, law of population. It is only for plants and animals that there is a law of population in the abstract, and that only in so far as man does not interfere with them.' This statement shows that Marx held that the dangers of rapid population growth were due to capitalism, and that all population problems would disappear under communist methods of production. There is considerable doubt today if this is true, but communist leaders accept Marx's philosophy. However, they also accept control of population growth for the valid reason that it offers true emancipation to women. This approach is particularly shown by China, as will be seen later.

In other nations family planning as such is unacceptable, but it is welcomed when it is offered in existing programmes of maternity and child health. The argument is that if births are spaced, both the health of the mother, and that of her last born child, are improved. This is particularly important in nations where the newborn child displaces the last born at the breast. If taboos exist about what foods may be eaten after weaning, the displaced child is at high risk of developing protein malnutrition, and kwashiorkor. Family planning, linked with maternity and child health care, implies family welfare in the broad sense. Family welfare is an acceptable goal of the leaders and people of several African nations, whilst birth control is not, and indeed is opposed on political grounds. This

343

statement simplifies the African experience. In the Islamic nations north of the Sahara, family planning is accepted and acceptable, as it is in the independent nations which were previously under British colonial rule. In the former French and Spanish colonies, and in the existing Portuguese colonies, birth control is not permitted, but family welfare (including family spacing) is becoming an important concept. In the two nations of Africa which were never under colonial rule, Ethiopia and Liberia, family planning is accepted but not encouraged, whilst in the white minority dominated nations of Southern Africa family planning is encouraged, but not fully accepted by the African majority.

In most Asian nations, family planning is encouraged as part of Governmental policies to control the rate of population growth, and considerable efforts are being made to increase the number of accepters. In Singapore and Mauritius, for example the free discussion of population dynamics and birth control is encouraged. In the majority of Asian nations a more direct approach to birth control may be made without shocking the cultural norms of the people.

In still other nations, the most suitable approach may be to seek to eliminate all unwanted births both outside and within marriage. Such an aim implies that widespread contraceptive knowledge and appliances are made available for women (and men) within the community. This is the currently favoured approach of those interested in population problems in Britain and in the U.S.A. In these two nations the reproductive growth rate is 0·5 and 0·9 per cent per annum respectively, implying a population doubling time of 145 and 85 years. And in both nations the population growth rate is falling as increasing numbers of women in the 15 to 24 age group decide to have no more than 2 children. Amongst most national leaders in both countries there is a desire to obtain a still lower reproductive growth rate, and a way in which this might be achieved with little disturbance would be to eliminate unwanted pregnancies. In the U.S.A., it has been calculated that between 1960 and 1965 about 900,000 births each year were unwanted, and calculations in Britain showed that about 150,000 unwanted births occurred annually between 1965 and 1969. These figures may be underestimated. Jaffe, writing about the situation in the

344

U.S.A., suggests that the majority of these births could have been prevented if several measures were intensified. These are, to increase educational programmes in family planning, population dynamics, family life and sexuality in schools, to remove the legal, administrative and cultural barriers which prevent birth control measures being provided to unmarried persons, to ensure that such measures are readily and easily available through a network of family planning services to those married persons who desire them, and to repeal anti-abortion laws so that abortion is available to those women who become pregnant by ill-luck or ill-management.

3

For a birth control campaign to succeed it is essential to mount a programme of information in which the full use is made of radio and newspapers. In this campaign the advantages of family planning are stressed. This has the effect of making the whole programme legitimate and acceptable to traditionally conservative people. For greater impact, trained informed workers must start to talk to couples on an informal, person-to-person, basis. There is a distinct advantage in using existing communication networks. This means that, where possible, local people are involved, and local key people are activated to do the work. The information campaign requires to be repeated at intervals, but with variations, otherwise its impact is diminished.

In many affluent nations, despite superficial sophistication and so-called civilization, there are taboos on discussion of sexuality. These taboos need to be broken so that education can also be given in schools, and community centres, in concepts of family welfare, and the relationship to it of population growth, human sexuality and family planning.

In most of the developed nations, the predominantly Judeo-Christian ethic tends to regard sexuality as a forbidden topic for discussion in schools. The argument is advanced that sexuality, family life and family planning are matters for parents to tell their children, despite the obvious fact that the majority of parents are insufficiently informed themselves, or unwilling to communicate with their children. It is held that teachers, in

345

the last years of primary school and the first years of secondary school, are incapable of teaching such a 'delicate' matter, and this is the period when the information should be given to the children. This argument is, in part, true, but teachers training programmes can be altered easily to include the subject, and 'in-service' courses can be arranged for graduate teachers without undue difficulty.

The main problem is that the adults, not the children, are embarrassed that sexuality should be taught at school. When they hear the word 'sex' they react like Pavlov's dog at food. It makes them salivate with disgust. Children are much more rational, and are anxious to know about sexuality. Yet, even today, in most so-called advanced nations, discussions about sexuality are banned in schools. And this is occurring at a time when each year one baby in ten is born to an unmarried mother.

Social workers in Australia, Britain and the U.S.A. who interview unmarried mothers, report again and again that their clients were misinformed about contraception, or had had constraints which had prevented them obtaining contraceptives. They report further that most unmarried girls are relatively ignorant about human reproduction, about sexuality and about sexual responsibility. In a large number of cases pregnancy occurred because of lack of knowledge. It would seem that this disgraceful situation could, and should, be remedied rapidly.

The objectives should be two-fold. Firstly, to ensure that every child in the country, starting at the age of 8, is given information about human sexuality, about human reproduction, and about sexual responsibility. This information should be given in courses of human biology, which would continue through the last years of primary school and through high school. The courses would include information on population problems, on ecology and on the environment, but throughout the course, human sexuality and sexual responsibility would receive stress. And since sexual responsibility implies avoidance of unwanted pregnancies, contraceptive technology would be discussed.

There are old ladies of both sexes who will attack this suggestion claiming that it will lead to moral decay, to promiscuity and to a weakening of the national moral fibre. There is no objective evidence that this is so. They will also claim that this sort of knowledge should be imparted to children by their parents. This may be so, in an ideal society. But in most Western societies most parents fail. Most parents feel that sex is something sinful, that the human body is obscene and that any mention of sexuality is indecent. In this there is a generation chasm. Misinformation about sexuality is exchanged inside and behind the lavatories of every primary school in the country. Misinformation about sexual responsibility is exchanged in every sports changing room in every secondary or high school (public or private school) in the country. It would seem more sensible to give accurate information within the schoolroom, rather than permit the existing pattern of miseducation to persist.

In the developing nations the situation is more complicated. In the traditional extended family, human sexuality was observable and in tribal societies puberty rites included information about sexuality, and sexual responsibility. With increasing urbanization, the impact of the extended family is diminishing and the transmission of sexual information has become limited. The remedy is difficult. Not only is there a shortage of trained teachers, particularly teachers trained to conduct courses in family welfare, but not all children (and especially not all girls) obtain formal primary education, and only a few continue to secondary education. Since there is little premarital sexuality, it can be argued that the information would be forgotten by the time it was needed. Experience in the few nations which have introduced programmes suggest that this is not so. A further argument is that the school is not an appropriate place for the transmission of such knowledge. The objective of education is to transmit a limited knowledge, and to enable the child to obtain some academic skills. Yet schools in many developing nations have additional objectives, one being to enhance the potential of the individual as well as helping society as a whole. Already in many nations, the elements of hygiene, nutrition and agricultural skills are taught. Family welfare, including population dynamics and family planning, could be introduced with little difficulty, except that a curriculum, already crowded, would be filled still more, unless some other subject was given less teaching time.

Clearly, much thought must be given in each nation, by educational leaders and others, on the desirability of modifying existing curricula to permit the introduction of courses of instruction in population dynamics, human sexuality and family planning and their relationship to family welfare. No outsider can help except in an advisory capacity, but indigenous doctors and other health workers in the field of family welfare can be of great assistance to educational planners. And it is likely that the effect of such programmes, in primary and secondary schools, would yield considerable benefits by making the concepts which lead to a reduced birth rate more readily acceptable.

The goals of such an educational programme do not necessarily include information about specific family planning methods, although it may. However, if the 35 to 45 per cent of the population under the age of 15 in the developing nations, and the 20 to 30 per cent in the developed nations, are made aware of concepts affecting population control, birth control and family welfare, the technical data required later will be more readily accepted, and the methods more readily adopted.

In the developing nations, particularly, the information obtained in schools needs to be supplemented by further information given in community centres, to pregnant women during the prenatal period and in child health care clinics. This is because so many girls fail to obtain schooling, or drop out before the information has been given.

During pregnancy the women are 'captive' and are more likely to accept instructional information because they are thinking about the care of their unborn child. In the developing nations, particularly in rural areas, the traditional midwife can play a valuable part in spreading family planning information, and in reinforcing information previously obtained. The importance of using child health clinics to inform mothers about family planning is emphasized by the finding that ten times as many mothers attend such clinics as go to postnatal clinics.

The third essential of a successful campaign is to encourage the participants to promote the method they had adopted. People are more likely to try a method if an acquaintance has already used it successfully. This is an adaptation of the well-known sales trick of producing satisfied customers. This method

348

is encouraged if a well-developed 'after sales service' is provided. Many women who have decided to use oral contraceptives or who have had an intra-uterine contraceptive device inserted, experience side-effects and require reassurance that these will pass, and that they are innocuous. Such women may become disappointed or dissatisfied participants unless they have the opportunity to discuss their problems with sympathetic, un-hurried, uncondescending health workers. For a campaign to succeed it is essential that health workers involved in family planning programmes are trained in this area of communication. As the then Population Council Representative in Korea, Paul Hartman, wrote in 1965, 'In the most practical sense, service is our most important product'. It has been argued that this service should extend to problems of infertility and child health. There is considerable incentive in many developing nations to integrate family planning services in maternity and child health services, to offer a service of family welfare.

4

The evidence, stressed repeatedly through this book, is that the world must seek to reduce the rate of population growth to zero, so that each nation obtains a stable population in as short a time as possible. Even if all resources were mobilized, even if all pronatalist attitudes changed, even if mankind suddenly became rational, the 2-child family is unlikely to be the norm in the developed nations before 1995 and in the developing nations for a further 10 to 20 years. Many of those who will want to have children after 1995 are already born, so that further growth of the world's population after the 2-child family has been generally adopted, will occur. The age structure of the population, which was discussed in Chapter 3, makes it inevitable, in the absence of famine, pestilence or war, that the world will ultimately have a population of at least 10,000 million, and perhaps one of 15,000 million. Provided the affluent nations accept a lower standard of living, so that the hungry nations may reduce their poverty, unemployment and malnutrition; provided we use ecologically sensible methods for the production of food and manufactured goods; provided we take action to reduce environmental pollution, mankind can just cope with this plethora of people. It will be painful, and hard. It is essential that the population really stabilizes at a 2-child family as soon as possible, and that couples are encouraged to have one or no children. This means going beyond birth control. To go beyond birth control, men and women will have to accept, one hopes unselfishly, that knowledge about sexuality, freely available, easily obtained contraceptives, and 'back-up' legal safe abortion, may not be sufficient. More may be needed.

The extra element needed is motivation. And voluntary motivation may not be enough.

Psychologists believe that most humans live in a system of rewards and punishments, one or other of which is obtained after any action. Break the law and you are punished; act in accordance with conventional custom and you are rewarded. Buck the system and you will probably have sanctions imposed upon you. Men, therefore, tend to act to obtain the reward and to avoid being punished.

To many people, who are socially responsible in other ways, any suggestion that they should limit the size of their family is considered an infringement of their liberties. Their right to choose the size of their family must not be interfered with. The appeal to their reason appears to be insufficient, their motivation is based on a pronatal cultural inheritance, when children were a sign of a man's virility and a safeguard against a lonely old age. Today's exploding population growth rate, and its probable consequences, make this pronatalist attitude obsolete.

One would like to believe that man is rational. The evidence of the twentieth century indicates that he is not. He is emotional, he is aggressive, he is prejudiced, he is selfish. Were he rational and unselfish he would see the twin problems of exponential population growth and exponential ecologically unbalanced economic growth. And he would act by reducing both.

But he is irrational, and if he persists it may be necessary to apply rewards and sanctions to ensure a reduction in the rate of population growth. For the measures beyond birth control to be acceptable and effective, the rewards must be obvious, the sanctions administratively simple. And since we live in a money economy, perhaps they should have an economic character.

The objective is to replace each death with a new birth, but to discourage profligate fertility. Since, on average, the two-child family meets this objective, maternity allowances, paid maternity leave, children's allowances and educational subsidies should continue to be paid for the two children needed. In other words, the parents would be rewarded.

But any births above the two would be discouraged by sanctions. These sanctions must not penalize any children above two, who are alive, or who have been conceived, prior to their imposition. The children are innocent of their parents' anti-social act, and must have the full opportunity to develop their potential.

The sanctions must also be equitable and avoidable. This means that all the available contraceptives must be freely advertised and freely available, and that legally induced abortion must be available as a 'back-up'. It also implies that all the people are educated about population dynamics, human reproduction and sexual responsibility.

So that the sanctions are equitable it means that a couple should be sure that their existing, or proposed, children should have a very high chance of reaching adult life. This implies education in nutritional practices and health measures, and the provision of high quality medical care in pregnancy and for child health, which is free at the point of consumption.

For the sanctions to be equitable, it also implies that adequate social support for the aged is guaranteed, so that their current reliance (even in many affluent nations) on financial support from their children is reduced, or eliminated. This means that a nation should provide realistic retirement pensions and health care even if it means diverting capital from the conspicuous consumption activities of armaments (most nations), subsidies for ailing uneconomic uncompetitive industry (Australia); the prestige projects of the space race (U.S.A. and U.S.S.R.); or nuclear development (France).

The sanctions would also require to be publicized widely so that adolescents and those couples about to marry and become potential parents may make a choice. And so that there would be a real choice, there should be the opportunity by education, and job opportunities, for women to take roles alternative, or supplementary, to marriage and domesticity, so that child-bearing faced competition, beyond the kitchen.

The first specific sanction would relate to the retirement pension. Only those couples who restricted their children to two or less would be entitled to the full pension. Each child above two would reduce the pension payable. A couple could choose. There would be no compulsion. The equity of the proposal is that as the community largely bears the cost of educating and providing health care for children, it should not be doubly burdened by providing a full pension for a socially selfish couple.

To reward further those choosing to have only two children, interest-bearing insurance bonds could be established. Should either parent die, the bond would provide financial support to the surviving spouse and any child still undergoing education. Should the couple remain childless, or have only the target number of children, the insurance would be payable in full when the wife reached the age of 45. The amount would be considerable. But if the couple had more than two children, the amount would be reduced for each additional child by 50 per cent or some such figure.

It is realized that this does not solve the problem of the baby born out of wedlock, or of the couple who have a desire for a son, and fail to get him in the target number of pregnancies. One suggestion for dealing with this dilemma is the decichild coupon. Every girl on reaching the age of 15 would be entitled to 20 child coupons. If she decided to have two children she would give up 10 child coupons after each birth. But 10 per cent of women do not marry, and 15 per cent of couples fail to have children, so that a woman wanting more than two children could buy child coupons from those prepared to sell. A woman who had more than two children because of her purchase of child coupons from other women, would not have the insurance or the retirement pension reduced. Equally, an unmarried mother who did not wish to keep her child, would surrender 10 decichild coupons on its birth, but would gain 10 coupons from its adoptive mother.

There are, of course, many other strategies. In fact, Bernard Berelson, the Director of The Population Council, lists twenty-nine and then rejects them all in favour of voluntary family planning.

I would like to believe that people knowing the facts of the exponential rate of population growth and knowing its consequences, would be sufficiently involved in mankind to voluntarily control their fertility, and to have no more than two children. I would like to believe that Governments would enable them to achieve their desire by providing contraceptive information and appliances freely, and easily available to all who need them.

But it may not be enough, and on this the penultimate day of exponential population growth, perhaps we will have to look beyond birth control.

5

One nation, and a vital one, in the world today seems to have made a large dent on their rate of population growth. That nation is China.

Because of its relative isolation from other nations until recently, the Chinese experience in family planning has not been widely reported. Yet, as China is the world's most populous nation, her experience is of exceptional importance.

The objective of China's national family planning programme is to secure healthy mothers and healthy children, to create time during which women can work and study, to provide facilities for the education of all children, and to regulate family size because of its impact on the economy.

Because it was realized that the earlier the age of marriage, the higher the fertility, efforts have been made to raise the age at marriage. In China, as a whole, the average age of women at marriage is now 25 in the urban areas, and 23 in the rural areas. Before marriage, there is considerable mingling of the sexes, but without any obvious sexuality. Companionship appears to be possible without copulation and conception.

To delay, or to prevent pregnancy, China has made available a whole range of birth control devices, and has widely publicized their use. The people have the knowledge that their leaders, from Chairman Mao Tse-Tung down, approve of family spacing. The Chinese have also ensured that the contraceptives are readily, and easily, available to all who want them. These services are provided free.

Condoms are available at no cost from family planning workers, or can be purchased. Oral hormonal contraceptives and IUDs are widely available at no cost, and widely used. Injectable hormonal contraceptives are being offered increasingly. Abortion is available (with certain restrictions) in the urban hospitals and in each of the 70,000 commune hospitals. Most are performed using the suction curette which was developed in China. For couples who wish for permanent methods of fertility control, vasectomy and tubal ligation is available, often under acupuncture analgesia.

What marks the outstanding nature of China's family planning programme is the strong emphasis given to the initiative and self-reliance of the people themselves. The programme relies on an infrastructure of education, considered rational discussion and the free availability of all birth control methods. There is no element of compulsion in the programme, nor have the sanctions mentioned earlier been required.

The self-reliance of the programme has been emphasized by the Western Pacific Regional Secretary of the International Planned Parenthood Federation (a non-political organization), who visited China in April, 1972. Mr. Katagiri points out that the clinical investigations, and adoption of new techniques, are based on studies made in the major hospitals. In many cases the doctors, nurses and social workers (who are over 90 per cent women) have been the first to try the new methods. 'This method of testing new techniques is both a socially responsible one, because this group of people will be best trained to observe adverse side-effects early, and is also of great motivational significance because it means that the methods which are passed on to the community have been tried by the workers, and they themselves have confidence in them.'

Perhaps even more significant, in a predominantly rural nation, is the unique core of health workers, 'the bare-foot doctors', who are recruited from the community in which they will work. They are given training in health techniques, including birth control. As they belong to the community they are readily able to communicate with their neighbours. They initiate educational sessions, and do 'face to face' motivation. They have contraceptives available for immediate distribution, and have been trained to put an IUD in the womb of a woman

354

who chooses the method. In addition, they counsel the patients, and assist the qualified doctors in legal abortions, in sterilizations and in introducing IUDs. They are always available to answer questions and to reduce doubts about family planning.

The success of China's campaign cannot yet be fully assessed, because of lack of data, but it seems that considerable progress has been made to reach the target of a less than 1 per cent per annum population growth rate by the year 2000.

Mr. Katagiri said on leaving China, 'Under the guidance of Chairman Mao, more than 700 million people in China are doing an experiment never before attempted in human history, an experiment not only in family planning, but also in every aspect of human existence. Mankind awaits the results.'

Not only in China, but in all the nations of this very small planet, mankind's survival depends on a rational approach to population control. But with good sense, and a bit of luck, we who live on this small planet will survive. If we act now. The choice lies in our hands.

References and Notes

Page | Chapter 1: The Problem of People

19–22   MEADOWS, D. *Limits to Growth*. Potomac, Washington, 1972.

21   BOYD, R. 'World Dynamics—a note'. *Science*, **178,** 517, 1972.

22   *pre-man around Lake Rudolph:* Leakey, R. Report in *The Australian*, 10 November, 1972.

23   LEOPOLD, A. C., and ARDREY, R. 'Toxic Substances in Plants and Food Habits of Early Man'. *Science*, **176,** 512, 1972.

24   *man not naturally aggressive*: Lomax, A., and Berkowitz, N. 'The Evolutionary Taxonomy of Man'. *Science*, **177,** 228, 1972.

26–7   World Bank Sector Working Paper: 'Population Planning'. Washington, 1972.

28   *aid given by affluent nations*: Hayter, T. *Aid as Imperialism*. Penguin, London, 1971.

29–33   U.N. *The World Population Situation in 1970*. U.N., New York, 1971.

31   CALDWELL, J. C. *Family planning in Sub Saharan Africa*. Mimeographed, Australian National University, 1972.

32   *Family Planning by China*: see reference for pages 326, 353.

34–6   TITMUSS, R., ABEL SMITH, B., and LYNES, T. *Social Policies and Population Growth in Mauritius*. Allen and Unwin, London, 1968.

Chapter 2: Population Dynamics

General References

BOGUE, D. J. *Principles of Demography*. Wiley, New York, 1969.

THOMPSON, W. S., and LEWIS, D. T. *Population Problems*, 5th ed. McGraw-Hill, New York, 1965.

39–42   GLASS, D. V. (ed.) *Introduction to Malthus.* Watts and Co.,
         London, 1953.
44–5   U.N. *Principles and Recommendations for National Censuses.*
         U.N., New York, 1958.

Chapter 3: Births . . . and . . . Deaths

         General Reference: BARCLAY, G. W. *Techniques of Popula-
         tion Analysis.* Chapman and Hall, London, 1958.
60–61   *Myths about semen:* Carstairs, G. M. *The Twice Born.*
         Indiana Univ. Press, 1957.
65–8   *The Irish famine:* information mainly from Woodham-
         Smith, C., in *The Great Hunger.* Hamish-Hamilton,
         London, 1962.
74   'Underestimates of infant mortality (in Indonesia)':
         Ruzicka, L. Paper given to the 4th Asian Population
         Conference, Tokyo, 1972.

Chapter 4: Don't Let My Baby Die!

84   *The definition of perinatal mortality.* This is complicated
         because two definitions are used. The Eighth Revision
         Conference of the International Classification of Dis-
         eases of the WHO, held in 1965, defined the perinatal
         period as extending from the 28th week of gestation to
         the 7th day of life. However, the Conference encouraged
         nations to collect pertinent data from the 20th week of
         pregnancy up to the 28th day of life. About half the
         nations in the European Region of the WHO, and a
         few in other Regions, have adopted the recommenda-
         tion and report fetal deaths occurring at 28 weeks, or
         more, of gestation, and deaths of live born infants
         occurring in the first week after birth. A total of 41 out
         of 132 nations report perinatal mortality ratios. A very
         few nations, or parts of nations, notably in the U.S.A.,
         some Canadian provinces, and the State of New South
         Wales, in Australia, report perinatal mortality ratios
         which include fetal deaths of at least 20 completed
         weeks' gestation, or at least 400 g weight (in some cases
         500 g weight) and infant deaths occurring within a
         period of 28 days after birth. It can be seen that two
         definitions of perinatal mortality are current.

    1) The extended perinatal mortality ratio, which is
       defined as: Fetal deaths of infants weighing 500 g or
       more at birth, and all neonatal deaths occurring
       from the day of birth up to the end of the 28th day
       of life, expressed as a ratio per 1,000 total births.

2) The standard perinatal mortality is the number of stillbirths (deaths of fetuses weighing 1,000 g or more) + the number of babies dying in the first 7 days of life (more exactly in the first 167 hours of life) per 1,000 births.

85   World Health Organization. 'The Prevention of Perinatal Mortality and Morbidity.' *Tech. Rep. Ser.*, **457**, Geneve, 1970.

85   *Perinatal mortality investigations in Britain*: see Butler, N. R., and Alberman, E. D. *Perinatal Problems*. Livingstone, Edinburgh, 1969.

88   BAIRD, D. 'Perinatal Mortality'. *Lancet*, **1**, 54, 1969.

Chapter 5: Off to Philadelphia

100–103 This montage is based on information mainly obtained from C. Woodham-Smith's *The Great Hunger*.

103   WALFORD, C. 'The famines of the world'. *Royal Statistical Society Journal*, **41**, 433, 1878.

104   *the origin of agriculture*: Harlen, J. R. 'Agricultural Origins: Centres and Non-centres'. *Science*, **174**, 468, 1971.

108   *content to live together etc.* Report of the New York Association for Improving Conditions of the Poor, Seventh Annual Report, 1850.

109–12 BORRIE, W. D. 'The Great Migrations' in *The Growth and Control of Population*. Weidenfeld and Nicholson, London, 1970.

112–15 *migration to Australia*, see Australian Institute of Political Science. *How Many Australians—Immigration and Growth*. Angus and Robertson, Sydney, 1971.

116   *urbanization in the U.S.A.: Population and the American Future*, Signet, 1972.

117   *housing shortages*: Ward, B., and Dubois, R. *Only One Earth*. Deutsch, London, 1972.

118   *urban crime*: Watt, K. E. F. 'The Costs of Urbanization'. *The Ecologist*, **2**, 20, 1972.

120   MUMFORD, L. *The Culture of Cities*. Secker and Warburg, London, 1940.

120   *Report of Select Committee . . . on Tenant Houses*. Documents of the Assembly of the State of New York, No. 205, 80th Session, 1857.

Chapter 6: The Hungry World

122–3 PAYNE, P. R., and WATERLOW, J. C. 'Relative Energy Requirements for Maintenance, Growth and Physical Activity'. *Lancet*, **2**, 210, 1971.

References

123   *F.A.O., Energy and protein requirements: F.A.O. Nutritional Meeting Report 52.* F.A.O., Rome, 1973.
Indian Council for Medical Research. Report 1966.

125   *Calorie protein malnutrition in children under 5*: 'The State of Food and Agriculture, 1972', page 24–8. F.A.O., Rome, 1972.

126   *Incidence of calorie protein malnutrition*: 'A Statistical Appraisal of the Protein Problem'. Paper given to 4th Session of F.A.O. Statistics Advisory Committee. F.A.O., Rome, 1969.
'Widespread incidence of protein calorie malnutrition'. Joint F.A.O./W.H.O. Committee on Nutrition, Geneve, 1970.

126–7 *Increased agricultural inputs 1951–1971*: 'The State of Food and Agriculture, 1972', p. 11–16. F.A.O., Rome, 1972.

129   *U.S. agricultural production, 1949–1968:* COMMONER, B. 'The Environmental Cost of Economic Growth' quoted in his book *The Closing Circle*, p. 149, and 'Future Percentage of U.S. agricultural workers', *Population and the American Future*, Signet, 1971, p. 30.

129   'A Blueprint for Survival', *The Ecologist*, **2,** 1, 1972.

137   *nitrites in the U.S.A.*: Wolff, I. A., and Wasserman, A. E. *Science*, **177,** 15, 1972.

137   *nitrites in Israel*: Shuval, H. *Scopus*, **26,** 17, 1972.

138   *D.D.T. in use*: Report of the Secretary's Commission on Pesticides and Their Relationship to Environmental Health. U.S. Dept. of H.E.W., 1969, p. 471.

139   *D.D.T. in malaria control*: Report by the Center for the Study of Natural Systems, St. Louis, U.S.A., **4,** 5, 1971.
'Alternate Insecticides for Control'. *Bull. W.H.O.*, **44,** 1971.

139   BORLAUG, N. 'McDougall Memorial Lecture': to 16th Governing Conference of the F.A.O. in Rome, 8 November, 1971, and *Ceres*, **5,** 21, 1972.

140   DORST, J. 'The age of agricultural chemical warfare is over'. *Ceres*, **1,** 31, 1972.

141   *Tungru virus:* Whitcombe, E., 'Development projects and environmental disruption'. *Soc. Sci. inform.* **II** (I), 29.

142   *the social consequences of the green revolution:* Thapar, A., in *Ceres*, **5,** 36, 1972, and Roy, P., in *Ceres*, **5,** 40, 1972.

143   WHITCOMBE, ELIZABETH: *Agrarian Conditions in Northern India*, Vol. I. Univ. California Press, Berkeley, California, 1971.

144   HUNT, A. O. *Agricultural reform in India*. London, Madras, 1899 (quoted by Dr. Whitfield).

147   RYTHER, J. H. 'Photosynthesis and Food Production from the Sea'. *Science*, **166,** 72, 1969.

References

Page

149   IDYLL, C. P. 'Farming the Sea'. *Ceres* **5,** 43, 1972.

150   PAYNE, R. 'Among Wild Whales'. *The New York Zoo logical Society Newsletter.* November, 1968.

153   NIXON, R. 'Acceptance Address when elected Republican candidate for the U.S. Presidency'. Miami, 24 August 1972.

153   MAYER, J. 'Towards a National Food Policy'. *Science,* **176** 237, 1972.

154   SWIFT, JONATHAN. *Gulliver's Travels.*

Chapter 7: A Precarious Ecological Balance

157–8   *Lake Erie:* See, for example, B. Commoner's *The Closing Circle,* Chapter 5. Cape, London, 1971.

158–9   *pollution in Rhine, and European lakes:* Loftar, T. 'The Ocean have become the sinks of the world'. *Ceres,* **5,** 35, 1972.

158–9   WEICHART, G. 'Pollution of the North Sea', in *Ambio,* **2** 99, 1973.

159–60   *Minamata tragedy:* Irukayama, K. 'The Pollution of Minamata Bay and Minamata Disease'. *Advances in Water Pollution Research,* **3,** 1967.

160   *Aswan High Dam and disease: British Medical Journal,* **1,** 63 1973.

164   COMMONER, B. *The Closing Circle.* Cape, London, 1971.

165   EHRLICH, P. R., and HOLDREN, J. P. 'One Dimensional Ecology'. *The Ecologist,* **8,** 11, 1972.

168   HAMMOND, A. C. 'Solar Energy—the largest resource' *Science,* **177,** 1088, 1972.

169   WEINBERG, ALVIN. 'Social Institutions and Nuclear Energy'. *Science,* **177,** 27, 1972.

173   KIRKBY, ELISABETH. 'Mid-Atlantic Avalanche'—a paper read to the International Federation of Women in Radio and Television. Brussels, 1970.

175   *the cargo cult:* See, for example, Worsley, P. *The Trumpet Shall Sound,* 2nd Edition. MacGibbon and Kee, London, 1968.

180   COALE, A. J. in *The Population Dilemma* (ed. Hauser). Spectrum, 1969.

181   U.N. Committee for Development Planning. *Ceres,* **5,** 13, 1972.

182   *The Third World to rethink:* Corea, G. 'A Third Style for Asia'. *Ceres,* **5,** 9, 1972.

Chapter 8: A Plethora of People

185   STYCOS, J. M., and MCEWAN, T. *Human Fertility in Latin America.* Cornell Univ. Press, N.Y., 1968.

References

Page

188–94 For a description of the medical aspects of England's demographic transition, see, for example, McKeown, T., *Medicine in Modern Society*. Allen and Unwin, London, 1965.

202 World Bank Report, 'Population and Progress'. Washington, 1972.

204 KEYFITZ, N. 'On the momentum of population growth'. *Demography*, **8**, 71, 1971.

205 *Zero population growth:* U.S. Bureau of the Census. 'The Two-child Family and Population Growth'. U.S. Government Printing Office, Washington D.C., 1971.

207 LAPHAM, R. J., and MAUDLIN, W. P. 'National Family Planning Programs—Review and Evaluation'. *Studies in Family Planning*, **3**, 30, 1972.

Chapter 9: A Child by Choice

General Reference: HINES, N. E. *A Medical History of Contraception*, 2nd edition. Harper, New York, 1929.

212 PLACE, F. 'To the Married of Both Sexes of the Working People'. A Handbill. 1822.

213 *disguised infanticide:* Langer, W. L. 'Europe's Initial Population Explosion'. *American Historical Review*, **69**, 1, 1963.

213 DISRAELI, B. 'Sybill'. Oxford Univ. Press, London, 1950.

216 *'comstockery':* Freyer, P. *The Birth Controllers*. Secker and Warburg, London, 1965.

217 SANGER, M. *An Autobiography*. Norton, New York, 1932.

222 *contraceptives and promiscuity:* Jordan, J. A., and Studd, J. W. W., in *Psychosomatic medicine in Obstetrics and Gynaecology* (edited, Morris, N.), Karger, London, 1972; and Newton, J., *British Medical Journal*, **2**, 642, 1972.

223 *Contraceptives in N.H.S. from 1974:* See *British Medical Journal*, **2**, 4, 1973.

224 PINCUS, E. *Proceedings 5th International Conference Planned Parenthood*. Tokyo, Japan, 1955.

Chapter 10: Contraception

228 *The Pearl index:* Pearl, R. 'Contraception and Fertility in 2,000 Women'. *Human Biology*, **4**, 363, 1932.

228 LASAGNA, L., in *Public Health and Population Change* (edited Sheps, M. C., and Ridley, J. C.). Univ. Pittsburgh Press, 1965.

230 POTTS, M. 'Human Fertility in Global Perspective'. *J. Bio. Social Science*, Supp. 3, 49, 1971.

References

Page

231 GORER, G., in *Sex and Marriage in England and Wales*.
     Nelson, London, 1972.

232 TIETZE, C. 'Advances in Family Planning'. *Excerpta
     Medica*, **VI,** 117, 1971.

234 *vasectomy effects:* Presser, H. 'Voluntary sterilization'.
     Reports on Population/Family Planning 5.1.1970.

237 *the calendar method:* Brayer, F. T. *et alia*. 'Birth control by
     the calendar method'. *Fertility and Sterility*, **20,** 279, 1969.

239 *the mucus method:* Billings, J. J. 'The ovulation method'.
     Advocate Press, Melbourne, Australia, 1969.

240 *the predictable ovulation method:* Boutselis, J. G. *et alia*. 'Con-
     trol of Ovulation Time'. *American Journal of Obstetrics
     and Gynaecology*, **112,** 171, 1971.

240 *the safe period in Latin America:* see Stycos, J. M., in *Ex-
     ploding Humanity* (ed. Reiger, H., and Falls, J. B.).
     Anansi, Toronto, Canada, 1969.

Chapter 11: Avoiding Unwanted Pregnancy

249 KUTCHERA, L. K. 'Postcoital contraception'. *Journal
     American Medical Association*, **218,** 562, 1971.

252 GOLDZIEHER, J. W. *et alia*. 'A placebo-controlled
     double blind cross over investigation of the side effects
     commonly attributed to oral contraceptives'. *Fertility
     and Sterility*, **22,** 609, 1971.

253 VESSEY, M. P., and DOLL, R. *British Medical Journal*, **2,**
     65, 1969.

254 DRILL, V. A., and CALHOUN, D. 'Oral contraceptives and
     thromboembolic disease'. *Journal American Medical
     Association*, **219,** 593, 1972.

259 *efficiency of oral contraceptives:* The Swedish Study. Ruten-
     skold, M., in *Acta Obstetrica et Gynaecologica Scandinavia*,
     50, 203, 1971.

261 *the history of the IUD:* see, for example, Guttmacher, A. F.
     Journal Reproduction and Fertility, **10,** 115, 1965.

Chapter 12: Where England Went Wrong

273 DEVEREAUX, G. *A Study of Abortion in Primitive Societies*.
     Julian Press, New York, 1955.

275 *Moral attitudes to abortion:* Shapiro, H. C., in *Abortion in a
     Changing World*, Vol. I (ed. Hall), p. 183. Colombia
     Univ. Press, London, 1970.

280 FORSSMAN, H., and THUWE, I. *Acta Psychiatrica Scandin-
     avia*, **42,** 71, 1966.

282 *affront to a woman's dignity:* Mehlen, K. H. 'Abortion in
     Eastern Europe', in Hall: *Abortion in a Changing World*
     p. 302, *op. cit.*

283   COLE, M., in *Abortion in Britain*. Pitman Medical, London, 1966.

287–9 *debate about abortion in Britain:* Horden, A. *Legal Abortion—The English Experience*. Pergamon, London, 1971.

289   Royal College of Obstetricians and Gynaecologists. 'An inquiry into the first year's working of the Abortion Act'. *British Medical Journal*, **2**, 529, 1970.

290   SIMMS, M., in *Nova*, page 83, October, 1971.

292   *the illogicality of the Abortion Act:* British Medical Association. 'Memorandum to the Inquiry into the Working of the Abortion Act'. *British Medical Journal*, **1**, supp. p. 31, 1972.

294   BEAZLEY, J. M., and HAERI, A. D. 'Termination of pregnancy refused'. *Lancet*, **1**, 1059, 1971.

295   KUMMER, J. M., in Hall: *Abortion in a Changing World*, p. 96, *op. cit.*

Chapter 13: Death in the Afternoon

301   EDGAR, T. 'Ignaz Phillip Semmelweiss'. *Annals Medical History*, **1**, 74, 1939.

308   Ministry of Health, England and Wales. 'Confidential Reports into Maternal Deaths'.

310   *high risk of dying in pregnancy:* Klein, M. D., and Karten, I. 'Maternal deaths: a health and socioeconomic challenge'. *American Journal of Obstetrics & Gynecology*, **110**, 299, 1971.

314   *the model of Singapore:* Lean, T. H. 'Maternal deaths in Singapore'. *Transactions 4th Asian Congress of Obstetrics and Gynaecology*, 1969.

Chapter 14: Unwanted, Often Unwelcome

319   *Age at puberty:* see, for example, Tanner, J. M. 'Earlier Maturation in Man'. *Scientific American*, **218**, 21, 1968.

323   WALLACE, H. M. 'Teenaged Pregnancy'. *American Journal of Obstetrics and Gynecology*, **92**, 1125, 1965.

       SEMMENS, J. P., and LAMERS, W. M. *Teenage Pregnancy*. Thomas, Springfield, 1968.

325   PAAVOLA, A. 'The illegitimacy rate and other factors influencing pregnancy and delivery of unmarried mothers'. *Acta Obstetrica et gynaecologica Scandinavica*, **47**, Supp. 3, 1968.

325   *cost of 'illegitimate' children:* Observer, 27 February, 1972.

326   *China:* see, 'Health and Family Planning Services in the Chinese People's Republic' by Faundes, A., and Luukkainen, T., in *Studies in Family Planning*, **3** (7 Supp.), 165, 1972.

327   *a diet which consists of potato chips etc.*: Marchetti, A. A., and Menaker, J. S. 'Pregnancy in adolescence'. *American Journal of Obstetrics and Gynecology*, **59,** 1013, 1950.

329   BOWLBY, J. *Maternal care and mental health.* W.H.O., Geneve, 1952.

329   YOUNG, L. *Out of Wedlock.* McGraw-Hill, New York, 1954.

330   WEIR, S. 'A Study of Unmarried Mothers in Scotland'. Scottish Home and Health Department, Edinburgh, 1971.

333   CRELLIN, E. *et alia. Born Illegitimate—Social and Educational Implications.* National Foundation for Educational Research, London, 1971.

333   *effect of separation from the mother on the emotional development of the child:* see Rutter, M. 'Parent–child separation', in *Journal of Child Psychology and Psychiatry*, **12,** 233, 1970; and
CALDWELL, B. *et alia.* 'Infant day care and attachment', *American Journal Orthopsychiatry*, **40,** 3, 1971.

Chapter 15: Beyond Birth Control

338   *KAP studies:* see Berelson, B., in *Family Planning and Population Programs* (ed. Berelson). Univ. Chicago Press, 1966.

340   MADDOX, J. *The Doomsday Syndrome.* Macmillan, London, 1972.

341   *the problem of population control in Latin America:* see, for example, Stycos, J. M., and McEwan, T. *Human Fertility in Latin America.* Cornell Univ. Press, New York, 1968.

344   JAFFE, F. S. 'Towards the Reduction of Unwanted Pregnancy'. *Science*, **174,** 119, 1971.

350   *need to go beyond family planning:* see Davis, K. C.,' Population Policy—will current programs succeed?'. *Science*, **158,** 730, 1967; and
BERELSON, B., 'Beyond Family Planning'. *Science*, **163,** 533, 1969.

352   *pensions as a reward for reduced fertility:* see Spengler, J. J., 'Population Problem—in search of a solution'. *Science*, **166,** 1234, 1969; and
RIDKER, R. G., and MUSCAT, R. J., 'Incentives to Family Welfare and Fertility Reduction'. *Studies in Family Planning*, **4,** 1, 1973.

352   *decichild coupons:* Kenneth Boulding. *The Meaning of the 20th Century.* Harper and Row, New York, 1964.

353   *the model of China:* see Katagiri. *I.P.P.F. Medical Bulletin,* June, 1972, and China reference, Chapter 14.

Index